D0204833

MUSIC
TRANSLATION
DICTIONARY

ABOUT THE COMPILER

Carolyn Doub Grigg received her Ph.D. in music theory from the University of Miami, Coral Gables, Florida. She has served as an orchestra director and a librarian; she is presently at work on a bibliography of double reed literature.

MUSIC TRANSLATION DICTIONARY

AN ENGLISH
CZECH
DANISH
DUTCH
FRENCH
GERMAN
HUNGARIAN
ITALIAN
POLISH
PORTUGUESE
RUSSIAN
SPANISH
SWEDISH
VOCABULARY
OF MUSICAL
TERMS

COMPILED BY
CAROLYN
DOUB
GRIGG

GREENWOOD PRESS
Westport, Connecticut • London, England

Library of Congress Cataloging in Publication Data

Grigg, Carolyn Doub.
    Music translation dictionary.

    Bibliography: p.
    Includes indexes.
    1. Music—Terminology. 2. Music—Dictionaries—
Polyglot. I. Title.
ML108.G855   780'.3   78-60526
ISBN 0-313-20559-0

Library of Congress Catalog Card Number: 78-60526
ISBN: 0-313-20559-0

First published in 1978

Greenwood Press, Inc.
51 Riverside Avenue, Westport, Connecticut 06880

Printed in the United States of America

10 9 8 7 6 5 4 3 2 1

Dedicated to
the memory of
GEORGE F. JOHNSON

CONTENTS

INTRODUCTION

The enormous growth and ramification of all musical fields, accompanied by a corresponding increase in the volume of publications, has created the need for a tool that will endow professional and amateur interpreters with the efficacy to understand one another more readily. The problem of the communication of ideas among peoples of different cultures is not new. For a long time the use of scholarly Latin, and later the use of Italian as a universal musical language, solved that problem for musicians of the Western world. Now, however, with the spread of Western music to all parts of the world, the rise of internationally sponsored musicological research, and the increase in travel, experts and students alike need to understand terms in many languages.

In nearly all languages and fields, the existing technical dictionaries are deplorably inadequate as working tools; there are no musical-term dictionaries in many idioms. In addition, there is a scarcity of technical translators. The only way to increase their output is to provide them with better implements—dictionaries. What is needed, especially in the world of music, is an aid to facilitate the reading of books and articles dealing with the problems and quests of the field and the interpretation of musical scores.

Although Coover in his *Music Lexicography* lists more than 1,300 musical dictionaries, nearly all are very much out-of-date, and most are quite limited in the number of terms translated. Usually translations are possible only to the language in which the dictionary was written. The exception is Smith's *A Dictionary of Musical Terms in 4 Languages*, which lists equivalents across a two-page spread. Its classified arrangement, however, is unhandy for translation work and it has no indexes. The *Music Translation Dictionary* is a true polyglot dictionary that has numbered, indexed entries, contains translations of terms into those languages where there is regular musical research and current musical publishing activity, and provides an index of these terms in all those languages. Hopefully it will help fill the needs of musical translators.

In the *Music Translation Dictionary* can be found ninety-one possible bilingual music dictionaries among its thirteen languages, which are, in the order in which they appear in the dictionary: English, Czech, Danish, Dutch, French, German, Hungarian, Italian, Polish, Portuguese, Russian, Spanish, and Swedish. All the translator has to do is locate the word he wants to translate in the index, which will indicate a number that refers him to an entry in the dictionary where that term may be instantaneously translated into any of the other twelve languages at a glance.

Terms for the *Music Translation Dictionary* were compiled by collecting all English word entries from several of the most popular music dictionaries and from musical scores. It became apparent that most dictionaries waste space by the inclusion of many forms of the same base word, by the use of terms in many contexts, and by the inclusion of plurals, Latin terms, similar spellings, and self-evident variations that increase the list unnecessarily and that may be a hindrance rather than a help. The list was reduced to include only adjective, infinitive, and noun forms as entries, wherever possible. Derivatives not found in the *Dictionary* may be obtained by adding prefixes and suffixes to, or changing the endings of, entries. Therefore many more terms are translatable than the 16,900 appearing in the *Dictionary*; more than 50,000 terms with musical meaning may be derived from those listed. Translations to the foreign languages were made from two-way dictionaries, musical-term dictionaries in the foreign languages, and personal interviews with professional musicians fluent in those languages. Examples of inclusions and exclusions are: 1) *to analyze*, but not *analysis*; 2) *to diminish*, but not *diminishing*; 3) *to detach*, but not *detached*; 4) *dignity*, but not *dignified*; and 5) *elegant*, but not *elegantly*. When English nouns and infinitives can be confused, such as *pedal* and *to pedal*, both forms are included. English verbs are listed by main word: *play, to*; *pedal, to*; and *sing, to*.

The *Dictionary* is arranged alphabetically in English. English is indicated by AAA (so that a computer would print it first), and each entry is numbered from 1 to 1300. However, in the index, English is abbreviated ENG. The index is abbreviated word-by-word, so that whenever a term contains more than one word, it may be found where the first word stops; but when an entry contains a comma, it may be found at the end of the list of entries that contain those letters that occur before the comma; for example, *i stället* comes before *ianychar*, and *en, dans* is after *enyelegni*. Russian appears transliterated in both the dictionary and the index.

By including so many languages and terms, the *Dictionary* may be used by peoples in most areas of the world and should be indispensable to translators and interpreters, writers and abstractors, scholars meeting language research tool requirements, performers and conductors, and students, providing all of them with a terminological apparatus for the utilization and dissemination of a planned, uniform, international terminology.

BIBLIOGRAPHY

Adeline, Jules. *The Adeline Art Dictionary*. Translated from the French by Adeline, with a supplement of new terms by Hugo G. Beigel, Ph.D. English edition, 1891. Second printing, 1967. New York: Frederick Ungar Publishing Company, 1967.

Akhmanova, Ol'ga Sergeevna. *Russko-angliĭskiĭ Slovar'*. Moscow: Sovetskaĭa entsiklopediĭa, 1964.

Amer, Christine. *Musicians Handbook of Foreign Terms*. New York: Schirmer, 1971.

Anglicko-česky a Česko-anglický Kapesní Slovnik. 1st edition. Prague: Státní Pedagogické Nakl., 1960.

Bergman, Peter M., compiler. *The Concise Dictionary of 26 Languages in Simultaneous Translation*. New York: Bergman Publishers, 1968.

Berkman, Al. *Singers' Glossary of Show Business Terms*. Hollywood, California: Wilshire Book Company, 1961.

Betteridge, Harold T., editor. *The New Cassell's German Dictionary*, *German-English. English-German*. Based on editions by Karl Breul. New York: Funk & Wagnalls, c. 1971.

Biagioni, Luigi. *Italienische Musikterminologie in Deutschen Übertragung*. Cologne: P. J. Tonger, 1929.

Bizonfy, Ferencz. *English-Hungarian Dictionary*. Ninth enlarged edition. Cleveland: Liberty Publishing Company, 1948.

Blom, Eric, compiler. *Everyman's Dictionary of Music*. New York: E. P. Dutton & Co., 1962.

Blomgren, Axel S. *Svensk-Engelsk Ordbok*. Lund, Sweden: Gleerups Forlag, 1939.

Böhm, László. *Zenei Müszótár*. Budapest: Zenemükiadó Vállalat, 1952.

Borba, Tomás, and Graça, Fernando Lopes. *Dicionario de Música*. Illustrated. Vol. I, A-H. Lisbon: 1945.

Bosch, Abraham Ten. *Ten Bosch' Viertalig Technisch Woordenboek*. 2 Vols. Deventer: N. V. Uitgevers-Mattschappij AE. E. Klewer, n.d.

Bouman, Leon C. *Vreemde Woorden in de Muziek*. Amsterdam: Seyffardt's Muziekhandel, 1950.

Boyer, Abel. *Boyer's Royal Dictionary*. Abridged. In two parts: I. French and English and II. English and French. Edinburgh: Bell & Bradfute, 1814.

Bratli, Carl Georg Valdeman Jensen. *Spansk-Dansk Ordbog*. With a foreword by
Holger Sten. Copenhagen: Forfatterens Forlag, 1947.

Büchen, Ernst. *Wörterbuch der Musik*. Weisbaden: Dieterich, 1955.

Bulas, Kozimierz, and Whitfield, Francis J. *The Kościuszko Foundation Dictionary*.
English-Polish, Polish-English. New York: The Kościuszko Foundation, 1960.

Bulle, Oscar, and Rigutini, Giuseppe. *Dizionario Italiano-Tedesco, Tedesco-Italiano*.
2 Vols. Leipsig: Bernard Tauchnitz, 1930. Milan: Ulrico Hoepli, 1930.

Caha, Jan, and Krámský, Jiří. *English-Czech Dictionary*. 1st edition. Prague: State
Pedogogical Publishing House, 1960.

Cassell's English-Dutch, Dutch-English Dictionary. Compiled by F. P. H. Prick van
Wely. 4th edition. London: Cassell, 1960.

Cassell's French-English, English-French Dictionary. New edition completely revised
by J. L. Manchon. New York: Funk & Wagnalls, 1951.

Cassell's Italian Dictionary, Italian-English, English-Italian. Compiled by Piero
Rebora. New York: Funk & Wagnalls, 1959.

Cassell's Spanish Dictionary, Spanish-English, English-Spanish. Edited by Edgar
Allison Peers, and others. New York: Funk & Wagnalls, 1966.

Coover, James B. *Music Lexicography, Including a Study of Lacunae in Music
Lexicography and a Bibliography of Music Dictionaries*. Denver: Bibliographic
Center for Research, 1958.

Cowles, Barbara, compiler. *Bibliographers' Glossary of Foreign Words and Phrases:
An Alphabet Compiled from Twenty Languages*. New York: R. R. Bowker
Company, 1935.

Crowell's Spanish-English and English-Spanish Dictionary. By Gerd A. Gillhoff.
New York: Crowell, 1963.

Csíkvári, Antal. *Zenei Kistukor*. Budapest: Zenemükiadó Vállalat, 1959.

Cuyás, Arturo. *Appleton's New Cuyás English-Spanish and Spanish-English Dictionary*. Revised edition by Catherine B. Avery. New York: Appleton-Century-
Crofts, 1966.

Danielsson, Bror. *Modern Engelsk-Svensk-Ordbok*. Stockholm: Bokforlaget Prisma,
1970.

Diccionario Manual Español-Ruso. Compiled by M. Gisbert and V. A. Nizskiï.
Moscow: Ediciones de Estado de Diccionarios Extranjeros y Nacionales, 1962.

Dizionario Italiano-Russo. Compiled by N. Skvorzova and B. Maizel. Moscow:
Casa Editrice Statale, 1963.

Doua, A. *Dictionar Technic Poliglot*. Bucharest: Editura Technica, 1967.

Duden Pictorial Encyclopedia in Five Languages. New York: Frederick Ungar Publishing Company, 1943.

Elwes, Alfred. *A Dictionary of the Portuguese Language in Two Parts: I. Portuguese-English and II. English-Portuguese*. London: The Technical Press, Ltd.,
1943.

Ernolv, Carl Josua. *Svensk-Engelsk Ordbog*. Stockholm: P. A. Norstedt, 1942.

Ferreira da Silva, J. B. *Vocabulario Musical, Contendo por Ordem Alfabetico,
Cerca de Doze Mil Palavras e Frases Alemãs, Arabes, Espanholas, Francescas,
Gregas, Hebraicas, Italianas e Latinas*. Rio de Janeiro: Casa Arthur Napoleão,
Sampaio, Araujo, c. 1921.

Foss, Gunnar. *Musikridtryk*. Copenhagen: P. Haase & Son, 1925.

Franco, Alvaro. *Dicionário Inglês-Português, Português-Inglés*. 6th edition. Rio de Janeiro: Livraria do Globo, 1947.

Galperin, Il'ia Romanovich. *New Russian-English Dictionary*. Moscow: Soviet Encyclopedia Publishing House, 1972.

Ganshina, Klavdiia Aleksandrovna. *Dictionaire Franais-Russe*. 16th edition. Moscow: Soviet Edts., 1971.

Gardner, A. L. "Technical Translating Dictionaries." *Journal of Documentation* 6 (March 1950): 25-31.

Gerkens, Karl Wilson. *Handbook of Musical Terms*. Boston: Oliver Ditson Company, 1927.

Golovinskii, M. *A New English-Russian and Russian-English Dictionary*. New York: David McKay Company, 1936?

Grzebieniowski, Tadeusz. *A Concise Polish-English Dictionary*. Warsaw: Wiedza Powszechna, 1963.

Harrap's New Standard French and English Dictionary. Edited by J. E. Mansion. Completely revised and enlarged edition. Revised and edited by R. P. L. Ledésert and Margaret Ledésert. New York: Scribner, 1972.

Harrap's Standard German and English Dictionary. Edited by Trevor Jones. London: Harrap, 1963.

Heath's Standard French and English Dictionary. Edited by J. E. Mansion. Boston: Heath, 1961-62.

Hemel, Victor van. *Woordenboekje der Muzikale Vormen,* ten Behoeve van Operaen Koncertbezoekers, Radioluisteraars, Muziekstuderenden. 2nd edition. Antwerp: Cupido-uitg., 1954.

Houaiss, Antonio. *The New Appleton Dictionary of the English and Portuguese Languages*. New York: Appleton-Century-Crofts, 1964.

IAsel'man. IU. S. *Russko-Ispanskii Slovar'*. Moscow: Gosudarstvennoe Izdatel'stvo Inostrannykh i Natsional'nykh Slovarei, 1948.

Jacobs, Arthur. *A New Dictionary of Music*. London: Cassell and Company, Ltd., 1961.

Jungberg, Carl Gustaf. *Svenskt och Engelskt Handlexicon*. Stockholm: L. J. Hiertas Förlag, 1869.

Karmannyi Cheshsko-Russkii Slovar'. Sostavili D. A. Dlugi and B. G. Raevskii. Moscow: Gos. Izd-vo Inos-trannykh i Natsional'nykh Slovarei, 1963.

Karmannyi Russko-Datskii Slovar'. Sostavili N. I. Krymova and A. IA. Emzina. Moscow: Sovetskaia entsiklopediia, 1964.

Karre, Karl, and others. *English-Swedish Dictionary*. 3rd. revised edition. Stockholm: Svenska Bokförlaget Norstedts, 1953.

Kecki, Feliks. *Podręszny Slownik Encyklopedyczno Muzyczny*. Warsaw: By the author, 1930?

Kel'in, Fedor Viktorovich. *Ispansko-Russkii Slovar'*. Moscow: Gos. Izd-vo Inos-trannykh i Natsional'nykh Slovarei, 1961.

Koch, Willi A. *Musiches Lexikon*. Stuttgart: Alfred Kroner Verlag, 1956.

Kolster, T. A. *Technical Dictionary*. English-Spanish, Spanish-English. Caracas, Venezuela: T. A. Kolster, n.d.

Kramers, Jacob. *Kramers' Dutch Dictionary*. English-Dutch and Dutch-English. Edited by F. P. H. Prick van Wely. 17th revised edition. New York: Dover Publications, 1946.

Langenscheidt's New Muret-Sanders Encyclopedic Dictionary of the English and German Languages. Completely revised. Edited by Otto Springer. New York: Barnes & Noble, 1962.

Langenscheidt's Standard Dictionary of the English and Spanish Languages by C. C. Smith, G. A. Davies and H. B. Hall. New York: Barnes & Noble, 1966.

Larson, Anton Laurentius. *A Dictionary of the Dano-Norwegian and English Languages*. 4th edition. Copenhagen and Christiana: Gyldendal Publishing House, 1910.

Leidecker, K. F. "How to Write a Technical Dictionary." *Library Journal* 63 (August 1947): 1096-97.

Le Grand, Raymond. *La Musique Expliqée*. Edition Français-Anglais. Music Made Easy. Paris: R. Breton, c.1950.

Leuchtmann, Horst, and Schick, Phillipine. *Langenscheidt's Fachworterbuch Music*. English. Berlin and Munich: Langenscheid KG, 1964.

McLaughlin's Danish-Norwegian-English Dictionary in Two Parts. Danish-Norwegian-English and English-Danish-Norwegian. New edition revised and improved by J. R. Ainsworth Davis. Philadelphia: David McKay Company, 1941.

Magnussen, Johannes Julius Claudi. *McKay's Modern Danish-English, English-Danish Dictionary*. New York: David McKay Company, 1954.

Mayer, Ralph. *A Dictionary of Art Terms and Techniques*. New York: Thomas A. Crowell Company, 1969.

Michaelis, Henriette. *A New Dictionary of the Portuguese and English Languages*. New York: Frederick Ungar Publishing Company, 1945.

Milanova, D. E. *Shvedsko-Russkiĭ Slovar'*. Moscow: Gos. Izd-vo Inostrannykh i Natsional 'nykh Slovareĭ, 1959.

Müller, Vladimer Karlovich, compiler. *English-Russian Dictionary*. 7th edition. New York: E. P. Dutton & Company, 1965.

Nash, Rose. *Multilingual Lexicon of Linguistics and Philology*. English, Russian German and French. Coral Gables, Florida: University of Miami Press, 1968.

Neues Taschen Wörterbuch der Schwedischen und Deutschen Sprache. Leipzig: O. Holtz, 1892.

New International French-English and English-French Dictionary. Chicago: Wilcox & Follett Company, 1943.

Newmark, Maxim. *Dictionary of Science and Technology in English, French, German, Spanish*. New York: Philosophical Library, 1943.

Nöjd, Ruben. *McKay's Modern English-Swedish and Swedish-English Dictionary*. New York: David McKay Company, 1967.

Országh, László. *Angol-Magyar Szótár*. 2 Vols.: A-M, N-Z. 4th edition. Budapest: Akadémiai Kiadó, 1974.

Osicka, Antonin, and Poldauf, Ivan. *Anglicko-Český Slovník*. Prague: Academia Nakladaletsvi Československé Akademie Ved, 1970.

Ouseg, H. L., compiler. *International Dictionary in 21 Languages*. New York: Philosophical Library, 1962.

Pavliuchenko, S. A. *Kratikiĭ Muzykal'nyi Slovar'*. Moscow: Gos. Muzykal'noe Izd-vo, 1950.

Pleijel, G. *Populart Musiklexikon*. Stockholm: 1945.

Portygal'sko-Russkiı Slovar'. Sostavili S. M. Starets, and E. N. Feershteĭn. Moscow: Gos. Izd-vo Inostrannykh i Natsional'nykh Slovareı, 1961.

Réau, Louis. *Dictionaire Polyglotte des Termes d'Art et d'Archeologie*. Paris: Presses Universitaires de France, 1953.

Reiss, Jósef Wladyslaw. *Podreczna Encyklopedia Muzyki*. Kraków, Wiedza, Zawód, Kultura, 1949.

Renier, Fernand Gabriel. *Dutch-English and English-Dutch Dictionary*. London: Routledge & Kegan Paul, Ltd., 1949.

Richardson, Elbert L., editor. *McKay's Modern Portuguese-English and English-Portuguese Dictionary*. New York: David McKay Company, 1958.

Robertson, Richard. *Diccionario Inglés-Español y Español-Inglés*. Barcelona: R. Sopena, 1964.

Russko-Angliĭshiĭ Slovar'. Sostavili A. M. Taube. Moscow: Sov. Entsiklopediıa, 1970.

Russisch-Nederlands Woordenboek, door J. Peirot. Moscow: Stattsuitgeverij voor Woordemboeken im Vreemde en Nationale Talen, 1961.

Sacher, Jack, editor. *Music A to Z*. Based on the work of Rudolf Steven. New York: Grosset & Dunlop, 1963.

Salvá y Pérez, Vicente. *Diccionario Moderno Español-Francés, Francés-Español*. Paris: Casa Editorial Garnier Hermanos, 1966.

Sandved, Kjell Bloch. *Musikkens Verden, Music fra A-Z*. Revised edition and revision by Vagn Kappel. Subeditor: K. Claussen. Alphabetically arranged with about 2,000 illustrations. Copenhagen: Musikens Verden, 1955.

Sarda, Antonio. *Léxico Technólogico Musical en Varios Idiomas*. Madrid: Unión Musical Española, c. 1929.

Schoen, Th., and Noeli, T. *Langenscheidt's Diccionario Manual*. Berlin: Casa Editorial, 1961.

Scholes, Percy A. *The Concise Oxford Dictionary of Music*. 2nd edition, edited by John Owen Reed. London: Oxford University Press, 1964.

Segal, Louis. *New Complete Russian-English Dictionary*. New York: Hafner Publishing Company, Inc., 1948.

Sezhenskii, K. *Kraktii Slovar' Muzykal'nykh Terminov,* Moscow: Gos. Muzykal'noe Izd-vo, 1950.

Sinzig, Petrus, Father. *Dicionário Musical*. Rio de Janeiro: Livraria Kosmos, 1947.

Smith, William James, editor. *A Dictionary of Musical Terms in Four Languages*. London: Hutchinson, 1961.

Stainer, Sir John, and Barrett, W. A. *Dictionary of Musical Terms*. Revised edition. London: Novello, 1889.

Stanislawski, Jan. *The Great English-Polish Dictionary*. Warsaw: Wiedza Powszechna State Publishing House, 1964.

Taylor, James Lumpkin. *A Portuguese-English Dictionary*. Stanford, California: Stanford University Press, 1970.

Van Nostrand's Concise Student Dictionary; French-English, English-French. By Jean-Pauyl Vinay, Pierre Daviault and Henry Alexander. Princeton, New Jersey: Van Nostrand, 1962.

Vladov, L. R. *Portygal'sko-Russkiĭ Slovar'*. Sostavili L. R. Vladov, B. A. Nokonov, H. G. Sotnikov, pod red. S. i B. Brandão. Moscow: Gos Izd-vo Inostrannykh i National'nykh Slovareĭ, 1950.

Vannes, René. *Essai de Terminologie Musicale*. Thann: Alsatia, 1925.

Votoček, Emil. *Hudební Slovní Cizích Výrazů a Rčení.* Hudební Matice Umělecké Besedy, 1946.

Werda, C., pseudo. *Muzikaal Handwoordenboek*. With an introduction by R. Ghesquiere. Turnhout: Brepols, 194-.

Westrup, Jack Allen, and Harrison, L. F. *The New College Encyclopedia of Music*. New York: W. W. Norton & Company, Inc., 1960.

Wevers, B. J., and Verhoeff, P. J. *Standaard Groot Engels-Nederlands Woordenboek*. Antwerp/Utrecht: Standaard Uitgeverij, 19--?.

Williams, Edwin Bucher. *Dictionary of Spanish and English*. New York: Holt, Rinehart and Winston, 1963.

DICTIONARY

1AAA ABANDON
1CZE ODEVZDANOSŤ
1DAN HENGIVENHED
1DUT OVERGAVE
1FRE ABANDON
1GER HINGEBUNG, HINGABE
1HUN ODAADÁS
1ITA ABBANDONO
1POL NIEDBALE
1POR ABANDONO
1RUS OSTAVLENIE
1SPA ABANDONO
1SWE HÄNGIVELSE

2AAA ABBREVIATE, TO
2CZE ZKRÁTITI
2DAN FORKORTE
2DUT VERKORTEN
2FRE ABRÉGER
2GER ABKÜRZEN
2HUN RÖVIDÍTNI
2ITA ABBREVIARE
2POL SKRACAĆ
2POR ABREVIAR
2RUS SOKRASHCHAT'
2SPA ABREVIAR
2SWE FÖRKORTA

3AAA ABDOMEN
3CZE BŘICHO
3DAN UNDERLIV
3DUT BUIK
3FRE ABDOMEN
3GER UNTERLEIB
3HUN ALTEST
3ITA ADDOME
3POL BRZUCH
3POR ABDÔMEN
3RUS BRIUSHKO
3SPA ABDOMEN
3SWE ABDOMEN

4AAA ABOVE
4CZE NAD, NAHOŘE
4DAN OVER
4DUT BOVEN
4FRE AU-DESSUS
4GER ÜBER, OBER
4HUN FELETT(E)
4ITA SOPRA
4POL PONAD
4POR SOBRE
4RUS NAD
4SPA SOBRE
4SWE ÖVER

5AAA ABSOLUTE
5CZE ABSOLUTNÍ
5DAN ABSOLUT
5DUT ABSOLUUT
5FRE ABSOLU
5GER ABSOLUT
5HUN ABSZOLUT
5ITA ASSOLUTO
5POL ABSOLUTNY
5POR ABSOLUTO
5RUS ABSOLIUTNYI
5SPA ABSOLUTO
5SWE ABSOLUT

6AAA ACCELERATE, TO
6CZE ZRYCHLITI
6DAN ACCELERERE
6DUT BESPOEDIGEN
6FRE ACCÉLÉRER
6GER BESCHLEUNIGEN
6HUN GYORSÍTNI
6ITA ACCELERARE
6POL PRZYŚPIESZAĆ
6POR ACELERAR
6RUS USKORIAT'
6SPA ACELERAR
6SWE PÅSKYNDA

7AAA ACCENT
7CZE AKCENT, PRIZVUK
7DAN BETONING
7DUT ACCENT
7FRE ACCENT
7GER BETONUNG, AKZENT
7HUN HANGSÚLY
7ITA ACCENTO
7POL AKCENT
7POR ACENTO
7RUS AKTSENT
7SPA ACENTO
7SWE BETONING

8AAA ACCENT, TO
8CZE AKCENTOVATI
8DAN ACCENTUERE, BETONE
8DUT ACCENTUEREN
8FRE ACCENTUER
8GER BETONEN, AKZENTUIEREN
8HUN HANGSÚLYOZNI
8ITA ACCENTARE
8POL AKCENTOWAĆ
8POR ACENTUAR
8RUS AKTSENTIROVAT'
8SPA ACENTUAR
8SWE BETONA

9AAA ACCIDENTAL(S)
9CZE POSUVKA
9DAN LØSE FORTEGN
9DUT ACCIDENTEN
9FRE ACCIDENTS
9GER ACCIDENTALEN
9HUN ACCIDENS
9ITA ACCIDENTI
9POL AKCYDENCYJNY
9POR ACIDENTE(S)
9RUS AL'TERATSIIA
9SPA ACCIDENTE(S)
9SWE ACCIDENTALER

10AAA ACCOMPANIMENT
10CZE DOPROVOD
10DAN AKKOMPAGNEMENT
10DUT ACCOMPAGNEMENT
10FRE ACCOMPAGNEMENT
10GER BEGLEITUNG
10HUN HANGKISÉRET
10ITA ACCOMPAGNAMENTO
10POL AKOMPANIAMENT
10POR ACOMPANHAMENTO
10RUS AKKOMPANEMENT
10SPA ACOMPAÑAMIENTO
10SWE ACKOMPANJERA

11AAA ACCOMPANY, TO
11CZE DOPROVÁZETI
11DAN AKKOMPAGNERE
11DUT ACCOMPAGNEREN
11FRE ACCOMPAGNER
11GER BEGLEITEN
11HUN KISÉRNI
11ITA ACCOMPAGNARE
11POL AKOMPANIOWAĆ
11POR ACOMPANHAR
11RUS AKKOMPANIROVAT'
11SPA ACOMPAÑAR
11SWE ACKOMPANJA

12AAA ACCORDION
12CZE FYSHARMONIKA
12DAN TRAEKHARMONIKA
12DUT TREKHARMONICA
12FRE ACCORDÉON
12GER ZIEHHARMONIKA
12HUN HARMONIKA
12ITA FISARMONICA, ACCORDION
12POL AKORDEON
12POR ACORDEÃO
12RUS AKKORDEON
12SPA ACORDEÓN
12SWE ACCORDION, DRAGSPEL

13AAA ACERBITY
13CZE KYSELOST
13DAN BITTERHED
13DUT WRANGHEID
13FRE ACERBITÉ
13GER HERBHEIT
13HUN FANYARSÁG
13ITA ACERBITÀ
13POL CIERPKOŚĆ
13POR ACERBIDADE
13RUS TERPKOST'
13SPA ACERBIDAD
13SWE BITTERHET

14AAA ACOUSTICS
14CZE AKUSTIKA
14DAN AKUSTIK
14DUT AKOESTIEK
14FRE ACOUSTIQUE
14GER AKUSTIK
14HUN HALLÁSTAN
14ITA ACUSTICA
14POL AKUSTYKA
14POR ACÚSTICA
14RUS AKUSTIKA
14SPA ACÚSTICA
14SWE AKUSTIK

15AAA ACT
15CZE AKT
15DAN AKT
15DUT AKTE
15FRE ACTE
15GER AKT
15HUN CSELEKEDET
15ITA ATTO
15POL AKT
15POR ATO
15RUS AKT
15SPA ACTO
15SWE AKT

16AAA ACTIVE
16CZE AKTIVNÍ
16DAN AKTIV
16DUT ACTIEF
16FRE ACTIF
16GER TÄTIG
16HUN TEVEKENY
16ITA ATTIVO
16POL AKTYWNY
16POR ATIVO
16RUS AKTIVNYÏ
16SPA ACTIVO
16SWE AKTIV

17AAA ADAPT, TO
17CZE PŘIZPŮSOBITI
17DAN AFPASSE
17DUT ADOPTEREN
17FRE ADAPTER
17GER BEARBEITEN
17HUN HOZZÁ ALKALMAZ
17ITA ADDATTARE
17POL PRZYSTOSOWAĆ
17POR ADAPTAR
17RUS PRISPOSOBLIAT'
17SPA ADAPTAR
17SWE AVPASSA

18AAA ADD, TO
18CZE PŘIPOJITI
18DAN ADDERE
18DUT TOEVOEGEN
18FRE AJOUTER
18GER HINZUFÜGEN
18HUN HOZZÁJÁRULNI
18ITA AGGIUNGERE
18POL DODAWAĆ
18POR ADICIONAR
18RUS PRIBAVLIAT'
18SPA ADICIONAR
18SWE ADDERA

19AAA ADJUNCT
19CZE PŘIPOJENÍ, PŘÍDAVEK
19DAN TILBEHØR
19DUT TOEGEVOEGD
19FRE ADJOINT
19GER NEBEN
19HUN SEGÉD, TÁRS
19ITA AGGIUNTA
19POL ADIUNKT
19POR ADJUNTO
19RUS AD'IUNKT
19SPA ADJUNTO
19SWE TILLBEHÖR

20AAA AEOLIAN
20CZE EOLINA
20DAN AEOLUS
20DUT AEOLISCH
20FRE ÉOLIEN
20GER ÄOLISCH
20HUN EOL
20ITA EOLIO
20POL EOLSKI
20POR EÓLIO
20RUS EOLIISKII
20SPA EÓLICA, EOLIA
20SWE EOLISK

21AAA AERO-
21CZE AERO-
21DAN AERO-, LUFT-
21DUT AERO-
21FRE AÉRO-
21GER AERO-
21HUN AERO-
21ITA AERO-
21POL AERO-
21POR AERO-
21RUS AERO-
21SPA AERO-
21SWE LUFT-

22AAA AFECTED, MINCING
22CZE AFEKTOVĚ, STROJENÝ
22DAN AFFEKTERET
22DUT GEAFFECTEERD
22FRE AFFECTÉ
22GER AFFEKTIERT
22HUN MESTERKELT
22ITA AFFECTATO
22POL AFEKTOWANY
22POR AFECTADO
22RUS AFFEKTIROVANNYI
22SPA AFECTADO
22SWE AFFEKTÉRT

23AAA AFFABLE
23CZE MILÝ
23DAN BEHAGELIGT, TILTALENDE
23DUT BELEEFD, VOORKOMEND
23FRE AFFABLE
23GER GEFÄLLIG, FREUNDLICH
23HUN KELLEMESEN
23ITA AFFABILE
23POL POGODNIE Z WDZIĘKIEM
23POR AFÁVEL
23RUS PRIVETLIVYI
23SPA AFABLE
23SWE VANLIGT, INTAGANDE

24AAA AFFECTIONATE
24CZE VZRUŠENÍ
24DAN MED LIDENSKABELIGT
24DUT HARTELIJK, WARM
24FRE AFFECTUEUSEMENT
24GER AFFECTVOLL
24HUN SZERETŐ
24ITA AFFETTUOSO
24POL AFEKTACJI, NAMIETNIE
24POR AFECTUOSO
24RUS NEZHNO
24SPA AFECTUOSO
24SWE LIDELSEFULLT

25AAA AFTER
25CZE PO, ZA
25DAN EFTER
25DUT NA
25FRE APRÈS, ENSUITE
25GER NACH
25HUN UTÁN
25ITA DOPO
25POL PO
25POR DEPOIS
25RUS ZA
25SPA DESPUÉS
25SWE EFTER

26AAA AGAIN
26CZE JEŠTĚ
26DAN IGEN, ENDNU EN GANG
26DUT NOG EENS
26FEW ENCORE
26GER NOCH
26HUN ISMÉT
26ITA ANCORA
26POL PONOWNIE, ZNOWU
26POR EM RETÔRNO, DE VOLTA
26RUS SNOVA
26SPA AÚN, TODAVÍA
26SWE IGEN, ANNU EN GÅNG

27AAA AGAINST
27CZE KONTRA-
27DAN KONTRA-
27DUT TEGEN-
27FRE CONTRE-
27GER GEGEN-
27HUN ELLEN-, KONTRA-
27ITA CONTRA-
27POL KONTRA-
27POR CONTRA-
27RUS KONTRA-
27SPA CONTRA-
27SWE KONTRA-

28AAA AGILE
28CZE HYBNÝ, AGILNÍ
28DAN HURTIG, BEHAENDIG
28DUT VLUG, VAARDIG
28FRE AGILE
28GER BEHEND
28HUN MOZGÉKONY
28ITA AGILE, AGEVOLE
28POL ZWINNIE
28POR ÁGIL
28RUS LOVKIÏ
28SPA ÁGIL
28SWE LÄLLRÖRLIG

29AAA AGITATED
29CZE VZRUŠENĚ
29DAN UROLIGT, HEFLIGT
29DUT ONRUSTIG, BEWOGEN
29FRE AGITÉ
29GER BEWEGT
29HUN IZGETOTT
29ITA AGITATO
29POL GWAŁTOWNIE
29POR AGITADO
29RUS VOZBUZHDENNO
29SPA AGITADO
29SWE UPPRÖRT

30AAA AGOGIC
30CZE AGOGICKÝ
30DAN AGOGISK
30DUT AGOGIEK
30FRE AGOGIQUE
30GER AGOGIK
30HUN AGOGIKA
30ITA AGOGICO
30POL AGOGIKA
30POR AGÓGICO
30RUS AGOGICA
30SPA AGÓGICO
30SWE AGOGIK

31AAA AGREEABLE
31CZE PŘÍJEMNÝ
31DAN BEHAGELIG
31DUT AANGENAAM
31FRE AGRÉABLE
31GER ANGENEHM
31HUN EGYBEHANGZÓAN
31ITA AGGRADEVOLE
31POL MIŁY
31POR AGRADÁVEL
31RUS SOGLASNYÏ
31SPA AGRADABLE
31SWE ANGENÄM

32AAA AIR, TUNE
32CZE ÁRIE, PÍSEŇ
32DAN ARIE
32DUT ARIA
32FRE AIR
32GER ARIE, LIED
32HUN ÉNEK, ÁRIA
32ITA ARIA
32POL ARIA, PIEŚŇ
32POR ÁRIA
32RUS ARIÏA
32SPA AIRE
32SWE ARIA, SÅNG

33AAA ALEATORY
33CZE ALEATORNÍ
33DAN UVIS
33DUT UVIS
33FRE ALÉATOIRE
33GER ALEATORISCH
33HUN VÉLETLEN
33ITA ALEATORIO
33POL PRZYPADLOWY
33POR ALEATÓRIO
33RUS ALEATORICHESKAIA
33SPA ALEATORIO
33SWE ALEATORISK

34AAA ALL
34CZE VŠICHNI
34DAN ALLE
34DUT ALLEN
34FRE TOUT
34GER ALLE
34HUN MINDEN
34ITA TUTTI
34POL WSZYSCY
34POR TODO
34RUS VES', VSIAKII
34SPA TODO
34SWE ALLA

35AAA ALLEGORY
35CZE ALEGORIE
35DAN ALLEGORI
35DUT ALLEGORIE
35FRE ALLÉGORIE
35GER ALLEGORIE
35HUN JELKÉP
35ITA ALLEGORIA
35POL ALEGORIA
35POR ALEGORIA
35RUS ALLEGORIIA
35SPA ALEGORÍA
35SWE ALLEGORI

36AAA ALLEMAND, ALMAN
36CZE ALEMANDA
36DAN ALLEMANDE
36DUT ALLEMANDE
36FRE ALLEMANDE
36GER ALLEMANDE
36HUN ALLEMANDE
36ITA ALLEMANDA
36POL ALLAMANDE
36POR ALEMANDA
36RUS ALLEMANDA
36SPA ALEMANDA
36SWE ALLEMANDE

37AAA ALMOST
37CZE SKORO
37DAN LIGESOM
37DUT BIJNA
37FRE PRESQUE, QUASI
37GER GLEICHSAM
37HUN MINTEGY
37ITA QUASI
37POL NIEMAL
37POR QUASE
37RUS KAK BY
37SPA CASI
37SWE NÄSTAN

38AAA ALONE
38CZE SÁM
38DAN ALENE
38DUT ALLEEN
38FRE SEUL, SOLO
38GER ALLIEN, SOLO
38HUN EGYEDÜL
38ITA SOLO
38POL SAM
38POR SÓ
38RUS ODIN
38SPA SOLO
38SWE ENSAM

39AAA ALREADY
39CZE JIŽ, UŽ
39DAN ALLEREDE
39DUT AL
39FRE DÉJÀ
39GER SCHON
38HUN MÁR
39ITA GIÀ
39POL JUZ
39POR JÁ
39RUS UZHE
39SPA YA
39SWE REDAN

40AAA ALSO
40CZE TAKÉ, TÉŽ
40DAN OGSÅ
40DUT OOK
40FRE AUSSI, ENCORE
40GER NOCH(MALS)
40HUN NYELV
40ITA ANCHE
40POL TAKŻE
40POR TAMBÉM
40RUS TOZHE
40SPA TAMBIÉN, ADEMÁS
40SWE OCKSÅ

41AAA ALTERATION
41CZE ALTEROVÁNÍ
41DAN FORANDRING
41DUT ALTERATIE
41FRE ALTERATION
41GER VERÄNDERUNG
41HUN ALTERÁCIÓ
41ITA ALTERAZIONE
41POL ALTERACJA
41POR ALTERAÇÃO
41RUS ALTERATSIIA
41SPA ALTERACIÓN
41SWE FÖRÄNDRING

42AAA ALTERNATE, TO
42CZE STŘÍDATI
42DAN AFVEKSLENDE
42DUT AFWISSELEN
42FRE ALTERNER
43GER ALTERNIEREN
42HUN FELVÁLTANI
42ITA ALTERNARE
42POL ZMIENIAĆ
42POR ALTERNAR
42RUS CHEREDOVAT'
42SPA ALTERNAR
42SWE OMVÄXLANDE

43AAA ALTER, TO
43CZE ALTEROVATI
43DAN FORANDRE
43DUT VERANDEREN
43FRE ALTÉRER
43GER ALTERIEREN
43HUN MÓDOSÍTNI
43ITA ALTERARE
43POL ZMIENIAĆ
43POR ALTERAR
43RUS IZMENIAT'
43SPA ALTERAR
43SWE FÖRÄNDRA

44AAA ALWAYS
44CZE STÁLE, POŘÁD
44DAN STEDSE
44DUT STEEDS, ALTIJD
44FRE TOUJOURS
44GER IMMER
44HUN MINDIG
44ITA SEMPRE
44POL ZAWSZE
44POR SEMPRE
44RUS VSE VREMIA
44SPA SIEMPRE
44SWE ALLTID

45AAA AMIABLE
45CZE ROZTOMILÝ
45DAN ELSKVAERDIG
45DUT LIEFELIJK
45FRE AIMABLE
45GER ANGENEHM, LIEBLICH
45HUN KEDVESEN, GYENGÉDEN
45ITA AMABILE
45POL POGODNIE
45POR AMÁVEL
45RUS LIUBEZNYĬ
45SPA AMABLE
45SWE ÄLSKVÄRT

46AAA AMOROUS
46CZE ZAMILOVANÝ, MILOSTNÝ
46DAN ØMT, INDERLIGT
46DUT VERLIEFD, TEDER
46FRE AMOUREUX
46GER INNIG, ZÄRTLICH
46HUN GYENGÉDEN
46ITA AMOROSO
46POL MIŁOSNIE
46POR AMOROSO
46RUS LIUBOVNO
46SPA AMOROSO
46SWE FÖRÄLSKAD

47AAA AMORPHOUS
47CZE AMORFNÍ
47DAN AMORF
47DUT AMORF
47FRE AMORPHE
47GER AMORPH
47HUN ALAKTALAN
47ITA AMORFO
47POL AMORFICZNY
47POR AMORFO
47RUS AMORFNYĬ
47SPA AMORFO
47SWE AMORF

48AAA AMPLIFY, TO
48CZE ROZŠIŘOVATI
48DAN UDVIDE
48DUT WIJDTE
48FRE AMPLIFIER
48GER ERWEITERN
48HUN BŐVITENI
48ITA AMPLIFICARE
48POL ROZSZERZAĆ
48POR AMPLIFICAR
48RUS RASCHIRIAT'
48SPA AMPLIAR
48SWE UTVIDGA

49AAA AMPLITUDE
49CZE AMPLITUDA
49DAN VIDDE
49DUT WIJDTE
49FRE AMPLITUDE
49GER AMPLITUDE
49HUN BŐVITÉS
49ITA AMPLITUDINE
49POL AMPLITUDA
49POR AMPLITUDA
49RUS AMPLITUDA
49SPA AMPLITUD
49SWE VIDD

50AAA ANALYZE, TO
50CZE ANALYZOVATI
50DAN ANALYSERE
50DUT ANALYSEREN
50FRE ANALYSER
50GER ANALYSIEREN
50HUN TAGLALNI, ELEMEZNI
50ITA ANALIZZARE
50POL ANALIZOWAĆ
50POR ANALISAR
50RUS ANALIZIROVAT'
50SPA ANALIZAR
50SWE ANALYSERA

51AAA AND
51CZE E(D)
51DAN OG
51DUT EN
51FRE ET
51GER UND
51HUN ÉS
51ITA E(D)
51POL I
51POR E
51RUS I
51SPA Y
51SWE OCH

52AAA ANGRY
52CZE ROZHNĚVANÝ
52DAN VREDAGTIG
52DUT BOOS, WOEDEND
52FRE BOURRASQUE
52GER ZORNIG
52HUN HARAGOS
52ITA ADIRATA
52POL GNIEWNY
52POR IRADO
52RUS GNEV
52SPA IRACUNDA
52SWE FÖRARGLIG

53AAA ANGUISH
53CZE ÚZKOST
53DAN SMERTE
53DUT ONRUSTIG
53FRE ANGOISSE
53GER SCHMERZ, ANGST
53HUN SZORONGATÁS
53ITA ANGOSCIA
53POL MĘKA
53POR ANGÚSTIA
53RUS MUKA, BOL'
53SPA ANGUSTIA
53SWE SMÄRTA

54AAA ANIMATED
54CZE ŽIVÝ
54DAN VARME
54DUT BEZIELT
54FRE ANIMÉ
54GER BELEBT
54HUN ÉLÉNK
54ITA ANIMATO
54POL Z ŻYCIEM
54POR ANIMADO
54RUS OZHIVLĔNNO
54SPA ANIMADO
54SWE LIVAKTIG

55AAA ANNOTATION
55CZE POZNÁMKA
55DAN NOTERING
55DUT ANNOTATIE
55FRE ANNOTATION
55GER ANMERKUNG
55HUN MEGJEGYZÉS
55ITA ANNOTAZIONE
55POL ANNOTACJA
55POR ANNOTAÇÃO
55RUS ANNOTATSIIA
55SPA ANOTACIÓN
55SWE ANNOTATION

56AAA ANNUAL
56CZE ROČNÍ
56DAN ÅRLIG
56DUT JAARLIJKS
56FRE ANNUEL
56GER JÄHRLICH
56HUN ÉVI, ÉVENKÉNT
56ITA ANNUALE
56POL ROCZNY
56POR ANUAL
56RUS GODOVOĬ
56SPA ANUAL
56SWE ÅRLIG

57AAA ANSWER
57CZE ODPOVĚD
57DAN SVAR
57DUT ANTWOORD
57FRE RÉPONSE
57GER ANTWORT
57HUN FELELET
57ITA RISPOSTA
57POL ODPOWIEDŹ
57POR RESPONSO
57RUS RISPOSTA
57SPA REPUESTA, RESPONSO
57SWE SVAR

58AAA ANTECEDENT
58CZE PŘEDCHÁZEJÍCÍ
58DAN FORUDGÅENDE
58DUT VOORAFGAAND(E)
58FRE ANTECÉDENT
58GER VORHERGEHEND
58HUN MEGELŐZŐ
58ITA ANTECEDENTE
58POL ANTECEDENCJA
58POR ANTECEDENTE
58RUS ANTETSEDENT
58SPA ANTECEDENTE
58SWE FÖREGÅENDE

59AAA ANTHEM, ANTIPHON(E)
59CZE ANTIFONA
59DAN KIRKESANG, HYMNE
59DUT KERKZANG, BEURTZANG
59FRE ANTIPHONIE
59GER ANTIPHON(IE)
59HUN KERETVERS
59ITA ANTIFONA
59POL ANTYFONA
59POR ANTIFONO
59RUS HYMN, PENIE
59SPA ANTÍFONO
59SWE ANTIFONI

60AAA ANTHOLOGY
60CZE ANTOLOGIE
60DAN ANTOLOGI
60DUT ANT(H)OLOGIE
60FRE ANTHOLOGIE
60GER ANTHOLOGIE
60HUN ANTOLÓGIA
60ITA ANTOLOGIA
60POL ANTOLOGIA
60POR ANTOLOGIA
60RUS ANTOLOGIIA
60SPA ANTOLOGÍA
60SWE ANTOLOGI

61AAA ANTI-
61CZE ANTI-
61DAN ANTI-
61DUT TEGEN-
61FRE ANTI-
61GER GEGEN-
61HUN ELLEN-
61ITA ANTI-
61POL ANTY-
61POR ANTI-
61RUS ANTI-
61SPA ANTI-
61SWE ANTI-

62AAA ANTICIPATION
62CZE ANTICIPACE
62DAN ANTICIPATION
62DUT ANTICIPATIO
62FRE ANTICIPATION
62GER ANTIZIPATION
62HUN ANTICIPÁTIÓ
62ITA ANTICIPAZIONE
62POL ANTYCYPACJA
62POR ANTICIPATION
62RUS OZHIDANIE
62SPA ANTICIPACIÓN
62SWE INTRÄDANDE I FÖRTID

63AAA ANVIL
63CZE KOVADLINA
63DAN AMBOLT
63DUT AANBEELD
63FRE ENCLUME
63GER AMBOSS
63HUN ÜLLŐ
63ITA INCUDINE
63POL KOWADŁO
63POR BIGORNA, INCUDE
63RUS NAKOVAL'NIA
63SPA YUNQUE, BIGORNETA
63SWE STÄD

64AAA ANXIOUS
64CZE ÚZKOSTNĚ
64DAN AENGSTELIG
64DUT ONRUSTIG
64FRE ANXIEUX
64GER ÄNGSTLICH
64HUN FÉLÉNK
64ITA ANGOSCIOSO
64POL NIESPOKOJNIE
64POR ANSIOSO
64RUS TREVOZHNYĬ
64SPA ANSIOSO
64SWE ÄNGSLIG

65AAA APPENDIX
65CZE DODATEK, PŘÍVĚSEK
65DAN BILAG
65DUT AANHANGEL
65FRE APPENDICE
65GER ANHANG
65HUN FÜGGELÉK
65ITA APPENDICE
65POL APENDYKS, DODATEK
65POR APÊNDICE
65RUS APPENDIKS
65SPA APÉNDICE
65SWE BIHANG

66AAA APPLAUSE
66CZE POTLESK, SOUHLAS
66DAN APPLAUS
66DUT APPLAUS
66FRE APPLAUDISSEMENTS
66GER APPLAUS
66HUN MEGTAPSOLÁS
66ITA APPLAUSO
66POL APLAUZ, OKLASKI
66POR APLAUSO
66RUS APLODISMENTY
66SPA APLAUSO
66SWE APPLÅDER

67AAA APPRECIATION
67CZE OCENĚNÍ
67DAN VURDERING
67DUT VAARDERING
67FRE APPRECIATION
67GER WÜRDIGUNG
67HUN MÉLTÁNYLÁT
67ITA APPREZZAMENTO
67POL OCENA
67POR APRECIÇÃO
67RUS OTSENIT'
67SPA APRECIO
67SWE VÄRDERING

68AAA ARABESK
68CZE ARABESKA
68DAN ARABESK
68DUT ARABESK
68FRE ARABESQUE
68GER ARABESKE
68HUN ARABDÍSZ
68ITA ARABESCA
68POL ARABSKI
68POR ARABÊSCO
68RUS ARABESKA
68SPA ARABESCO
68SWE ARABESK

69AAA ARCHIVE(S)
69CZE ARCHÍV
69DAN ARKIV
69DUT ARCHIEF
69FRE ARCHIVES
69GER ARCHIV
69HUN LEVÉLTÁR
69ITA ARCHIVIO
69POL ARCHIWUM
69POR ARGUIVOS
69RUS ARKHIV
69SPA ARCHIVOS
69SWE ARKIV

70AAA ARDOR
70CZE ŽÁR, ŽHAVOST
70DAN HEDE
70DUT HITTE
70FRE ARDEUR
70GER HITZE, EIFER
70HUN HÉV
70ITA ARDORE
70POL ŻAR
70POR ARDOR
70RUS ZHAR
70SPA ARDOR
70SWE HETTA

71AAA ARM
71CZE PAŽE, RÁMĚ
71DAN ARM
71DUT ARM
71FRE BRAS
71GER ARM
71HUN KAR
71ITA BRACCIO
71POL RAMIĘ
71POR BRAÇO
71RUS RUKA
71SPA BRAZO
71SWE ARM

72AAA ARPEGGIATE, TO
72CZE ARPEDŽOVATI
72DAN ARPEGGERE
72DUT HARPACHTEN
72FRE ARPÉGER
72GER ARPEGGIEREN
72HUN HÁRFÁZNI
72ITA ARPEGGIARE
72POL GRAC ARPEDZDJO
72POR ARPEJAR
72RUS BRAT' ARPEDZHIO
72SPA ARPEGIAR
72SWE SPELA HARPMASSIGT

73AAA ARPEGGIO
73CZE ARPEDŽO
73DAN HARPEGGIO
73DUT HARPACTIG
73FRE ARPÈGE
73GER VON ARPEGGIARE
73HUN TÖRT AKKORD
73ITA ARPEGGIO
73POL ARPEDZDJO
73POR ARPEJO
73RUS ARPEDZHIO
73SPA ARPEGIO
73SWE HARPMÄSSIGT

74AAA ARRANGE, TO
74CZE UPRAVITI
74DAN ARRANGERE
74DUT ARRANGEREN
74FRE ARRANGER
74GER ARRANGIEREN
74HUN ÁTIRNI
74ITA ARRANGIARE, RIDURRE
74POL ARANŻOWAĆ
74POR ARRANHAR
74RUS ARANZHIROVAT'
74SPA ARREGLAR
74SWE ARRANGERA

75AAA ARRANGEMENT
75CZE ÚPRAVA
75DAN ARRANGEMENT
75DUT ZETTING
75FRE ARRANGEMENT
75GER ARRANGEMENT
75HUN ÁTÍRÁS
75ITA RIDUZIONE
75POL ARANZACJA
75POR ARRANJO
75RUS ARANZHIROVKA
75SPA ARREGLO
75SWE ARRANGEMANG

76AAA ART
76CZE UMĚNÍ, ŠIKOVNOST
76DAN KUNST
76DUT ARS, KUNST
76FRE ART
76GER KUNST
76HUN MŰVÉSZET
76ITA ARTE
76POL SZTUKA
76POR ARTE
76RUS ISKUSSTVO
76SPA ARTE
76SWE KONST

77AAA ARTICULATE, TO
77CZE ARTIKULOVATI
77DAN ARTIKULERE
77DUT ARTICULEREN
77FRE ARTICULER
77GER ARTIKULIEREN
77HUN ARTIKULÁLNI
77ITA ARTICOLARE
77POL ARTYKUŁOWAĆ
77POR ARTICULAR
77RUS ARTIKULIROVAT'
77SPA ARTICULAR
77SWE ARTIKULERA

78AAA AS
78CZE JAKO
78DAN LIGESOM
78DUT HOE, ZOALS
78FRE COMME, PRESQUE
78GER WIE
78HUN UGY
78ITA COME (SE), QUASI
78POL JAK
78POR COMO
78RUS KAK
78SPA COMO
78SWE LIKSOM

79AAA ASCEND, TO
79CZE STOUPATI
79DAN STIGE OP
79DUT OPGAAN, BEKLIMMEN
79FRE ASCENSIONNER
79GER AUFSTEIGEN
79HUN FELMENNI
79ITA ASCENDERE
79POL PODNIEŚĆ
79POR ASCENDER
79RUS PODNIMAT'SÍA
79SPA ASCENDER
79SWE BESTIGA

80AAA ASPERITY
80CZE DRSNOST
80DAN BARSKHED
80DUT RUWHEID
80FRE ÂPRETÉ
80GER RAUHEIT, SCHROFFHEIT
80HUN ZORDONSÁG
80ITA ASPERITÀ
80POL OSTROŚĆ
80POR ASPEREZA, ASPERIDADE
80RUS REZKOST'
80SPA ASPEREZA
80SWE STRÄVHET

81AAA ASPIRATE, TO
81CZE ASPIROVATI
81DAN INDAANDE
81DUT AANGEBLAZEN
81FRE ASPIRER
81GER ASPIRIEREN
81HUN BEHEZETESEN
81ITA ASPIRARE
81POL ASPIROWAĆ
81POR ASPIRAR
81RUS VDYZHAT'
81SPA ASPIRAR
81SWE LÄNGTA

82AAA ASSOCIATE, TO
82CZE DRUŽOVATI
82DAN FORBUNDEN
82DUT VERBINDEN
82FRE ASSOCIER
82GER VERBÜNDEN
82HUN EGYESULNI
82ITA ASSOCIAR
82POL POŁĄCZYĆ
82POR ASSOCIAR
82RUS ASSOTSIIROVAT'
82SPA ASOCIAR
82SWE FÖRBUNDEN

83AAA AT
83CZE NA
83DAN PA
83DUT TOT
83FRE À
83GER IN, AN, BEI
83HUN -N, -ON, -EN
83ITA A
83POL NA
83POR A
83RUS NA
83SPA A(L)
83SWE PÅ

84AAA ATTACK
84CZE ÚTOK
84DAN ANGREB
84DUT AANVAL
84FRE ATTAQUE
84GER ATTACKE, EINSATZ
84HUN MEGTAMÁDÁS
84ITA ATTACCA
84POL ATAK
84POR ATAQUE
84RUS ATAKA
84SWE ANGREEP

85AAA ATTACK, TO
85CZE ZAČÍTI, SPUSTITI
85DAN ANGRIBE
85DUT AANVALLEN
85FRE ATTAQUER
85GER ANGREIFFEN
85HUN MEGTÁMADNI
85ITA ATTACCARE
85POL ATAKOWAĆ
85POR ATACAR
85RUS ATAKOVAT'
85SPA ATACAR
85SWE ANGRIPA

86AAA AT WILL
86CZE PO VŮLE
86DAN EFTER BEHAG
86DUT NAAR GOEDDUNKEN
86FRE À VOLONTÉ
86GER NACH BELIEBEN
86HUN TETSZÉS SZERINT
86ITA A PIACERE
86POL DOWOLNIE
86POR A VONTADE
86RUS PO ZHELANIIU
86SPA A VOLUNTAD
86SWE EFTER BEHAG

87AAA AUDACIOUS
87CZE SMĚLÁ, ODVÁŽNÁ
87DAN DRISTIG
87DUT DURF
87FRE AUDACIEUX
87GER KÜHN, HERZHAFT
87HUN MERÉSZEN
87ITA AUDACE
87POL ŚMIAŁY
87POR AUDACIOSO
87RUS SMELYĬ
87SPA AUDAZ
87SWE DRISTIG

88AAA AUDIENCE
88CZE AUDIENCE
88DAN AUDIENS
88DUT AUDIËNTIE
88FRE AUDIENCE
88GER AUDIENZ
88HUN MEGHALLGATÁS
88ITA UDIENZA
88POL AUDIENCJA
88POR AUDIÊNCIA
88RUS AUDIENTSIIA
88SPA AUDIENCIA
88SWE AUDIENS

89AAA AUGMENT, TO   93AAA AUTHOR
89CZE ZVĚTŠITI   93CZE AUTOR
89DAN FORØGE   93DAN FORFATTER
89DUT VERMEERDEREN   93DUT AUTEUR
89FRE AUGMENTER   93FRE AUTEUR
89GER VERMEHREN, WACHSEN   93GER SCHRIFTSTELLER
89HUN SZAPORÍTANI   93HUN SZERZŐ
89ITA AUMENTARE   93ITA AUTORE
89POL DODOWAĆ, AUGMENT DO   93POL AUTOR
89POR AUMENTAR   93POR AUTOR
89RUS UVELICHIVAT'   93RUS AVTOR
89SPA AUMENTAR   93SPA AUTOR
89SWE FÖRÖKA   93SWE FÖRFATTARE

90AAA AUGMENTATION   94AAA AWAKEN, TO
90CZE AUGMENTATIVUM   94CZE PROBUDITI
90DAN FORØGELSE   94DAN VAEKKE
90DUT AUGMENTATIO   94DUT WEKKEN
90FRE AUGMENTATION   94FRE ÉVEILLER
90GER AUGMENTATION   94GER ERWACHEN, ERWECKEN
90HUN AUGMENTÁCIÓ   94HUN FELEBREDNI
90ITA AUMENTAZIONE   94ITA SVEGLIARE
90POL AUGMENTACJA   94POL PRZEBUDZIĆ
90POR AUMENTAÇÃO   94POR DESPERTAR
90RUS SUVELICHENIE   94RUS BUDIT'
90SPA AUMENTACIÓN   94SPA DESPERTAR
90SWE FÖRSTORING   94SWE VAKNA

91AAA AURAL   95AAA BABY GRAND
91CZE UŠNÍ   95CZE MALÉ KŘÍDLO
91DAN HØRELSE   95DAN KABINETSFLYGEL
91DUT OOR   95DUT KLEINE VLEUGEL
91FRE AURICULAIRE   95FRE PIANO DEMI-QUEUE
91GER HÖRBAR   95GER STUTSFLÜGEL
91HUN FÜLI   95HUN ZONGORASZO
91ITA DELL' ORECCHIO   95ITA PIANO A MEZZACODA
91POL AURALNY   95POL MAŁY FORTEPIAN
91POR AURICULAR   95POR PIANO A 1/4 DE CAUDA
91RUS USHNOĬ   95RUS KABINETNYĬ ROIAL'
91SPA AURICULAR   95SPA PIANO DE MEDIA COLA
91SWE HÖRSEL-   95SWE KABINETTSFLYGEL

92AAA AUTHENTIC   96AAA BACKGROUND
92CZE AUTENTICKÝ   96CZE POZADÍ
92DAN AUTENTISK   96DAN BAGGRUND
92DUT AUTHENTIEK   96DUT ACHTERGRUND
92FRE AUTHENTIQUE   96FRE FOND
92GER AUTHENTISCH   96GER HINTERGRUND
92HUN HITELES, AUTENTIKUS   96HUN HÁTTÉR
92ITA AUTENTICA   96ITA S FONDO
92POL AUTENTYCZNY   96POL TŁO
92POR AUTHÊNTICO   96POR FUNDO
92RUS AUTENTICHNYĬ   96RUS FON
92SPA AUTENTICA   96SPA FONDO
92SWE AUTENTISK   96SWE BAKGRUND

97AAA BAGATELLE   101AAA BALLAD(E)
97CZE BAGATELA   101CZE BALADA
97DAN BAGATEL   101DAN BALLADE
97DUT BAGATEL(LA)   101DUT BALLADE
97FRE BAGATELLE   101FRE BALLADE
97GER KLEINIGKEIT   101GER BALLADE
97HUN POTOMSÁG   101HUN REGEDAL
97ITA BAGATTELLA   101ITA BALLATA
97POL BAGATÉL   101POL BALLADA
97POR BAGATELA   101POR BALADA
97RUS BEZDELKA, MELOCH'   101RUS BALLADA
97SPA BAGATELA   101SPA BALADA
97SWE BAGATELL   101SWE BALLAD

98AAA BAGPIPE(S)   102AAA BALLET
98CZE DUDY   102CZE BALET
98DAN SAEKEPIBE   102DAN BALLET
98DUT DOEDELZAK, ZAKPIJP   102DUT BALLET
98FRE CORNEMUSE   102FRE BALLET
98GER DUDELSACK, SACKPFEIFE   102GER BALLETT
98HUN DUDA   102HUN TÁNCZJÁTÉK
98ITA CORNAMUSA   102ITA BALLETTO
98POL DUD(Y)   102POL BALET
98POR CORNAMUSA   102POR BAILADO
98RUS VOLYNKA   102RUS BALET
98SPA GAITA, CORNAMUSA   102SPA BAILETE, BAILETO
98SWE SÄCKPIPA   102SWE BALETT

99AAA BALANCE, TO   103AAA BAMBOO
99CZE BALANCOVATI, HOUPATI   103CZE BAMBUS
99DAN BALANCERE   103DAN BAMBUS
99DUT BALANCEREN   103DUT BAMBOE
99FRE BALANCER   103FRE BAMBOU
99GER BALANCIEREN   103GER BAMBUS
99HUN HANGREMEGTETÉS   103HUN BAMBUSZNÁD
99ITA BILANCIARE   103ITA BAMBÙ
99POL BALANSOWAĆ   103POL BAMBUS
99POR BALANGAR   103POR BAMBU
99RUS BALANSIROVAT'   103RUS BAMBUK
99SPA BALANCEAR   103SPA BAMBÚ
99SWE BALANCERA   103SWE BAMBURÖR

100AAA BALL   104AAA BAND
100CZE BÁL, PLES   104CZE HUDEBNÍ SBOR, KAPELA
100DAN BAL   104DAN MUSIKKORPS
100DUT BAL   104DUT MUZIEKCORPS
100FRE BAL   104FRE BANDE
100GER BALL, TANZ   104GER BANDA, KAPELLE
100HUN TÁNC   104HUN BANDA, ZENETÁRSASÁG
100ITA BALLO   104ITA BANDA
100POL BAL   104POL BANDA, KAPELA
100POR BAILA   104POR BANDA
100RUS BAL   104RUS ORKESTR
100SPA BAILE   104SPA BANDA
100SWE DANS   104SWE MUSIKKÅR

105AAA BANJO   109AAA BARCAROLLE
105CZE BENDŽO   109CZE BARKAROLA
105DAN BANJO   109DAN BARCAROLE
105DUT NEGERGITAAR   109DUT BARCAROLLE
105FRE BANJO   109FRE BARCAROLLE
105GER NEGERGUITARRE   109GER BARCAROLE, BARKAROLE
105HUN GITÁRSZERU HANGSZER   109HUN GONDOLIERA
105ITA CHITARRA DEI NEGRI   109ITA BARCAROLA
105POL RODZAJ GITARY   109POL BARKAROLA
105POR BANJO   109POR BARCAROLA
105RUS BANDZHO   109RUS BARKAROLA
105SPA BANJO   109SPA BARCAROLA, BARAROLOA
105SWE BANJO   109SWE BARKAROL

106AAA BANTER, TO   110AAA BARD
106CZE LAŠKOVATI   110CZE BARD
106DAN SKAEMTE, SPØGE   110DAN BARDE
106DUT SCHERTSEN   110DUT BARD
106FRE BADINER   110FRE BARDE
106GER SCHERZEN   110GER BARDE
106HUN INCSELKEDVE   110HUN BARD, DALNOK
106ITA MOTTEGIARE   110ITA BARDO
106POL ZAŻARTOWAĆ   110POL BARD
106POR BURLAR   110POR BARDO
106RUS SHUTIT'   110RUS BARD
106SPA BURLAR   110SPA BARDO
106SWE SKÄMTA   110SWE BARD

107AAA BAR   111AAA BARITONE
107CZE TAKT   111CZE BARYTON
107DAN TAKT   111DAN BARYTON
107DUT MATTSTREEP   111DUT BARITON
107FRE MESURE, BARRE   111FRE BARYTON
107GER TAKT(STRICH)   111GER BARITON
107HUN ÜTEM   111HUN BARITON
107ITA BARRA, BATTUTA   111ITA BARITONO
107POL TAKT   111POL BARYTON
107POR BARRA   111POR BARÍTONO
107RUS BAR'ER   111RUS BARITON
107SPA BARRA   111SPA BARÍTONO
107SWE TAKT(STRECK)   111SWE BARYTON

108AAA BARBAROUS   112AAA BAROQUE
108CZE BARBARSKÝ   112CZE BAROKNÍ
108DAN BARBARISK   112DAN BAROK
108DUT BARBAARS   112DUT BAROK
108FRE BARBARE   112FRE BAROQUE
108GER BARBARISCH   112GER BARO(C)K
108HUN KEGYETLEN   112HUN BAROK
108ITA BARBARO   112ITA BAROCCO
108POL BARBARZYŃSKI   112POL BAROK
108POR BÁRBARO   112POR BAR(R)OCO
108RUS VARVARSKIŸ   112RUS BAROKKO
108SPA BÁRBARO   112SPA BARROCO
108SWE BARBARISKT   112SWE BAROK, SÄLLSOMT

113AAA BARREL-ORGAN
113CZE KOLOVRÁTEK
113DAN LIREKASSE
113DUT DRAAIORGEL
113FRE ORGUE DE BARBARIE
113GER LEIERKASTEN, DREHORGEL
113HUN KINTORNA
113ITA ORGANETTO A CILINDRO
113POL KATARYNKA
113POR REALEJO
113RUS SHARMANKA
113SPA ORGANILLO
113SWE POSITIV

114AAA BASS
114CZE BAS
114DAN BAS
114DUT BAS
114FRE BASSE, BAS
114GER BASS
114HUN BASSZUS
114ITA BASSO
114POL BAS
114POR BAIXO
114RUS BAS
114SPA BAJO
114SWE BAS

115AAA BASSET-HORN
115CZE BASETOVÝ ROH
115DAN VENTILHORN
115DUT BASSETHOORN
115FRE COR DE BASSET
115GER BASSETTHORN
115HUN BASSZETKÜRT
115ITA CORNO DI BASSETTO
115POL KLARNET ALTOWY
115POR CLARINETE ALTO
115RUS KLARNET BASOVYÏ
115SPA CLARINETTE ALTO
115SWE VENTILHORN

116AAA BASSOON
116CZE FAGOT
116DAN FAGOT
116DUT FAGOT
116FRE BASSON
116GER FAGOTT
116HUN FAGOTT
116ITA FAGOTTO, BASSONE
116POL FAGOT
116POR FAGOTE
116RUS FAGOT
116SPA BAJÓN, FAGOTE
116SWE FAGOTT

117AAA BATON, STICK
117CZE TAKTOVKA
117DAN TAKTSTOK
117DUT MATTSTOK
117FRE BÂTON
117GER TAKTSTO(C)K
117HUN KARMESTERI PÁLCA
117ITA BACCHETTA, BASTONE
117POL PAŁECZKA
117POR BATUTA
117RUS PALKA, PALOCHKA
117SPA BATUTA
117SWE TAKTPINNE, BATTONG

118AAA BATTERY
118CZE BATERIE, BUBNOVÁNÍ
118DAN BATTERI
118DUT BATTERIE
118FRE BATTERIE
118GER BATTERIE
118HUN ÜTEG
118ITA BATTERIA
118POL BATERIA
118POR BATERIA
118RUS BATEREÍA
118SPA BATERÍA
118SWE BATTERI

119AAA BEAT
119CZE TAKT
119DAN SLAG
119DUT MATTSLAG
119FRE BATTEMENT
119GER SCHLAG, TAKTTEIL
119HUN ÜTES
119ITA BATTIMENTO, BATTUTO
119POL TAKT
119POR BATIDA
119RUS TAKT
119SPA BATIDA
119SWE TAKTSLAG

120AAA BEAT A DRUM, TO
120CZE BÍTI BUBEN
120DAN SLAA PAA TROMME
120DUT SLAAN, UITSLAAN
120FRE BATTRE LE TAMBOUR
120GER SCHLAGEN
120HUN A SZÍV DOBOG
120ITA SONARE IL TAMBURO
120POL BIĆ NA BUBEN
120POR BATER
120RUS BIT' V BARABAN
120SPA BATIR
120SWE LJUDA

121AAA BEAT TIME, TO
121CZE DÁVATI TAKT
121DAN SLAA TAKT
121DUT DE MATT SLAAN
121FRE BATTRE LA MESURE
121GER TAKTIEREN
121HUN TAKTUST JELEZ
121ITA BATTERE LA MISURE
121POL WYBIJAĆ TAKT
121POR BATER O COMPASSO
121RUS OTBIVAT' TAKT
121SPA BATIR EL COMPAS
121SWE SLÅ TAKTEN

122AAA BEAUTY
122CZE KRÁSA
122DAN SKØNHED
122DUT SCHOONHEID
122FRE BEAUTÉ
122GER SCHONHEIT
122HUN SZÉPSÉG
122ITA BELLEZZA
122POL PIĘKNO
122POR BELEZA
122RUS KRASOTA
122SPA BELLEZA, HERMOSURA
122SWE SKÖNHET

123AAA BEFORE
123CZE PŘED
123DAN FØR
123DUT VÓÓR
123FRE AVANT
123GER VORHER
123HUN ELŐTT
123ITA AVANTI
123POL PRZED
123POR ANTES
123RUS VPEREDI
123SPA ANTES
123SWE FÖRE

124AAA BEGIN, COMMENCE, TO
124CZE ZAČITI
124DAN BEGYNDE
124DUT BEGINNEN
124FRE COMMENCER
124GER ANFANGEN
124HUN KEZDENI
124ITA COMINCIARE
124POL ZACZYNAĆ
124POR COMEÇAR
124RUS NACHINAT'
124SPA EMPEZAR, COMENZAR
124SWE BEGYNNA

125AAA BELL
125CZE ZVON
125DAN KLOKKE
125DUT KLOK
125FRE CLOCHE
125GER GLOCKE
125HUN CSONGÓ
125ITA CAMPANA, PADIGLIONE
125POL DZWON(EK)
125POR CAMPAINHA
125RUS ZVONOK
125SPA CAMPANA
125SWE KLOCKA

126AAA BELL(OF INSTRUMENT)
126CZE OZVUČNÍK, ROZTRUB
126DAN LYDSTYK
126DUT BEKER
126FRE PAVILLON
126GER SCHALLTRICHTER
126HUN KERTIHÁZ
126ITA CAMPANE
126POL DZWONKI
126POR PAVILHÃO
126RUS PAVIL'ON
126SPA PABELLON
126SWE KYRKKLOCKE, KLOCKOR

127AAA BELLOWS
127CZE MĚCH
127DAN BLAESEBAELG
127DUT BLASSBALG
127FRE SOUFFLETS
127GER BLASEBALG
127HUN FUVÓ
127ITA SOFFIETTO, MANTICE
127POL MIECH
127POR FOLE
127RUS MEKHÝ
127SPA FUELLE
127SWE BLÅSBÄLG

128AAA BELOW
128CZE POD
128DAN UNDER
128DUT ONDER
128FRE SOUS
128GER UNTER
128HUN ALUL
128ITA SOTTO
128POL POD CZEM
128POR ABAIXO
128RUS POD
128SPA DEBAJO
128SWE UNDER

129AAA BINARY
129CZE DVOJDÍLNÝ, PODVOJNÝ
129DAN BINAER
129DUT BINAIR
129FRE BINAIRE
129GER BINÄR
129HUN KÉT
129ITA BINARIO
129POL DWÓJKOWY
129POR BINÁRIO
129RUS DVOĬNOĬ
129SPA BINARIO
129SWE DUBBEL-

130AAA BIPARTITE
130CZE DVOJSTRANNÝ
130DAN TVEDELT
130DUT TWEEDELIG
130FRE BIPARTI
130GER ZWEITEILIG
130HUN KÉTRÉSZŰ
130ITA BIPARTITO
130POL DWUDZIELNY
130POR BIPARTIDO
130RUS DVUKHCHASTNAĬA
130SPA BIPARTIDO
130SWE TVETALIG

131AAA BITTER
131CZE HOŘKÝ
131DAN BITTER
131DUT BITTER
131FRE AMER
131GER BITTER
131HUN KESERÜ
131ITA AMARO
131POL GORZKI
131POR AMARGOR
131RUS GORKIĬ
131SPA AMARGO
131SWE BITTER

132AAA BIZARRE, ODD
132CZE BIZÁRNÍ
132DAN BIZAR
132DUT BIZAR
132FRE BIZARRE
132GER BIZARR
132HUN BIZARR
132ITA BIZZARRO
132POL BIZARRO
132POR ESTRAMBOTICO
132RUS STRANNYĬ
132SPA BIZARRO
132SWE BISARR

133AAA BLACK
133CZE ČERNÝ
133DAN SORT
133DUT ZWART
133FRE NOIRE
133GER SCHWARZ
133HUN FEKETE
133ITA NERO
133POL CZARNY
133POR NEGRO, PRÊTO
133RUS CHĚRNYĬ
133SPA NEGRA, PRIETO
133SWE SVART

134AAA BLARE, TO
134CZE HRÁTI KOVOVÝM TÓNEM
134DAN GJALDE
134DUT SCHALLEN, SCHETTEREN
134FRE CUIVRER LE SON
134GER SCHMETTERN, SCHALLEN
134HUN HARSOGATNI
134ITA SQUILLARE
134POL TRĄBIĆ
134POR CLANGORAR
134RUS TRUBY GREMIAT
134SPA RIMBOMBAR
134SWE SMATTRA

135AAA BLEND, TO
135CZE MÍCHATI
135DAN BLENDE
135DUT MENGEN
135FRE SE MÊLER
135GER VERMISCHEN
135HUN ÖSSZEKEVERNI
135ITA MISCHIARE, MESCOLARE
135POL MIESZAĆ
135POR MISTURAR
135RUS SMESHIVAT'
135SPA MEZCLAR
135SWE BLANDA

136AAA BLITHE
136CZE VESELÝ, RADOSTNÝ
136DAN MUNTER
136DUT VROLIJK
136FRE JOYEUX
136GER MUNTER, FRÖHLICH
136HUN VIDÁMAN
136ITA GAIO
136POL WESOŁY
136POR ALEGRE
136RUS VESĚLYĬ
136SPA ALEGRE
136SWE MUNTER

137AAA BLOW, TO
137CZE FOUKATI
137DAN BLAESE
137DUT BLAZEN
137FRE SOUFFLER
137GER ANBLASEN
137HUN FÚJNI
137ITA SOFFIARE, SONARE
137POL WIAĆ
137POR ASSOPRAR
137RUS DYSHAT)
137SPA SOPLAR
137SWE BLÅSA

138AAA BODY
138CZE TĚLESO
138DAN KORPS
138DUT CORPS
138FRE CORPS
138GER CORPS
138HUN TEST
138ITA CORPO
138POL CIAŁO
138POR CORPO
138RUS TELO
138SPA CUERPO
138SWE KROPP

139AAA BOISTEROUS
139CZE HLUČNÝ
139DAN STØJENDE
139DUT HEFTIG
139FRE BRUYANT
139GER LÄRMEND
139HUN ERŐSZAKOS
139ITA STREPITOSO
139POL BURZLIWY
139POR RUIDOSO
139RUS BURNYĬ
139SPA ESTREPITOSO, RUIDOSO
139SWE HÄFTIGT, VALDSAMT

140AAA BOLD
140CZE SMĚLÝ
140DAN DRISTIG
140DUT KOEN EN KRACHTIG
140FRE HARDI, AUDACIEUX
140GER KECK
140HUN MERÉSZEN
140ITA ARDITO
140POL ŚMIAŁY
140POR VALENTE
140RUS SMELYĬ
140SPA VALIENTE
140SWE DRISTIG

141AAA BOMBARDON
141CZE BOMBARDA, BOMBARDON
141DAN BOMBARDON
141DUT BOMBARDON, BASTUBA
141FRE BOMBARDON
141GER BOMBARDON
141HUN BASSZUS SZAXKÜRT
141ITA BOMBARDONE
141POL BOMBARDON
141POR BOMBARDÃO
141RUS BOMBARDA
141SPA BOMBARDÓN
141SWE BOMBARDON

142AAA BONE
142CZE KOST
142DAN KNOGLE
142DUT BEEN
142FRE OS
142GER BEIN, KNOCHEN
142HUN CSONT
142ITA OSSO
142POL KOŚĆ
142POR OSSO
142RUS KOST)
142SPA HUESO
142SWE KNOTA, BEN

143AAA BOTH
143CZE OBÅDVA
143DAN BADE
143DUT BEIDE
143FRE DEUX
143GER BEIDE
143HUN MINDKETTŐ
143ITA TUTT'E DUE
143POL OBA(J)
143POR AMBOS, OS DOIS
143RUS OBA
143SPA AMBOS, LOS DOS
143SWE BÅDA

144AAA BOUNCE, SPRING, TO
144CZE SKÁKATI
144DAN SPRINGE
144DUT SPRINGEN
144FRE SAUTER
144GER SPRINGEN
144HUN UGRANI
144ITA SALTARE
144POL SKAKAĆ
144POR SALTAR
144RUS SKAKAT)
144SPA SALTAR
144SWE SPRINGA

145AAA BOURDON(DRONE BASS)   149AAA BREATH
145CZE BURDON   149CZE DECH
145DAN BASSTRENG   149DAN ÅNDE
145DUT BOURDON   149DUT ADEM
145FRE BOURDON   149FRE RESPIRATION
145GER BOURDON, BUMMBASS   149GER ATEM
145HUN BORDÓ   149HUN LÉLEKZET
145ITA BORDONE   149ITA RESPIRO
145POL BURDONOWY   149POL DECH
145POR BORDAO   149POR RESPIRAÇÃO, ALENTO
145RUS TRUTEN'   149RUS DYKHANIE
145SPA BORDÓN   149SPA RESPIRO, ALIENTO
145SWE BORDUNA   149SWE ANDA

146AAA BOW   150AAA BREATHE, TO
146CZE SMYČEC   150CZE DÝCHATI
146DAN BUE   150DAN ÅNDE
146DUT STRIJKSTOK   150DUT ADEMEN
146FRE ARCHET   150FRE RESPIRER
146GER BOGEN   150GER ATMEN
146HUN HEGEDŰVONÓ, VONÓ   150HUN LÉLEKZENI
146ITA ARCHETTO, ARCO   150ITA RESPIRARE
146POL SMYCZEK   150POL ODDYCHAĆ
146POR ARCO   150POR RESPIRAR
146RUS SMYCHOK   150RUS DYSHAT'
146SPA ARCO   150SPA RESPIRAR
146SWE STRÅKEN   150SWE ANDA

147AAA BRACE   151AAA BREVE
147CZE ZÁVORKA   151CZE KRÁTKÝ
147DAN KLAMME   151DAN BREVIS
147DUT KLAMP   151DUT DUBBELE HELE NOOT
147FRE ACCOLADE   151FRE BRÈVE
147GER KLAMMER   151GER BREVIS
147HUN ACCOLADE   151HUN RÖVID
147ITA GRAPPA   151ITA BREVE
147POL AKOLADA   151POL CAŁE NUTY
147POR COLCHÊTE   151POR BREVE
147RUS SKOBKA   151RUS BREV
147SPA CORCHETE   151SPA BREVE
147SWE KLAMMER   151SWE BREV

148AAA BRASS   152AAA BRIDGE
148CZE MOSAZ   152CZE KOBYLKA
148DAN MESSING   152DAN STOL
148DUT KOPER   152DUT VIOOLKAM
148FRE CUIVRE   152FRE CHEVALET
148GER MESSING, BLECH   152GER STEG
148HUN RÉZFÚVOK   152HUN HEGEDŰLÁB
148ITA OTTONE   152UTA PONTICELLO
148POL MOSIĄDZ   152POL KOBYŁKA
148POR METAIS   152POR CAVALÊTE
148RUS DUZHOVYE   152RUS KOBYLKA
148SPA METAL   152SPA PUENTE
148SWE BLECH   152SWE STALL, FIOLSTALL

153AAA BRIGHT
153CZE JASNÝ
153DAN STRAALENDE
153DUT HELDER
153FRE ECLATANT
153GER HELL, KLAR
153HUN FÉNYESEN
153ITA BRILLANTE, CHIARO
153POL JASNY
153POR BRILHANTE
153RUS IARKIĬ
153SPA FULGENTE
153SWE GLÄNSANDE

154AAA BRILLIANT
154CZE SKVĚLÝ
154DAN GLIMRENDE
154DUT SCHITTEREND
154FRE BRILLANT
154GER KLINGEND
154HUN BRILLIÁNTKŐ
154ITA BRILLIANTE
154POL BRAWUROWO
154POR BRILHANTE
154RUS BLESTĬASHCHIĬ
154SPA BRILLANTE
154SWE BRILJANT

155AAA BRISK
155CZE ŽIVÝ
155DAN LIVLIG
155DUT LEVENDIG, VURIG
155FRE ÉVEILLÉ
155GER LEBHAFT
155HUN ÉLÉNKEN
155ITA BRIOSO
155POL ŻYWO
155POR VIVO
155RUS ZHIVOĬ
155SPA VIVO, BRIOSO
155SWE LIVLIG, ELD

156AAA BROAD
156CZE ŠIROKÝ
156DAN BREDT
156DUT BREED
156FRE LARGE
156GER BREIT, LANGSAM
156HUN SZÉLES
156ITA LARGO
156POL SZEROKI
156POR LARGO
156RUS PROTĬAZHNO
156SPA LARGO
156SWE BRETT

157AAA BRUSQUE
157CZE PŘÍKRÝ
157DAN BRYSK
157DUT BRUUSK
157FRE BRUSQUE
157GER BARSCH, SCHROFF, RAUH
157HUN NYERS
157ITA BRUSCO
157POL SZORSTKI
157POR BRUSCO
157RUS GRUBYĬ
157SPA BRONCO, RUDO
157SWE BRYSK

158AAA BUGLE
158CZE POLNICE
158DAN BUGELHORN, KLAPHORN
158DUT JACHTHOORN
158FRE BUGLE
158GER BÜGELHORN, JAGDHORN
158HUN BILLENTYŰSKÜRT
158ITA BIUCOLO
158POL TRĄBKA WOJSKOWA
158POR BUGLE
158RUS ROZHOK
158SPA BUGLE
158SWE BYGELHORN, JAKTHORN

159AAA BURDEN
159CZE RITORNEL
159DAN RITORNEL
159DUT REFREIN
159FRE RITOURNELLE
159GER RITORNELL
159HUN REFRÉN
159ITA RITORNELLO
159POL BORDUN
159POR ESTRIBILHO
159RUS RITURNEL)
159SPA RETORNELO
159SWE RITORNELL

160AAA BURLESK
160CZE BURLESKA
160DAN BURLESK
160DUT BURLESK
160FRE BURLESQUE
160GER BURLESK(E)
160HUN BURLESZK
160ITA BURLESCO
160POL BURLESKA
160POR BURLESCO
160RUS BURLESKA
160SPA BURLESCO
160SWE BURLESK

161AAA BUT
161CZE ALE
161DAN MEN
161DUT MAAR
161FRE MAIS
161GER ABER
161HUN DE, HANEM
161ITA MA
161POL ALE
161POR SEM
161RUS NO
161SPA PERO, SINO
161SWE MEN

162AAA CACOPHONY
162CZE NELIBOZVUK
162DAN KAKOFONI
162DUT KAKOFONIE
162FRE CACOPHONIE
162GER KAKOPHONIE
162HUN CACOPHYONY
162ITA CACOFONIA
162POL KAKOFONIA
162POR CACOFONIA
162RUS KAKOFONIA
162SPA CACOFONÍA
162SWE MISSLJUD

163AAA CADENCE
163CZE KADENCE
163DAN FALD, TONESLUTNING
163DUT KADENS
163FRE CADENCE
163GER KADENZ, TONSCHLUSS
163HUN KADENCIA
163ITA CADENZA
163POL KADENCJA
163POR CADÊNCIA
163RUS KADENTSIA
163SPA CADENCIA
163SWE KADENS

164AAA CALM
164CZE KLIDNÝ
164DAN ROLIGT
164DUT KALM
164FRE CALME
164GER RUHIG, STILL
164HUN NYUGODTAN
164ITA CALMO
164POL SPOKÓJ
164POR CALMA
164RUS SPOKOÝNYÝ
164SPA CALMA
164SWE LUGNT

165AAA CAMPANILE
165CZE ZVONEČEK
165DAN KLOKKE
165DUT KLOJE, KLOKKENSPEL
165FRE CAMPANIL(L)E
165GER GLOCKENTURM
165HUN HARANGJÁTÉK
165ITA CAMPANELLA
165POL DZWONEK
165POR CAMPANÁRIO
165RUS KAMPANELLA
165SPA CAMPANILLA
165SWE LITEN KLOCKA

166AAA CANE
166CZE PÍŠT'ALA
166DAN RØR
166DUT REIT
166FRE TUYAU
166GER ROHR
166HUN SÍP
166ITA ANCIA
166POL TRZCINA
166POR CANA
166RUS TROST'
166SPA CAÑO
166SWE RÖR

167AAA CANON
167CZE KÁNON
167DAN KANON
167DUT CANON
167FRE CANON
167GER KANON
167HUN KÁNON
167ITA CANONE
167POL KANON
167POR CÂNONE
167RUS KANON
167SPA CANON
167SWE KANON

168AAA CANTATA
168CZE KANTÁTA
168DAN KANTATE
168DUT CANTATE
168FRE CANTATE
168GER KANTATE
168HUN KANTÁTA
168ITA CANTATA
168POL KANTATA
168POR CANTATA
168RUS KANTATA
168SPA CANTATE, CANTADA
168SWE KANTAT

169AAA CANTICLE
169CZE VÁNOČNÍ KOLEDA
169DAN SALME
169DUT LOFZANG
169FRE CANTIQUE
169GER LOBGESANG, KIRCHENLIED
169HUN DAL
169ITA CANTICO
169POL KANTYCZKI
169POR CÂNTICO
169RUS HIMN
169SPA CÁNTICO
169SWE KORAL

170AAA CAPRICE
170CZE ROZMAR, VRTOCH
170DAN KAPRICE
170DUT GRIL
170FRE CAPRICE, BOUTADE
170GER LAUNE, GRILLE
170HUN SZÓSZERINT
170ITA CAPRICCIO
170POL KAPRYS
170POR CAPRICHO
170RUS KAPRICHCHIO
170SPA CAPRICHO
170SWE KAPRIS

171AAA CARESS, TO
171CZE LICHOTITI
171DAN KAERTEGNE
171DUT LIEFKOZEN
171FRE CÂLINER
171GER SCHMEICHELN
171HUN ENYELEGNI
171ITA ACCAREZZARE
171POL PIEŚCIĆ
171POR ACARICIAR
171RUS LASKAT'
171SPA ACARICIAR
171SWE SMEKA

172AAA CARILLON
172CZE ZVONKOVÁ HRA
172DAN KLOKKESPIL
172DUT KLOKKENSPEL
172FRE JEU DE CLOCHES
172GER GLOCKENSPIEL
172HUN HARANGJÁTÉK
172ITA SCAMPANIO, CAMPANETTA
172POL DZWONY ZEGAROWE
172POR CARRILHÃO
172RUS TREZVON
172SPA JUEGO DE TIMBES
172SWE KLOCKSPEL

173AAA CAROL
173CZE KOLEDA
173DAN SYNGE, SANG
173DUT KERSTLIEDJE
173FRE NOËL
173GER WEIHNACHTLIED
173HUN ÉNEK
173ITA CANTICO PER NATALE
173POL KOLĘDA
173POR CÂNTICO
173RUS ROZHDESTVO
173SPA VILLANCICO
173SWE LOVSÅNG, SÅNG

174AAA CASTANET(S)
174CZE KASTANĚTA(Y)
174DAN KASTAGNET
174DUT CASTAGNETTEN
174FRE CASTAGNETTES, NACAIRE
174GER KASTAGNETTEN
174HUN KASZTANYÉT
174ITA CASTAGNETTE, NACCHERE
174POL KASTANIETY
174POR CASTANHOLAS
174RUS KASTAN'ETY
174SPA CASTAÑUELAS, NARCARIOS
174SWE KASTANJETT(ER)

175AAA CATALOG
175CZE KATALOG
175DAN KATALOG
175DUT CATALOGUS
175FRE CATALOGUE
175GER VERZEICHNIS
175HUN KATALÓGUS, LAJSTROM
175ITA CATALOGO
175POL KATALOG
175POR CATÁLOGO
175RUS KATALOG
175SPA CATÁLOGO
175SWE KATALOG

176AAA CATALOG, TO
176CZE KATALOGIZOVATI
176DAN KATALOGISERE
176DUT CATALOGISEREN
176FRE CATALOGUER
176GER VERZEICHNEN
176HUN LAJSTROMOZ
176ITA CATALOGARE
176POL KATALOGOWAĆ
176POR CATALOGAR
176RUS KATALOGIZIROVAT'
176SPA CATALOGAR
176SWE KATALOGISERA

177AAA CELEBRATE, TO
177CZE SLAVITI
177DAN FEJRE
177DUT CELEBREREN
177FRE CELEBRER
177GER ZELEBRIEREN, FEIREN
177HUN ÜNNEPELNI
177ITA CELEBRARE
177POL CELEBROWAĆ
177POR CELEBRAR
177RUS PRAZDNOVAT'
177SPA CELEBRAR
177SWE FIRA

178AAA CELESTA
178CZE ČELESTA
178DAN CELESTA
178DUT CELESTE
178FRE CÉLESTE, CELESTA
178GER CELESTA
178HUN CSELESZTA
178ITA CELESTA
178POL CZELESTA
178POR CELESTA
178RUS CHELESTA
178SPA CELESTE
178SWE CELESTA

179AAA CENTRAL
179CZE STŘEDOVÝ
179DAN CENTRAL
179DUT CENTRAAL
179FRE CENTRAL
179GER ZENTRAL
179HUN KÖZPONTI
179ITA CENTRALE
179POL CENTRALNY
179POR CENTRAL
179RUS TSENTRAL'NYĬ
179SPA CENTRAL
179SWE CENTRAL

180AAA CHACONNE
180CZE ČAKÓNA
180DAN CHACONNE
180DUT CHACONNE
180FRE CHACON(N)E
180GER CHACONNE
180HUN CHACONNE
180ITA CIAC(C)ONA
180POL CHACONNE
180POR CHACONA, CHACOINA
180RUS CHAKONA
180SPA CHACONA
180SWE CHACONNE

181AAA CHAMBER
181CZE KOMORA
181DAN KAMMER
181DUT KAMER
181FRE CHAMBRE
181GER KAMMER
181HUN KAMARA
181ITA CAMERA
181POL KOMERA
181POR CÂMARA
181RUS KAMORA
181SPA CÁMARA
181SWE KAMMARE

182AAA CHANGE, TO
182CZE ZMĚNITI
182DAN FORANDRE
182DUT VERANDEREN
182FRE CHANGER
182GER VERÄNDERN, WECHSELN
182HUN VÁLTOZÁS
182ITA CAMBIARE
182POL ZMENIAĆ
182POR CAMBIAR
182RUS ZAMENIAT'
182SPA CAMBIAR
182SWE FÖRÄNDRA

183AAA CHANT
183CZE ZPEV
183DAN SANG, SYNGE
183DUT GESANG
183FRE CHANT
183GER GESANG
183HUN ÉNEK
183ITA CANTO FERMO, SALMO
183POL KANT
183POR CANTO
183RUS PETN', CHORAL
183SPA CANTO FIRME, LLANO
183SWE JÄMN SÅNG

184AAA CHANT, TO
184CZE ZPÍVATI
184DAN BESYNGE
184DUT BEZINGEN
184FRE CHANTER
184GER BESINGEN
184HUN ÉNEKELNI
184ITA SALMEGGIARE
184POL ŚPIEWAĆ
184POR DECANTAR
184RUS PET'
184SPA DISCANTAR
184SWE BESJUNGA

185AAA CHAPEL   189AAA CHEER
185CZE KAPELA   189CZE VESELOST
185DAN KAPEL   189DAN MUNTERHED
185DUT KAPEL, CHAPELLE   189DUT VROLIJKHEID
185FRE CHAPELLE   189FRE CHÈRE
185GER KAPELLE, CAPELLE   189GER MUNTERHEIT
185HUN KAPOLNA   189HUN ÖRÖM
185ITA CAPPELLA   189ITA ALLEGREZZA
185POL KAPLICA   189POL WESOŁOŚĆ
185POR CAPELA   189POR ÂNIMO
185RUS KAPELLA   189RUS VESELIE
185SPA CAPILLA   189SPA ÁNIMA
185SWE KAPELL   189SWE GLÄDJE

186AAA CHARACTERISTIC   190AAA CHEST(BODY)
186CZE VÝZNAČNÝ   190CZE HRUD'
186DAN KARAKTERISTISK   190DAN BRYST
186DUT KARAKTERISTIEK   190DUT BORST
186FRE CARACTÉRISTIQUE   190FRE POITRINE
186GER CHARAKTERISTISCH   190GER BRUST
186HUN JELLEMZŐ   190HUN DOB
186ITA CARATTERISTICO   190ITA PETTO
186POL CHARAKTERYSTYKA   190POL PIERŚ(I)
186POR CARATERÍSTICA   190POR PEITO
186RUS KHARAKTERNYĬ   190RUS GRUD'
186SPA CARACTERÍSTICA   190SPA PECHO
186SWE KARAKTERISTISK   190SWE BRÖST

187AAA CHARM, TO   191AAA CHIME
187CZE ČAROVATI   191CZE ZVONKOVÁ HRA
187DAN TRYLLE, TROLDE   191DAN KLOKKESPIL
187DUT BETOVEREN   191DUT GELUI
187FRE CHARMER   191FRE CARILLON
187GER BEZAUBERN, EINSINGEN   191GER GLOCKENSPIEL
187HUN ELBÁJOLNI   191HUN OSSZHANG
187ITA INCANTARE   191ITA SCAMPANATA
187POL CZAROWAĆ   191POL GRAĆ
187POR ENCANTAR   191POR CARRILHÃO
187RUS OCHAROVYVAT'   191RUS ZVON KOLOKOLOV
187SPA ENCANTAR   191SPA CAMPANA, REPIQUE
187SWE FÖRTROLLA   191SWE KLOCKSPEL

188AAA CHASE   192AAA CHIME, TO
188CZE LOV, HONBA   192CZE ZVONITI
188DAN JAGT   192DAN RINGE
188GER JACHT(STUK)   192DUT LIUDEN
188FRE CHASSE   192FRE CARILLONNER
188GER JAGD   192GER GLOCKEN LÄUTEN
188HUN VADÁSZAT   192HUN ZENEKARI HARANG
188ITA CACCIA   192ITA SCAMPANARE
188POL GONIĄ SIĄ, POŚCIG   192POL O DZOWNACH GRAĆ
188POR CAÇA   192POR CARRILHONAR
188RUS OKHOTA   192RUS TREZVONIT'
188SPA CAZA   192SPA CAMPANEAR
188SWE JAKT   192SWE RINGA

193AAA CHINREST
193CZE PODBRADEK
193DAN VIOLINPUDE
193DUT KINHOUDER
193FRE MENTONIÈRE
193GER KINNHALTER
193HUN ÁLLTARTÓ
193ITA BARBOZZA
193POL WKŁADAC POD BRODĘ
193POR SOPORTE DO QUEIXO
193RUS PODBORODNIK
193SPA BARBADA
193SWE HAKSTÖD

197AAA CHORD
197CZE AKORD
197DAN AKKORD, ACCORD
197DUT AKKOORD
197FRE ACCORD
197GER AKKORD
197HUN AKKORD
197ITA ACCORDO
197POL AKORD
197POR ACORDE
197RUS AKKORD
197SPA CUERDA, ACORDE
197SWE ACKORD

194AAA CHOIR, CHORUS
194CZE CHÓR, SBOR
194DAN KOR
194DUT KOOR
194FRE CHOEUR
194GER CHOR
194HUN ÉNEKKAR
194ITA CORO
194POL CHÓR
194POR CORO
194RUS KHOR
194SPA CORO
194SWE KÖR

198AAA CHOREOGRAPHY
198CZE CHOREOGRAFIE
198DAN KOREOGRAFI
198DUT CHOREOGRAFIE
198FRE CHORÉGRAPHIE
198GER TANZKUNST
198HUN TANC
198ITA COREOGRAFIA
198POL CHOREOGRAFJA
198POR COREOGRAFIA
198RUS KHOREOGRAFIĨA
198SPA COROGRAFÍA
198SWE KOROGRAFI

195AAA CHOKE, DAMP, TO
195CZE DUSITI, TLUMITI
195DAN STOPPE
195DUT VERSTOPPEN
195FRE ÉTOUFFER
195GER DÄMPFEN
195HUN MEGFOJTANI
195ITA SOFFOCARE, STROZZARE
195POL ZADUSIĆ
195POR ABAFAR
195RUS DUSHIT'
195SPA ABAFAR
195SWE DÄMPA

199AAA CHROMATIC
199CZE CHROMATICKÝ
199DAN KROMATISK
199DUT CHROMATISCH
199FRE CHROMATIQUE
199GER CHROMATISCH
199HUN KROMATIKUS
199ITA CROMATICO
199POL CHROMATYKA
199POR CROMÁTICO
199RUS KHROMATICHESKIĨ
199SPA CROMÁTICO
199SWE KROMATISK

196AAA CHORAL
196CZE CHORÁL
196DAN KORAL
196DUT KORAAL
196FRE CHORAL
196GER CHORAL
196HUN KAR-ÉNEK
196ITA CORALE
196POL CHORAL
196POR CORAL
196RUS KHORAL
196SPA CHORAL
196SWE KORAL

200AAA CHURCH
200CZE KOSTEL
200DAN KIRKE
200DUT KERK
200FRE ÉGLISE
200GER KIRCHE
200HUN EGYHAZ
200ITA CHIESA
200POL KOŚCIÓL
200POR IGREJA
200RUS TSERKOV'
200SPA IGLESIA
200SWE KYRKA

201AAA	CIRCLE	205AAA	CLASSIC
201CZE	KRUH	205CZE	KLASICKÝ
201DAN	CIRKEL	205DAN	KLASSISK
201DUT	CIRKEL	205DUT	KLASSIEK
201FRE	CERCLE	205FRE	CLASSIQUE
201GER	ZIRKEL, KREIS	205GER	KLASSISCH
201HUN	KÖR	205HUN	KLASSZIKUS
201ITA	CIRCULO, CIRCOLO	205ITA	CLASSICO
201POL	KRĄG	205POL	KLASYK
201POR	CICLO, CÍRCULO	205POR	CLÁSSICO
201RUS	KRUG	205RUS	KLASSICHESKAIA
201SPA	CÍRCULO	205SPA	CLÁSICO
201SWE	CIRKEL	205SWE	KLASSISK
202AAA	CLAPPER	206AAA	CLASSIFY, TO
202CZE	SRDCE	206CZE	KLASIFIKOVATI
202DAN	KLAPPER	206DAN	KLASSIFICERE
202DUT	KLAPPER	206DUT	CLASSIFICEREN
202FRE	BATTANT	206FRE	CLASSIFIER
202GER	GLOCKENKLÖPPEL	206GER	KLASSIFIZIEREN
202HUN	CSÖRGETYŰ	206HUN	OSZTÁLYOZNI
202ITA	BATACCHIO, BATTAGLIO	206ITA	CLASSIFICARE
202POL	SERCE	206POL	ZAKLASYFIKOWAĆ
202POR	BADALO	206POR	CLASSIFICAR
202RUS	KLAKÉR	206RUS	KLASSIFITSIROVAT'
202SPA	BADAJO	206SPA	CLASIFICAR
202SWE	KLÄPP	206SWE	KLASSIFICERA
203AAA	CLARINET	207AAA	CLAVICHORD
203CZE	KLARINET	207CZE	KLÁVESNICE
203DAN	KLARINET	207DAN	KLAVIKORD
203DUT	KLARINET	207DUT	KLAVECIMBEL
203FRE	CLARINETTE	207FRE	CLAVICORDE, CLAVIER
203GER	KLARINETTE	207GER	KLAVICHORD
203HUN	KLARINÉT	207HUN	KLAVIKORK
203ITA	CLARINETTO	207ITA	CLAVICORDIO
203POL	KLARNET	207POL	KLAWIKORD
203POR	CLARINETE	207POR	CLAVICÓRDIO
203RUS	KLARNET	207RUS	KLAVIKORDY
203SPA	CLARINETE	207SPA	CLAVICORDIO
203SWE	KLARINETT	207SWE	KLAVIKORD
204AAA	CLARION	208AAA	CLAVIER
204CZE	POLNICE	208CZE	KLAVIATURA
204DAN	TROMPET	208DAN	CLAVECIN
204DUT	KLAROEN, TROMPET	208DUT	CLAVIATUUR
204FRE	CLAIRON	208FRE	CLAVECIN, CLAVIER
204GER	TROMPETE	208GER	KLAVIATUR, TASTATUR
204HUN	JELZŐKÜRT	208HUN	ZONGORA
204ITA	CLARINO	208ITA	TASTATURA, TASTIERA
204POL	TRĄBKA	208POL	KLAVIER
204POR	CLARIM	208POR	TECLADO
204RUS	TRUBA	208RUS	KLAVIR
204SPA	CLARÓN	208SPA	TECLADO
204SWE	ÅLDERDOMLIG, KLARIN	208SWE	KLAVER

209AAA CLEAN, NEAT
209CZE ČISTÝ
209DAN REN
209DUT ZUIVER
209FRE NET
209GER NETT, REIN
209HUN TISZTA
209ITA NETTO
209POL CZYSTY
209POR NÍTIDO
209RUS CHISTYĬ
209SPA NETO
209SWE REN

210AAA CLEAR
210CZE JASNÝ
210DAN KLAR
210DUT KLAAR
210FRE CLAIR
210GER KLAR
210HUN VILÁGOS
210ITA CHIARO
210POL JASNY
210POR CLARO
210RUS ÎASNYĬ
210SPA CLARO
210SWE KLAR

211AAA CLEF
211CZE KLÍČ
211DAN NØGLE
211DUT SLEUTEL
211FRE CLEF
211GER SCHLÜSSEL
211HUN KULCS
211ITA CIAVE
211POL KLUCZ
211POR CLAVE
211RUS KLÎUCH
211SPA CLAVE, LLAVE
211SWE KLAV

212AAA CLIMAX
212CZE KLIMAX
212DAN KLIMAKS
212DUT STIJGING
212FRE GRADATION
212GER STEIGERUNG, ABSTUFUNG
212HUN FOKOZÁS
212ITA GRADAZIONE
212POL PUNKT KULMINACYJNY
212POR CLÍMAX
212RUS GRADATSIĬA
212SPA GRADATIÓN
212SWE KLIMAX

213AAA CLOSE
213CZE ZAVŘENÝ
213DAN SLUTTET
213DUT GESLOTEN
213FRE FERME
213GER GESCHLOSSEN
213HUN ZÁRT
213ITA CHIUSO
213POL ĆSICŁY
213POR CERRADO
213RUS ZAKRYTYĬ
213SPA CERRADO
213SWE SLUTEN

214AAA CLOSE, TO
214CZE ZAVŘITI
214DAN LUKKE
214DUT SLUITEN
214FRE FERMER
214GER SCHLIESSEN
214HUN ZÁRNI
214ITA CHIUDERE
214POL ZAWRZEĆ
214POR ENCERRAR
214RUS ZAKRYVAT'
214SPA CERRAR
214SWE SLUTA

215AAA COLD
215CZE CHLAD
215DAN KOLD
215DUT KOUD
215FRE FROID
215GER KALT
215HUN HIDEGEN
215ITA FREDDO
215POL CHŁOD
215POR FRIO
215RUS KHOLODNYĬ
215SPA FRÍO
215SWE KALL

216AAA COLLECT
216CZE KOLEKTA
216DAN KOLLEKT
216DUT COLLECIE
216FRE COLLECTE
216GER KOLLEKTE
216HUN KOLLEKTA
216TIA COLLETTA
216POL KOLEDA, KOLEKTA
216POR COLETA
216RUS SKLADCHINA
216SPA COLECTA
216SWE KOLLEKT

217AAA COLOR, TONE
217CZE BARVA
217DAN FARVE
217DUT KLEUR, VERSIERING
217FRE TIMBRE
217GER FARBE
217HUN HANGSZÍN
217ITA TIMBRO
217POL TEMBR
217POR CÔR
217RUS TIMBR
218SPA TIMBRE
217SWE KLANGFÄRG

218AAA COMIC
218CZE KOMICKÝ
218DAN KOMISK
218DUT KOMISCH, KLUCHTIG
218FRE COMIQUE
218GER KOMISCH
218HUN KOMIKUS
218ITA COMICO, BUFFO
218POL KOMETOWY
218POR CÔMICO
218RUS KOMICHESKIĬ
218SPA CÓMICO
218SWE KOMISK

219AAA COMMA
219CZE KOMMA
219DAN KOMMA
219DUT KOMMA
219FRE COMMA
219GER KOMMA
219HUN VESSZŐ
219ITA COMMA
219POL KOMA
219POR COMA
219RUS KOMMA
219SPA COMA
219SWE KOMMA

220AAA COMMODIOUS
220CZE POHODLNÝ
220DAN BEKVEM
220DUT GEMAKKELIJK
220FRE COMODE
220GER BEQUEM, GEMÄCHLICH
220HUN KÉNYELMES
220ITA COM(M)ODO
220POL SWOBODNIE
220POR CÔMODO
220RUS UDOBNYĬ
220SPA CÓM(M)ODO
220SWE MAKLIGT, BEKVÄMT

221AAA COMPASS
221CZE KOMPAS, ROZRAH
221DAN KOMPAS
221DUT KOMPAS
221FRE ÉTENDUE
221GER KOMPASS, UMFANG
221HUN HANGTERJEDELEM
221ITA TESSITURA, ESTENSIONE
221POL KOMPĄS
221POR COMPASSO
221RUS KOMPAS, TAKT
221SPA COMPÁS, EXTENSIÓN
221SWE KOMPASS

222AAA COMPLEMENT, TO
222CZE DOPLNITI
222DAN UDFYLDELSE
222DUT AANVULLEN
222FRE COMPLÉTER
222GER ERGANZEN
222HUN KIEGÉSZITENI
222ITA COMPLEMENTARE
222POL DOPEŁNIENIE
222POR COMPLEMENTAR
222RUS DOPOLNIAT'
222SPA COMPLEMENTAR
222SWE KOMPLETTERA

223AAA COMPLEX
223CZE KOMPLEXNÍ
223DAN KOMPLEKS
223DUT COMPLEX
223FRE COMPLEXE
223GER KOMPLEX
223HUN ÖSSZETETT
223ITA COMPLESSO
223POL KOMPLEKS
223POR COMPLEXO
223RUS KOMPLEKSNYĬ
223SPA COMPLEJO
223SWE KOMPLEX

224AAA COMPOSE, TO
224CZE KOMPONOVÁTI
224DAN KOMPONERE
224DUT COMPONEREN
224FRE COMPOSER
224GER KOMPONIEREN
224HUN KOMPONÁLNI
224ITA COMPONERE, COMPORRE
224POL KOMPONOWAĆ
224POR COMPOR
224RUS KOMPONOVAT'
224SPA COMPONER
224SWE KOMPONERA

225AAA COMPOSITION
225CZE KOMPONOVÁNÍ
225DAN KOMPOSITION
225DUT COMPOSITIE
225FRE COMPOSITION
225GER KOMPOSITION
225HUN SZERZEMÉNY
225ITA COMPOSIZIONE
225POL KOMPOZYCJA
225POR COMPOSIÇÃO
225RUS KOMPOZITSIIA
225SPA COMPOSICIÓN
225SWE KOMPOSITION

226AAA COMPOUND
226CZE SLOŽENÝ
226DAN SAMMENSAETTE
226DUT SAMMENGESTELD
226FRE COMPOSÉ
226GER ZUSAMMENGESETZT
226HUN ÖSSZETETT
226ITA COMPOSTI, DISPARI
226POL ZKOŽONY
226POR COMPOSTO
226RUS KOMPAUND
226SPA COMPUESTO
226SWE SAMMENSÄTTA

227AAA CONCERT
227CZE KONCERT
227DAN KONCERT
227DUT CONCERT
227FRE CONCERT
227GER KONZERT
227HUN HANGVERSENY
227ITA CONCERTO
227POL KONCERT
227POR CONCÊRTO
227RUS KONTSERT
227SPA CONCIERTO
227SWE KONSERT

228AAA CONCLUSION
228CZE ZÁVĚREČNÁ
228DAN SLUTNING
228DUT BESLUIT, CONCLUSIE
228FRE CONCLUSION, FIN
228GER SCHLUSS(SATZ)
228HUN KÖVETKEZTETÉS
228ITA FINE, CONCLUSIONE
228POL KONKLUZJA
228POR CONCLUSÃO
228RUS ZAVERSHENIE
228SPA CONCLUSIÓN
228SWE SLUT, AVSLUTNING

229AAA CONCORD
229CZE SHODA, SOUHLAS
229DAN ENDRÄKT
229DUT EENDRACHT
229FRE CONCORDE
229GER EINTRACHT
229HUN EGYETÉRTES
229ITA CONCORDANZA, CONCENTO
229POL ZGODA
229POR CONCÓRDIA
229RUS NASTRAIVAT', SOGLASIE
229SPA CONCORDIA, ACORDE
229SWE ENDRÄKT

230AAA CONDUCTOR
230CZE VEDOUCÍ, DIRIGENT
230DAN DIRIGENT
230DUT CONDUCTEUR
230FRE CONDUCTEUR, MAITRE
230GER DIREKTOR, DIRIGENT
230HUN VEZETŐSZÓLAM
230ITA CONDUTTORE
230POL KONDUKTOR
230POR CONDUTOR
230RUS KONDUKTOR
230SPA CONDUCTOR, MAESTRO
230SWE KONDUKTÖR

231AAA CONDUCT, TO
231CZE DIRIGOVATI, ŘÍDITI
231DAN FØRELSE
231DUT DIRIGEREN, LEIDEN
231FRE CONDUIRE
231GER FÜHREN
231HUN VEZETNI
231ITA CONDURRE, MENARE
231POL PROWADZIĆ
231POR CONDUZIR
231RUS DIRIZHIROVAT'
231SPA CONDUCIR
231SWE FÖRA

232AAA CONE
232CZE KUŽEL
232DAN KEGLE
232DUT KEGEL
232FRE CÔNE
232GER KEGEL
223HUN KÚP
232ITA CONO
232POL STOŽEK
232POR CONE
232RUS KONUS
232SPA CONO
232SWE KON, KÄGLA

233AAA CONNECT, TO
233CZE SPOJITI
233DAN BINDE
233DUT VERBINDEN
233FRE LIER
233GER BINDEN
233HUN KÖTNI
233ITA LEGARI
233POL ŁACZYĆ
233POR FAZER CONEXÃO
233RUS SOEDINIAT
233SPA CONECTAR
233SWE BINDA

234AAA CONSECUTIVE
234CZE NÁSLEDNÝ
234DAN PAAFØLGENDE
234DUT PARALLELEN
234FRE CONSÉCUTIF
234GER KONSEKUTIV
234HUN PÁRHUZAM
234ITA SEGUITO
234POL RÓWNOLEGŁE
234POR CONSECUTIVO
234RUS POSLEDUIUSHCHIĬ
234SPA CONSECUTIVO
234SWE PÅ VARANN FÖLJANDE

235AAA CONSEQUENT
235CZE PRŮVODČÍ
235DAN FOLGENDE
235DUT DE VOLGENDE
235FRE CONSÉQUENT
235GER FOLGEND, KONSEQUENT
235HUN KÖVETKEZETES
235ITA CONSEGUENTE
235POL KONSEKWENTY
235POR CONSEQUENTE
235RUS POSLEDOVATEL'NYĬ
235SPA CONSECUENTE
235SWE FÖLJANDE

236AAA CONSERVATORY
236CZE KONZERVATOŘ
236DAN KONSERVATORIUM
236DUT CONSERVATORIUM
326FRE CONSERVATOIRE
236GER KONSERVATORIUM
236HUN KONZERVATÓRIUM
236ITA CONSERVATORIO
236POL KONSERWATORJUM
236POR CONSERVATÓRIO
236RUS KONSERVATORIIA
236SPA CONSERVATORIO
236SWE KONSERVATORIUM

237AAA CONSOLING
237CZE ÚTĚŠLIVNÝ
237DAN TRØSTENDE
237DUT TROOSTEN
237FRE CONSOLANT
237GER TRÖSTLICH
237HUN VIGASZTALÓ
237ITA CONSOLANTE
237POL POCIESZAJĄCY
237POR CONSOLANTE
237RUS UTESHITEL'NYĬ
237SPA CONSOLANTE
237SWE TRÖSTA

238AAA CONSOLE
238CZE KONZOLA
238DAN KONSOL
238DUT CONSOLE
238FRE CONSOLE
238GER KONSOLE
238HUN JÁTÉKASZTAL
238ITA CONSOLLE
238POL KONSOLA
238POR CONSOLA, CONSOLO
238RUS KONSOL'
238SPA CONSOLA
238SWE KONSOL

239AAA CONSONANCE
239CZE SOUZVUK
239DAN SAMKLANG
239DUT GELIJKLUIDENDHEID
239FRE CONSONANCE
239GER WOHLKLANG
239HUN JÓHANGZAS
239ITA CONSONANZA
239POL KONSONANSOWY
239POR CONSONÂNCIA
239RUS KONSONANS
239SPA CONSONANCIA
239SWE KONSONANS

240AAA CONSONANT
240CZE KONSONUJÍCÍ
240DAN KONSONANT
240DUT GELIJKLUIDEND
240FRE CONSONANT
240GER KONSONANT
240HUN MÁSSALHANGZÓ
240ITA CONSONANTE
240POL KONSONANS
240POR CONSONANTE
240RUS SOZVUCHNYĬ
240SPA CONSONANTE
240SWE KONSONANT

241AAA CONSTANT
241CZE STÁLÝ
241DAN BESTANDIG
241DUT CONSTANT
241FRE CONSTANT
241GER BESTÄNDIG
241HUN ÁLLHATATOS
241ITA COSTANTE
241POL STAŁY
241POR CONSTANTE
241RUS POSTOJANNYĬ
241SPA CONSTANTE
241SWE BESTÄNDIG, KONSTANT

242AAA CONTINUE, TO
242CZE POKRAČOVATI
242DAN FORSAETTE
242DUT AANHOUDEN
242FRE CONTINUER
242GER FORTFAHREN
242HUN FOLYTATNI
242ITA CONTINUARE, SEGUITARE
242POL KONTYNUOWAĆ
242POR CONTINUAR
242RUS UCHREZHDAT'
242SPA CONTINUAR
242SWE FORTSÄTTA

243AAA CONTOUR
243CZE OBRYS
243DAN KONTUR
243DUT CONTOUR
243FRE CONTOUR
243GER KONTUR
243HUN KÖRRAJZ
243ITA CONTOURNO
243POL KONTUR
243POR CONTÔRNO
243RUS KONTUR
243SPA CONTORNO
243SWE KONTUR

244AAA CONTRA-
244CZE KONTRA-
244DAN KONTRA-
244DUT CONTRA-
244FRE CONTRE-
244GER KONTRA-
244HUN ELLEN-, KONTRA-
244ITA CONTRA-
244POL KONTRA-
244POR CONTRA-
244RUS KONTRA-
244SPA CONTRA-
244SWE KONTRA-

245AAA CONTRALTO
245CZE ALT
245DAN ALT
245DUT ALT(STEM)
245FRE CONTRALTO
245GER ALTSTIMME
245HUN ALTO
245ITA CONTRALTO
245POL ALT
245POR CONTRALTO
245RUS KONTRAL'TO
245SPA CONTRALTO
245SWE ALT

246AAA CONTRARY
246CZE OPAČNY
246DAN KONTRAER
246DUT TEGENGESTELD
246FRE CONTRAIRE, A L'ENVERS
246GER ENTGEGENGEFESST
246HUN ELLENKEZŐ
246ITA CONTRARIO, AL ROVESCIO
246POL PRZECIWNY
246POR CONTRÁRIO
246RUS PROTIVOPOLOZHNYĬ
246SPA CONTRARIO
246SWE MOTSATT

247AAA CONTRAST
247CZE KONTRAST
247DAN KONTRAST
247DUT KONTRAST
247FRE CONTRASTE
247GER GEGENSATZ
247HUN ELLENKESET
247ITA CONTRASTO
247POL KONTRAST
247POR CONTRASTE
247RUS KONTRAST
247SPA CONTRASTE
247SWE KONTRAST

248AAA CONVENIENT
248CZE PŘÍSLUŠNÝ
248DAN BEKVEM
248DUT GEMAKKELIJK
248FRE COMMODE
248GER BEQUEM
248HUN KÉNYELMESEN
248ITA COM(M)ODO
248POL WYGODNIE
248POR CONVENIENTE, CÓMODO
248RUS UDOBNYĬ
248SPA CONVENIENTE, CÓMODO
248SWE MAKLIGT

249AAA CONVERT, TO
249CZE KONVERTOVATI
249DAN FORVANDLE
249DUT CONVERTEREN
249FRE CONVERTIR
249GER VERWANDELN
249HUN ÁTVÁLTOZTATNI
249ITA CONVERTIRE
249POL ZAMIENIAĆ
249POR CONVERTER
249RUS KONVERTIROVAT'
249SPA CONVERTIR
249SWE OMVÄNDA

250AAA COPY, TO
250CZE KOPÍROVATI, OPISOVATI
250DAN AFSKRIVE
250DUT AFSCHRIJVEN
250FRE COPIER
250GER KOPIEREN, ABSCHREIBEN
250HUN MÁSOLNI
250ITA COPIARE
250POL KOPIOWAĆ
250POR COPIAR
250RUS KOPIROVAT'
250SPA COPIAR
250SWE KOPIERA

251AAA COPYRIGHT
251CZE NAKLADATELSKÉ PRÁVO
251DAN FORFATTERRET
251DUT KOPIJRECHT
251FRE DROITS D'AUTEUR
251GER VERLAGSRECHT
251HUN KIADÓI JOG
251ITA DIRITTI D'AUTORE
251POL PRAWO AUTORSKIE
251POR DIREITOS AUTORAIS
251RUS AVTORSKOE PRAVO
251SPA DERECHOS DE AUTOR
251SWE FORFATTARARVODE

252AAA CORNET
252CZE KORNET
252DAN KORNET
252DUT CORNET, ZINK
252FRE CORNETTE
252GER ZINK(E), KORNETT
252HUN KÜRTŐCSKE, CINK
252ITA CORNETTA
252POL KORNET
252POR CORNETIM, CORNETA
252RUS KORNET
252SPA CORNETA
252SWE KORNETT

253AAA CORNOPEON
253CZE VENTILOVÝ KORNET
253DAN KORNETT
253DUT CORNET À PISTONS
253FRE CORNET À PISTONS
253GER VENTILKORNETT
253HUN BILLENTYŰS KÜRT
253ITA CORNETTO A PISTÓNE
253POL KORNET
253POR CORNETA DE PISTŐES
253RUS KORNET-A-PISTON
253SPA CORNETA DE LLAVES
253SWE KORNETT

254AAA COTILLON
254CZE ŘADOVÝ TANEC
254DAN KOTILLON
254DUT COTILLON, KOTILLON
254FRE COTILLON
254GER KOTILLON
254HUN EREDETILEG EGYSZERŰ
254ITA COTILLON
254POL KOTYLION
254POR COTILHÃO
254RUS KOTIL'ON
254SPA COTILLON
254SWE KADRILJ

255AAA COUNT
255CZE POCET
255DAN TAELLING
255DUT TEL
255FRE COMPTE
255GER ZAHL
255HUN SZÁM
255ITA CONTO
255POL LICZENIE
255POR CONTA
255RUS SCHÉT
255SPA CUENTO
255SWE TAL

256AAA COUNT, TO
256CZE POČÍTATI
256DAN TAELLE
256DUT TELLEN
256FRE COMPTER
256GER ZAHLEN
256HUN SZÁMLÁLNI
256ITA CONTARE
256POL LICZYĆ
256POR CONTAR
256RUS SCHITAT'
256SPA CONTAR
256SWE BETALA

257AAA COUNTERPOINT
257CZE KONTRAPUNKT
257DAN KONTRAPUNKT
257DUT CONTRAPUNT
257FRE CONTREPOINT
257GER KONTRAPUNKT
257HUN ELLENPONT
257ITA CONTRAP(P)UNTO
257POL KONTRAPUNKT
257POR CONTRAPONTO
257RUS KONTRAPUNKT
257SPA CONTRAPUNTO
257SWE KONTRAPUNKT

258AAA COVERED
258CZE KRYTÝ
258DAN DAEKKE
258DUT BEDEKT
258FRE COUVERT
258GER BEDECKT
258HUN FEDÖ
258ITA COPERTO
258POL KOPERTA
258POR COBERTO
258RUS ZAKRYTYĬ
258SPA CUBIERTO
258SWE BETÄCKT

259AAA CRADLE
259CZE KOLÉBKA
259DAN VUGGE
259DUT WIEG
259FRE BERCEAU
259GER WIEGE
259HUN BÖLSCÓ
259ITA CULLA
259POL KOLEBKA
259POR BERÇO
259RUS KOLYBEL'
259SPA CUNA
259SWE VAGGA

260AAA CRISP
260CZE SUCHÝ
260DAN KRUSET
260DUT KROES
260FRE SEC, CRÊPÉS
260GER FRISCH, TROCKEN
260HUN ROPOGÓS, FRISS
260ITA SECCO, CREPO
260POL ŻYWO
260POR CRÊSPO
260RUS SVEZHIĬ
260SPA CRESPO
260SWE KRUSIG

261AAA CRITIC
261CZE KRITIK
261DAN KRITIKER
261DUT CRITICUS
261FRE CRITIQUEUR
261GER KRITIKER, KUNSTRICHTER
261HUN KRITIKA
261ITA CRITICO
261POL KRYTYK
261POR CRÍTICO
261RUS KRITIK
261SPA CRÍTICO
261SWE KRITIKER

262AAA CROSS, TO
262CZE KŘIŽITI
262DAN KORS
262DUT KRUISEN
262FRE CROISER
262GER BEKREUZEN
262HUN KERESZTEZNI
262ITA TRAVERSARE, INCROCIARE
262POL KRZYZOWAĆ
262POR CRUZAR
262RUS SKRESHCHVAT'
262SPA CRUZAR
262SWE I KORS

263AAA CUE
263CZE REPLIKA, ODPOVĚD
263DAN RÉPLICA
263DUT KEU
263FRE RÉPLIQUE
263GER KUSTOS
263HUN JELSZÓ
263ITA REPLICA
263POL REPLIKA
263POR DEIXO
263RUS REPLIKA
263SPA RÉPLICA
263SWE REPLIK

264AAA CURTAIN
264CZE DIVADELNÍ (OPONA)
264DAN FORHAENG
264DUT GORDIJN
264FRE RIDEAU
264GER VORHANG
264HUN FÜGGÖNY
264ITA CORTINA, SIPARIO
264POL KURTYNA
264POR PANO DE BÔCA, CORTINA
264RUS ZANAVES
264SPA TELON, CORTINA
264SWE FÖRHÄNGE

265AAA CYCLE
265CZE CYKLUS
265DAN CYKEL
265DUT CYCLUS
265FRE CYCLE
265GER ZYCLUS
265HUN KÖRZET
265ITA CICLO
265POL CYKL
265POR CICLO
265RUS TSIKL
265SPA CICLO
265SWE CYKEL

266AAA CYMBAL(S)
266CZE CYMBEL, TALÍŘE
266DAN CYMBEL
266DUT CYMBAAL, CYMBAL(UM)
266FRE CYMBALE(S)
266GER BECKE(N), SCHALE
266HUN CZIMBALOM, RÉZTÁNYER
266ITA PIATTO, PIATTI
266POL CZYNELE
266POR CYMBALO(S)
266RUS TSIMBALY
266SPA CÍMBALO, PLATILLOS
266SWE BÄCKEN

267AAA DACTYL
267CZE DAKTYL
267DAN DAKTYL
267DUT DACTYLUS
267FRE DACTYLE
267GER DACTYLO
267HUN VERSLÁB FAJTA
267ITA DATTILO
267POL DAKTYL
267POR DÁCTILO
267RUS DAKTIL
267SPA DÁCTILO
267SWE DAKTYL

268AAA DAMP, MUFFLE, TO
268CZE DUSITI
268DAN DAEMPER
268DUT DAMPEN, TEMPEREN
268FRE ÉTOUFFER
268GER DÄMPFEN
268HUN ELFOJTANI
268ITA SOFFOGAR
268POL TŁUMIĆ
268POR ABAFAR
268RUS DUSHIT'
268SPA ABAFAR, ENLUTAR
268SWE DÄMMARE

269AAA DANCE, TO
269CZE TANČITI
269DAN DANSE
269DUT DANSEN
269FRE DANSER
269GER TANZEN
269HUN TÁNCZOLNI
269ITA DANZARE, BALLARE
269POL TAŃCZYĆ
269POR DANÇAR
269RUS TANTSEVAT'
269SPA DANZAR, BAILAR
269SWE DANZA

270AAA DARK
270CZE CHMURNÝ, TEMNÝ
270DAN DUNKEL, MØRK
270DUT DONKER
270FRE SOMBRE, OBSCURE
270GER DUNKEL, DÜSTER, TRÜBE
270HUN FOJTVA
270ITA OSCURO, CUPO
270POL CIEMNY
270POR ESCURO
270RUS TĚMNYĬ
270SPA OSCURO, OBSCURO
270SWE MÖRK

271AAA DAWN
271CZE JITŘNÍ ZASTAVENIČKO
271DAN GRY
271DUT DAGERAAD
271FRE AUBADE
271GER DÄMMERUNG
271HUN HAJNAL
271ITA ALBA, MATTINATA
271POL ŚWIT
271POR ALVORADA
271RUS RASSVET
271SPA ALBA, ALBORADA
271SWE GRYNING

272AAA DEAF
272CZE DUŠENÝ, HLUCHÝ
272DAN DØV
272DUT DOOF
272FRE SOURD
272GER TAUB
272HUN SÜKET
272ITA SORDO
272POL GŁUCHY
272POR SURDO
272RUS GLUKHOĬ
272SPA SORDO
272SWE DÖV

273AAA DECEPTIVE
273CZE KLAMNÝ
273DAN SKUFFENDE
273DUT BEDRIEGLIJK
273FRE INTERROMPUE
273GER TRUG-
273HUN ÁLZÁRLAT
273ITA INGANNO
273POL ŁATWOWIERNY
273POR ENGANO
273RUS OBMAN
273SPA ENGAÑO
273SWE FELAKTIG

274AAA DECIDED
274CZE ODHODLANÉ
274DAN AFGJORT, BESTEMT
274DUT BESLISSNED
274FRE DÉCIDÉ, EN DEHORS
274GER BESTIMMT
274HUN HANGSÚLYOZVA
274ITA MARCATO, DECISO
274POL SŁANOWCZO
274POR DECIDIDO
274RUS RESHITEL'NO
274SPA DECIDIDO
274SWE BESTÄMT

275AAA DECISIVE
275CZE ROZHODNÝ
275DAN AFGØRENDE
275DUT BESLISSEND
275FRE DÉCISIF
275GER ENTSCHEIDEND
275HUN HATÁROZOTTAN
275ITA DECISIVO
275POL DECYDUJĄCY
275POR DECISIVO
275RUS RESHITEL'NYÏ
275SPA DECISIVO
275SWE AVGÖRANDE

276AAA DECLAIM, TO
276CZE DEKLAMOVATI
276DAN DEKLAMERE
276DUT DECLAMEREN
276FRE DÉCLAMER
276GER DEKLAMIEREN
276HUN DEKLAMALNI
276ITA DECLAMARE
276POL DEKLAMOWAĆ
276POR DECLAMAR
276RUS DEKLAMIROVAT'
276SPA DECLAMAR
276SWE DEKLAMERA

277AAA DECREASE, TO
277CZE ZMENŠOVATI
277DAN AFTAGEN
277DUT AFNEHMEN
277FRE DIMINUER
277GER ABNEHMEN
277HUN KEVESBEDNI
277ITA DECRESCERE
277POL ZMNIEJSZAĆ
277POR DECRESCER
277RUS UMEN'SHAT'
277SPA DECRECER
277SWE AVTA

278AAA DEEP
278CZE HLUBOKÝ
278DAN DYB
278DUT DIEP
278FRE PROFOND
278GER TIEF
278HUN MÉLY
278ITA PROFONDO
278POL GŁEBOKI
278POR PROFUNDO
278RUS GLUBOKIÏ
278SPA PROFUNDO
278SWE DJUP

279AAA DEFLECTION
279CZE ODCHYLKA
279DAN AFVIGELSE
279DUT AFWIJKING
279FRE DEFLEXION, DÉVIATION
279GER ABWEICHUNG
279HUN ELTÉRÉS
279ITA FLESSIONE
279POL ODCHYLENIE
279POR DESVIO
279RUS OTKLONENIE
279SPA DESVÍO
279SWE BÖJNING

280AAA DEGREE
280CZE STUPEŇ
280DAN GRAD
280DUT GRAAD, TOONTRAP
280FRE DEGRÉ
280GER GRAD, STUFE
280HUN HANGFOK
280ITA GRADO
280POL STOPIEŃ
280POR GRAU
280RUS STEPEN'
280SPA GRADO
280SWE GRAD

281AAA DELAY, TO
281CZE ZPOMALOVATI
281DAN FÖRHALE, OPSAETTE
281DUT UITSTELLEN
281FRE RETENIR, RETARDER
281GER VERZÖGERN, ZURÜCKHALTEN
281HUN KÉSLELTENI
281ITA RITARDARE
281POL ODKAŁADAĆ
281POR RETARDAR
281RUS ORKLADYVAT'
281SPA RETARDAR
281SWE ÅTERHÅLLA

282AAA DELICATE
282CZE JEMNÝ
282DAN DELIKAT, SMAGFULDT
282DUT DELICAAT
282FRE DÉLICAT(E)
282GER DELIKAT, ZART
282HUN FINOMAN
282ITA DELICATO
282POL DELIKATNY
282POR DELICADO
282RUS DELIKATNYĬ
282SPA DELICADO
282SWE DELIKAT

283AAA DELICIOUS
283CZE ROZKOŠNÝ
283DAN HEERLIJK
283DUT HEERLIJK
283FRE DÉLICIEUX
283GER ANMUTIG
283HUN FÖLSÉGES
283ITA DELIZIOSO
283POL ROZKOSZNY
283POR DELICIOSO
283RUS VOSKHITITEL'NYĬ
283SPA DELICIOSO
283SWE HÄRLIG

284AAA DELIGHT
284CZE ROZKOŠ
284DAN GLAEDE
284DUT GENOEGEN
284FRE DÉLICE
284GER VERGNÜGEN
284HUN GYÖNYÖRKÖDÉS
284ITA DELIZIA, DILETTO
284POL ROZKOSZ
284POR DELEITE
284RUS NASLAZHDENIE
284SPA DELEITE
284SWE GLÄDGE

285AAA DELIRIOUS
285CZE TŘEŠTIVÝ
285DAN DELIRERENDE
285DUT IJLEND
285FRE DÉLIRANT, EN DÉLIRE
285GER SCHWÄRMEND, WAHNSINN
285HUN ÖRGÖNVE
285ITA DELIRANTE, IN DELIRIO
285POL DOTKNIĘTY DELIRIUM
285POR DELIRANTE, DELIRIOSO
285RUS BREDIASHCHIĬ
285SPA DELIRANTE, DELIRIO
285SWE YRANDE, RASANDE

286AAA DERISIVE
286CZE ZMĚKČILE, PODDAJNĚ
286DAN SPOTTENDE
286DUT SPOTTEND
286FRE MOQUEUR
286GER SPÖTTISCH
286HUN GÚNYOLÓ
286UTA DERISIVO
286POL KPIĄCY, IRONICZNY
286POR DERRISÓRIO
286RUS SMECHNOĬ
286SPA IRRISORIO
286SWE SPEFULL

287AAA DERIVE, TO
287CZE ODVODITI
287DAN AFLEDE
287DUT AFLEIDEN
287FRE DÉRIVER
287GER ABLEITEN
287HUN SZÁRMAZTATNI
287ITA DERIVARE
287POL POCHODZIĆ
287POR DERIVAR
287RUS OTNOSIT'SIA
287SPA DERIVAR
287SWE AFLEDA

288AAA DESCANT
288CZE DISCANTUS
288DAN SOPRAN
288DUT DISCANT
288FRE DÉCHANT
288GER DISKANT
288HUN DISZKANT
288ITA SOPRANO
288POL DYSZKANT
288POR DESCANTE, DISCANTE
288RUS DISKANT
288SPA DISCANTE, TIPLE
288SWE DISKANT

289AAA DESCEND, TO   293AAA DETACH, TO
289CZE SESTOUPITI   293CZE ODDĚLOVATI, ODRÁŽETI
289DAN STIGE NED   293DAN DETACHERE
289DUT AFDALEN   293DUT DETACHEREN
289FRE DESCENDRE   293FRE DÉTACHER
289GER ABSTEIGEN   293GER ABTOSSEN
289HUN LESZÁLLANI   293HUN RÖVIDEBBÍTNI
289ITA SCENDERE, DISCENDERE   293ITA STACCARE
289POL SCHODZIĆ   293POL ODŁĄCZAĆ
289POR DESCER   293POR DESTACAR
289RUS SKHODIT'   293RUS OTDELIAT'
289SPA DESCENDER   293SPA DESTACAR, PICAR
289SWE NEDSTIGA   293SWE DETACHERA

290AAA DESIRE   294AAA DETERMINE, TO
290CZE TOUHA   294CZE URČITI
290DAN ØNSKE   294DAN DESTEMME
290DUT VERLANGEN   294DUT VASTSTELLEN
290FRE DÉSIR   294FRE DÉTERMINER
290GER SEHNSUCHT   294GER ENTSCHEIDEN
290HUN VÁGY   294HUN DÖNTENI
290ITA DESIDERIO   294ITA DETERMINARE
290POL ŻYCZYĆ   294POL DETERMINOWAĆ
290POR DESEJO   294POR DETERMINAR
290RUS ZHELANIE   294RUS OPREDELIAT'
290SPA DESEO   294SPA DETERMINAR
290SWE ÖNSKA   294SWE BESTÄMMA

291AAA DESK   295AAA DEVELOPMENT
291CZE HUDEBNÍ PULT   295CZE ROZVINOUTÍ
291DAN PULT   295DAN UDVIKLING
291DUT LESSENAAR   295DUT UITBREIDING
291FRE PUPITRE, LUTRIN   295FRE DÉVELOPPEMENT
291GER PULT, NOTENSTÄNDER   295GER DURCHFÜHRUNG
291HUN POLC   295HUN FELDOGOZÁS
291ITA LEGGIO   295ITA SVOLGIMENTO
291POL PULPIT   295POL PRZETWORZENIE CZYLI
291POR ATRIL, ESTANTE   295POR DESENVOLVIMENTO
291RUS PIUPITR   295RUS RAZVITIE
291SPA PUPITRE, FACISTOL   295SPA DESARROLLO
291SWE PULPET   295SWE UTVECKLING

292AAA DESPAIR   296AAA DEVOUT
292CZE ZOUFALSTVÍ   296CZE POKORNÝ
292DAN FORTVIVLE   296DAN FROM
292DUT WANHOOP   296DUT GODSDIENSTIG
292FRE DÉSESPOIR   296FRE DÉVOT, PIEUSEMENT
292GER VERZWEIFLUNG   296GER FROMM, ANDÄCHTIG
292HUN KÉTSÉGBEESÉS   296HUN ÁHÍTATOSAN
292ITA DISPERAZIONE   296ITA DEVOTO
292POL ROZPACZ   296POL NABOŻNIE
292POR DESESPÊRO   296POR DEVOTO
292RUS OTCHAIANIE   296RUS NABOZHNYÍ
292SPA DES(ES)PERACIÓN   296SPA DEVOTO
292SWE FÖRTVIVLAN   296SWE FROM

297AAA DEXTEROUS
297CZE OBRATNÝ
297DAN BEHAENDIG
297DUT DEHENDIG
297FRE ADROIT
297GER GEWANDT
297HUN ÜGYES
297ITA DESTRO
297POL ZRĘCZNY
297POR DESTRO
297RUS PROVORNYĬ
297SPA DIESTRO
297SWE HÄNDIG

298AAA DIA-
298CZE DIA-
298DAN DIA-
298DUT DIA-
298FRE DIA-
298GER DIA-
298HUN DIA-
298ITA DIA-
298POL DIA-
298POR DIA-
298RUS DIA-
298SPA DIA-
298SWE DIA-

299AAA DIALOG
299CZE ROZMLUVA
299DAN DIALOG
299DUT DIALOOG
299FRE DIALOGUE
299GER DIALOG
299HUN DIALÓGUS
299ITA DIALOGO
299POL DIALOGI
299POR DIÁLOGO
299RUS DIALOG
299SPA DIÁLOGO
299SWE DIALOG

300AAA DIAPASON
300CZE LADIČKA, ROZSAH TÓNOVÝ
300DAN TONEREGISTER
300DUT OCTAAF
300FRE DIAPASON, MONTRE
300GER DIAPASON, PRINZIPAL
300HUN EREDETILEG OKTAV
300ITA DIAPASON, PRINCIPALE
300POL DIAPAZON
300POR DIAPASÃO
300RUS DIAPAZON
300SPA DIAPASÓN, FACHADA
300SWE TONOMFÅNG

301AAA DIAPHRAGM
301CZE BRÁNICE
301DAN MELLEMGULV
301DUT DIAPHRAGMA
301FRE DIAPHRAGME
301GER DIAPHRAGMA
301HUN REKESZIZOM
301ITA DIAFRAMMA
301POL DIAFRAGMA
301POR DIAFRAGMA
301RUS DIAFRAGMA
301SPA DIAFRAGMA
301SWE MELLANGARDE

302AAA DIATONIC
302CZE DIATONICKÝ
302DAN DIATONISK
302DUT DIATONISCH
302FRE DIATONIQUE
302GER DIATONISCH(E)
302HUN DIATONIKUS
302ITA DIATONICO
302POL DIATONIKA
302POR DIATÔNICO
302RUS DIATONIKA
302SPA DIATÓNICO
302SWE DIATONISK

303AAA DICTATE, TO
303CZE DIKTOVÁNÍ
303DAN DIKTERE
303DUT DICTEREN
303FRE DICTER
303GER DIKTIEREN
303HUN DIKTÁLNI
303ITA DETTARE
303POL DYKTOWAĆ
303POR DITAR
303RUS DIKTOVAT'
303SPA DICTAR
303SWE DIKTERA

304AAA DICTION
304CZE DIKCE
304DAN DIKTION
304DUT DICTIE
304FRE DICTION
304GER DIKTION
304HUN ELŐADÁS
304ITA DIZIONE
304POL DYKCJA
304POR DICÇÃO
304RUS DIKTSIĬA
304SPA DICCIÓN
304SWE DIKTION

305AAA DIFFERENT
305CZE ROZLIČNÝ
305DAN FORSKELLIG
305DUT· VERSCHILLEND
305FRE DIFFÉRENT
305GER VERSCHIEDEN(E)
305HUN KÜLÖNBÖZŐ
305ITA DIFFERENTE
305POL RÓŻNY
305POR DIFERENTE
305RUS RAZLICHNYĬ
305SPA DIFERENTE
305SWE SKILJAKTIG

306AAA DIFFRACTION
306CZE ODCHÝLENÍ
306DAN DIFFRAKTION
306DUT DIFFRACTIE
306FRE DIFFRACTION
306GER DIFFRAKTION
306HUN FÉNYTÖRÉS
306ITA DIFFRAZIONE
306POL UGINANIE
306POR DIFRAÇÃO
306RUS DIFRAKTSIĬA
306SPA DIFRACCIÓN
306SWE BÖJNING

307AAA DIGNITY
307CZE DŮSTOJNOST
307DAN OPHØJE
307DUT WAARDIGHEID
307FRE DIGNITÉ
307GER WÜRDE
307HUN MÉLTÓSÁG
307ITA DIGNITÀ
307POL DOSTOJNOŚĆ
307POR DIGNIDADE
307RUS DOSTOINSTVO
307SPA DIGNIDAD
307SWE UPPHÖJA

308AAA DIMINISH, TO
308CZE ZMĚNŠITI
308DAN FORMINDSKE
308DUT VERMINDEREN, AFNEMEN
308FRE DIMINUER
308GER VERMINDERN, ABNEHMEN
308HUN SZŰKÍTNI
308ITA DIMINUIRE, SCEMARE
308POL ZMNIEJSZAĆ
308POR DIMINUIR
308RUS UMEN'SHAT'
308SPA DISMINUIR
308SWE FÖRMINSKA

309AAA DIMINUTION
309CZE ZMENŠOVÁNÍ, UBÝVÁNÍ
309DAN FORMINDSKELSE
309DUT VERKLEINING
309FRE DIMINUTION
309GER VERKLEINERUNG
309HUN KISEBBEDÉS
309ITA DIMINUZIONE
309POL DIMINUCJA
309POR DIMINUIÇÃO
309RUS UMEN'SHENIE
309SPA DIMINUCIÓN
309SWE FÖRMINSKNING

310AAA DIRECTOR
310CZE ŘEDITEL
310DAN DIRIGENT
310DUT DIRIGENT
310FRE DIRECTEUR
310GER INTENDANT
310HUN ZENEIGAZGATÓ
310ITA DIRETTORE
310POL DYRYGENT
310POR DIRETOR
310RUS DIREKTOR
310SPA DIRECTOR
310SWE DIREKTÖR

311AAA DIRECT, TO
311CZE DIRIGOVATI, ŘÍDITI
311DAN DIREKTE
311DUT RICHTEN
311FRE DIRIGER
311GER RICHTEN, DIRIGIEREN
311HUN IGAZGATI, VEZÉNYELNI
311ITA DIRIGERE
311POL DYRYGOWAĆ
311POR DIRIGIR
311RUS DIRIZHIROVAT'
311SPA DIRIGIR, CONDUCIR
311SWE RIKTA

312AAA DIRGE
312CZE ŽALOZPĚV
312DAN KLAGESANG
312DUT GRAFLIED, TREURZANG
312FRE NENIE, CHANT FUNÈBRE
312GER NÄNIE, GRABGESANG
312HUN GYÁSZÉNEK
312ITA NENIA, TRENODIA
312POL ŻAŁOBNE
312POR NENIA
312RUS NADGROBNAĬA PESNĬA
312SPA ENDECHA
312SWE SORGESÅNG

313AAA DISCORD
313CZE NESOUZVUK, DISONANCE
313DAN DISHARMONI
313DUT DISHARMONIE
313FRE DISCORDANCE
313GER DISKORD, DISSONANZ
313HUN HANGZAVAR
313ITA DISCORDIA
313POL NIEZGODA, DYSONANS
313POR DISCORDE
313RUS NEVERNYĬ STROĬ
313SPA DISCORDE
313SWE MISSLJUD, DISSONANS

314AAA DISMAL
314CZE PONURÝ, SMUTNÝ
314DAN TRIST
314DUT DUISTER
314FRE TRISTE
314GER DÜSTER
314HUN SZOMORÚ
314ITA TRISTE
314POL PONURY
314POR TRISTE
314RUS GNETUSHCHIĬ, UGRIUMYĬ
314SPA TRISTE
314SWE DYSTER

315AAA DISPLACE, TO
315CZE PŘEMÍSTITI
315DAN FLYTTE
315DUT VERPLAATSEN
315FRE DÉPLACER
315GER VERSETZEN
315HUN ELMOZDÍTNI
315ITA SPOSTARE
315POL PRZESUWAĆ
315POR DESLOCAR
315RUS PEREMESHCHAT'
315SPA DEPONER
315SWE FÖRSÄTTA

316AAA DISSONANCE
316CZE NESOUZVUK, NESHODA
316DAN DISSONANS
316DUT DISSONANT
316FRE DISSONANCE
316GER DISSONANZ
316HUN SZÉTHANGZAS
316ITA DISSONANZA
316POL DYSONANS
316POR DISSONANCIA
316RUS NEBLAGOZVUCHIE
316SPA DISONANCIA
316SWE MISSLJUD

317AAA DISSONANT
317CZE DISONUJÍCÍ
317DAN DISSONANTS
317DUT DISSONANT
317FRE DISSONANTE
317GER DISSONANT
317HUN SZÉTHANZÓ
317ITA DISSONANTE
317POL DYSONANS
317POR DISSONANTE
317RUS NESTROĬNYĬ
317SPA DISONANTE
317SWE MISSLJUDANDE

318AAA DISTANCE
318CZE VZDÁLENOST
318DAN ABSTAND
318DUT AFSTAND
318FRE DISTANCE
318GER ENTFERNUNG
318HUN TÁVOLSÁG
318ITA DISTANZA
318POL ODDALENIE
318POR DISTÂNCIA
318RUS DISTANTSIIA
318SPA DISTANCIA
318SWE AFSTÅND

319AAA DISTINCT
319CZE ODLIŠNÝ, ZŘETELNÝ
319DAN FORSKELLING
319DUT HELDER
319FRE DISTINCT
319GER DEUTLICH
319HUN VILÁGOSAN
319ITA DISTINTO
319POL ODRĘBNY
319POR DISTINTO
319RUS OTLICHNYĬ
319SPA DISTINTO
319SWE SKILNAD

320AAA DISTORTION
320CZE ZKROUCENÍ
320DAN FORVRIDNING
320DUT VERWRINGING
320FRE CONTORSION
320GER VERDREHUNG
320HUN SVÉTVÁLASZTÁS
320ITA DISTORSIONE
320POL SKRĘCENIE
320POR TORCEDURA
320RUS IZVRASHCHAT'
320SPA TORCEDURA
320SWE FÖRVRIDNING

321AAA DIVERSION
321CZE DIVERTIMENTO
321DAN UNDERHOLDNING
321DUT TUSSENSPEL
321FRE DIVERTISSEMENT
321GER DIVERTISSEMENT
321HUN SZÓRAKOZÁS
321ITA DIVERTIMENTO
321POL UCIECHA, ZABAWA
321POR DIVERSÃO
321RUS DIVERTISMENT
321SPA DIVERTIMIENTO
321SWE UPPEHÅLLNING

322AAA DIVIDE, TO
322CZE ROZDĚLITI
322DAN DELE
322DUT DELEN
322FRE DIVISER
322GER TEILEN
322HUN OSZTANI
322ITA DIVIDERE
322POL ROZDZIELAĆ
322POR DIVIDIR
322RUS RAZDELIAT'
322SPA DIVIDIR
322SWE DIVIDERA

323AAA DO, TO
323CZE ČINITI
323DAN GØRE
323DUT DOEN
323FRE FAIRE
323GER MACHEN
323HUN TENNI
323ITA FARE
323POL CZYNIĆ
323POR FAZAR
323RUS DELAT
323SPA HACER'
323SWE GÖRA

324AAA DODECÁPHONY
324CZE DODECAFONIE
324DAN TOLVTONSYSTEM
324DUT DODEKAKOFONIE
324FRE DODÉCAPHONIE
324GER DODEKAPHONIE
324HUN DODEKAFÓNIA
324ITA DODECAFONIA
324POL DODEKAFONIA
324POR DODECAFÓNIA
324RUS DODEKAFONIIA
324SPA DODECAFONÍA
324SWE DODEKAFONI

325AAA DOMINANT
325CZE DOMINANTA
325DAN DOMINANT
325DUT DOMINANT
325FRE DOMINANTE
325GER DOMINANTE
325HUN DOMINÁNS
325ITA DOMINANTE
325POL DOMINANTA
325POR DOMINANTE
325RUS DOMINANTA
325SPA DOMINANTE
325SWE DOMINANT

326AAA DORIAN
326CZE DORICKÝ, DORSKÝ
326DAN DORISK
326DUT DORISCH
326FRE DORIEN
326GER DORISCH
326HUN DÓR
326ITA DORIANO
326POL DORYCKA
326POR DÓRIO, DÓRICO
326RUS DORICHESKII
326SPA DÓRICO
326SWE DORISK

327AAA DOT
327CZE BOD
327DAN PUNKT
327DUT PUNT
327FRE POINT
327GER PUNKT, STICH
327HUN PONT
327ITA PUNTO
327POL PUNKTO
327POR PONTO
327RUS TOCHKA
327SPA PUNTILLO, PUNTO
327SWE PUNKT

328AAA DOUBLE, TO
328CZE ZDVOJITI
328DAN DUBLERE, FORDOBLE
328DUT VERDUBBELEN
328FRE REDOUBLER
328GER VERDOPPELN
328HUN KETTŐZNI
328ITA RADDOPPIARE
328POL DUBLOWAĆ
328POR DOBRAR
328RUS DUBLIROVAT'
328SPA DOBLAR
328SWE DUBBLERA

329AAA DOUBLE BASS
329CZE KONTRABAS
329DAN KONTRABAS
329DUT CONTRABAS
329FRE CONTREBASSE
329GER KONTRABASS
329HUN GORDON
329ITA CONTRABASSO
329POL KONTRABAS
329POR CONTRABAIXO
329RUS KONTRABAS
329SPA CONTRABAJO
329SWE KONTRABAS

330AAA DOXOLOGY
330CZE CHVALOZPĚV
330DAN LOVPRISNING
330DUT DOXOLOGIE
330FRE DOXOLOGIE
330GER DOXOLOGIE
330HUN DOXOLÓGIA
330ITA DOSSOLOGIA
330POL HYMN POCHWALNY
330POR DOXOLOGIA
330RUS SLAVOSLOVIE
330SPA GLORIA PATRI
330SWE DOXOLOGI

331AAA DRAG, TO
331CZE VLÉCI
331DAN SLAEBE
331DUT SLEPEN
331FRE TRAÎNER
331GER SCHLEPPEN
331HUN VONTATNI
331ITA TRAINARE, TRASCINARE
331POL WLEC SIĘ
331POR ARRASTAR
331RUS VLASHIT'
331SPA ARRASTRAR
331SWE SLÄPA

332AAA DRAMA
332CZE DRAMA
332DAN DRAMA
332DUT DRAMA, HANDELING
332FRE DRAMA
332GER DRAMA, SCHAUSPIEL
332HUN DRÁMA
332ITA DRAMMA
332POL DRAMAT
332POR DRAMA
332RUS DRAMA
332SPA DRAMA
332SWE DRAMA

333AAA DRAW OUT, TO
333CZE ROZŠIRITI, ZPOMALITI
333DAN UDBREDE
333DUT LANG AANHOUDEN
333FRE ELARGIR
333GER BREITER WERDEN
333HUN ELLASSULVA
333ITA SLARGARE
333POL ROZSZERZAĆ
333POR ALARGAR
333RUS RAZCHIRIAT'
333SPA ALARGAR
333SWE UTBREDA

334AAA DREAM, TO
334CZE SNÍTI
334DAN DRØMME
334DUT VERDROMEN
334FRE RÊVER
334GER TRÄUMEN
334HUN ÁLMODOZNI
334ITA SOGNARE
334POL ŚNIĆ
334POR SONHAR
334RUS SNIT'SIA
334SPA SOÑAR
334SWE DRÖMMA

335AAA DRONE
335CZE BURDON, KRYT
335DAN DRONE
335DUT REFREIN
335FRE FAUX-BOURDON
335GER DROHNE
335HUN BORDÓ
335ITA RITORNELLO, BORDONE
335POL REFREN,TRUTEN
335POR ZÂNGÃO
335RUS TRUTEN'
335SPA ZÁNGANO, ABEJÓN
335SWE BORDUNA

336AAA DRUM
336CZE BUBEN
336DAN TROMME
336DUT TROMMEL
336FRE TAMBOUR
336GER TROMMEL
336HUN DOB
336ITA TAMBURO
336POL BĘBEN
336POR TAMBOR
336RUS BARABAN
336SPA TAMBOR
336SWE TRUMMA

337AAA DRUMHEAD
337CZE KŮŽENABUBNU
337DAN TROMMESKIND
337DUT TROMMELVEL
337FRE PEAU DE TAMBOUR
337GER TROMMELFELL
337HUN DOBHÁRTYA
337ITA MEMBRANA
337POL SKÓRA NA BĘBNIE
337POR PELE DE TAMBOR
337RUS BARABANNAĬA KOZHA
337SPA PARCHE, PIEL
337SWE TRUMSKINN

338AAA DRUMSTICK
338CZE PALIČKA U BUBNU
338DAN TROMMESTIKKE, PALILLO
338DUT TROMMELSTOK
338FRE BAGUETTE
338GER TROMMELSTOCK
338HUN DOBVERŐ
338ITA BACCHETTA
338POL PAŁECZKA
338POR BAQUETA
338RUS PALOCHKA
338SPA BAQUETA
338SWE TRUMPINNE

339AAA DRY
339CZE SUCHÝ
339DAN TØR
339DUT KORT
339FRE SÈC
339GER TROCKEN
339HUN SZÁRAZ
339ITA SECCO
339POL SUCHO
339POR SÊCO
339RUS SUKHOĬ
339SPA SECO
339SWE TORRT

340AAA DUET
340CZE DUETO
340DAN DUET
340DUT DUET
340FRE DUETTE, DUETTO, DUO
340GER DUETT
340HUN DUETT
340ITA DUETTO, DUO
340POL DUET
340POR DUETO
340RUS DUET
340SPA DUETO, DUO
340SWE DEUTT

341AAA DULCIMER
341CZE CIMBÁL(U)
341DAN HAKKEBRAEDT
341DUT HAKKEBORD
341FRE TYMPANON
341GER HACKBRETT, ZIMBAL
341HUN CIMBALOM
341ITA SALTERIO TEDESCO
341POL CYMBAŁY
341POR SALTÉRIO, CÍTARA
341RUS PIMBALY
341SPA DULCÉMELE
341SWE HACKBRÄDE

342AAA DUMB, MUTE
342CZE NĚMÝ
342DAN STUM
342DUT STOM
342FRE MUET
342GER STUMM
342HUN NÉMA
342ITA MUTO
342POL NIEMY
342POR MUDO
342RUS NEMOĬ
342SPA MUDO
342SWE STUM

343AAA DUPLE
343CZE DVOJNÁSOBNÝ
343DAN DOBBELT
343DUT DUBBEL
343FRE DOUBLE
343GER DOPPELT, ZWEIFACH
343HUN KÉTSZERES
343ITA DOPPIO, DUPLA
343POL PODWÓJNY
343POR DUPLO
343RUS DVOĬNOĬ
343SPA DOBLE, DUPLO
343SWE DUBBEL

344AAA DUPLICATE, TO
344CZE ZDVOJITI
344DAN DUPLIKERE
344DUT VERDUBBELEN
344FRE FAIRE LE DOUBLE
344GER VERDOPPLEN
344HUN MEGKETTŐZNI
344ITA DUPLICARE
344POL PODWAJAĆ
344POR DUPLICAR
344RUS DUBLIROVAT'
344SPA DUPLICAR
344SWE FORDUBBLA

345AAA DURATION
345CZE TRVÁNÍ, DÉLKA
345DAN VARIGHED
345DUT DUUR
345FRE DURÉE
345GER DAUER
345HUN ELŐADÁSI IDŐ
345ITA DURATA
345POL TRWANIE
345POR DURAÇÃO
345RUS VREMIA
345SPA DURACIÓN
345SWE VARAKTIGHET

346AAA DYING (AWAY)
346CZE UBÝVAVĚ
346DAN DOENDE
346DUT STERVENDE
346FRE ETEINDRE, S'ÉTEIGNANT
346GER ERLÖSCHEND, VERTONEND
346HUN ELFOSZÓAN
346ITA MORENDO, PERDENDOSI
346POL ZAMIERAJĄC
346POR APAGANDO
346RUS VYMIRANIE
346SPA APAGANDO
346SWE BORTDÖENDE

347AAA DYNAMICS
347CZE DYNAMIKA
347DAN DYNAMIK
347DUT DYNAMIEK
347FRE DYNAMIQUE
347GER DYNAMIK
347HUN DINAMIKA
347ITA DINAMICA
347POL DYNAMIKA
347POR DINÂMICA
347RUS DINAMIKA
347SPA DINAMICA
347SWE DYNAMIK

348AAA EAGER
348CZE ŽHAVÝ
348DAN IVRIG
348DUT VURIG
348FRE ARDENTE, EMPRESSÉ
348GER GLÜHEND, FEURIG
348HUN LÁNGOLÓAN
348ARD ENTE
348POL OGNIŚCIE
348POR ANSIOSO, ÁVIDO
348RUS PYLAIUSHCHII
348SPA ANHELANTE
348SWE BRÄNNANDE

349AAA EAR
349CZE UCHO
349DAN ØRE
349DUT OOR
349FRE OREILLE
349GER OHR
349HUN FÜL
349ITA ORECCHIO
349POL UCHO
349POR ORELHA
349RUS UCHO
349SPA OREJA
349SWE ÖRA

350AAA EARDRUM
350CZE UŠNÍ BUBÍNEK
350DAN TROMMEHINDE
350DUT TROMMELVLIES
350FRE TYMPAN
350GER TROMMELFELL
350HUN DOBHÁRTYA
350ITA TIMPANO
350POL BĘBENEK
350POR TÍMPANO
350RUS BARABANNAIA PEREPONKA
350SPA TÍMPANO DEL OÍDO
350SWE TRUMHINNA

351AAA EBULLIENT
351CZE OHNIVÉ, KYPÍCÍ
351DAN KOGENDE
351DUT KOKEND
351FRE FOUGUEUSEMENT
351GER FEURIG
351HUN FORRONGÁS
351ITA EBOLLIMENTE
351POL KIPIĄCY
351POR EBULIENTE
351RUS KIPIASHCHII
351SPA FOGOSAMENTE
351SWE KOKANDE

352AAA ECCLESIASTIC
352CZE CÍRKEVNÍ
352DAN GEJSTLIG
352DUT KERKELIJK, GEESTELIJKE
352FRE ECCLÉSIASTIQUE
352GER GEISTLICHE , KIRCHLICH
352HUN EGYHÁZI
352ITA ECCLESIASTICO
325POL DUCHOWNY
352POR ECLESIÁSTICO
352RUS DUKHOVNYI, TSERKOVNYI
352SPA ECLESIÁSTICO
352SWE ECKLESIASTIK

353AAA ECHO
353CZE OZVĚNA, ECHO
353DAN EKKO
353DUT ECHO
353FRE ÉCHO
353GER ECHO
353HUN VIZZHANG, ECHO
353ITA EC(C)O
353POL ECHO
353POR ECO
353RUS EKHO
353SPA ECO
353SWE EKO

354AAA ECLOGUE
354CZE EKLOGA
354DAN HYRDEDIGT
354DUT HERDERSDICHT
354FRE ECLOGUE, ÉGLOGUE
354GER EKLOGE
354HUN PÁSZTORDAL
354ITA EGLOGA
354POL EKLOGA
354POR ÉCLOGA
354RUS EKLOGA
354SPA ÉGLOGA
354SWE EKLOG

355AAA EDIT, TO
355CZE VYDÁVATI, REDIGOVATI
355DAN UDGIVE
355DUT UITGAVE
355FRE ÉDITER
355GER EDIEREN, HERAUSGEBEN
355HUN KIADNI
355ITA CURARE
355POL WYDAWAĆ
355POR EDITAR
355RUS REDAKTIROVAT'
355SPA EDITAR
355SWE UTGIVA

356AAA EFFECT
356CZE ÚČINEK
356DAN VIRKNING
356DUT UITWERKING
356FRE EFFET
356GER EFFEKT, WIRKUNG
356HUN HATÁS
356ITA EFFETTO
356POL SKUTEK
356POR EFEITO
356RUS EFFEKT
356SPA EFECTO
356SWE VERKAN

357AAA EIGHT
357CZE OSM
357DAN OTTE
357DUT ACHT
357FRE HUIT
357GER ACHT
357HUN NYOLC
357ITA OTTO
357POL ÓSMY
357POR OITO
357RUS VOSEM'
357SPA OCHO
357SWE ÅTTA

358AAA EIGHTH NOTE, QUAVER
358CZE OSMINOVÁ NOTA
358DAN OTTENDEDELSNODE
358DUT TRILLER, 8STE NOOT
358FRE CROCHE
358GER ACHTELNOTE, TRILLER
358HUN NYOLCZADKÓTA
358ITA CROMA
358POL ÓSEMKA
358POR COLCHEIA
358RUS VOS'MAIA
358SPA CORCHEA
358SWE ÅTTONDELS NOT

359AAA ELECTRO-
359CZE ELEKTRO-
359DAN ELEKTRO-
359DUT ELECTRO-
359FRE ELECTRO-
359GER ELEKTRO-
359HUN ELEKTRO-
359ITA ELETTRO-
359POL ELEKTRO-
359POR ELEKTRO-
359RUS ELEKTRO-
359SPA ELECTRO-
359SWE ELEKTRO-

360AAA ELEGANT
360CZE ELEGANTNÍ
360DAN ELEGANT
360DUT ELEGANT, SIERLIJK
360FRE ÉLÉGANT
360GER ELEGANT, ZEIRLICH
360HUN VÁLASZTÉKOS
360ITA ELEGANTE
360POL WYTWORNIE
360POR ELEGANTE
360RUS ELEGANTNYĬ
360SPA ELEGANTE
360SWE ELEGANT, SIRLIGT

361AAA ELEGY
361CZE ELEGIE, ŽALOZPĚV
361DAN ELEGI
361DUT ELEGIE
361FRE ÉLÉGIE
361GER ELEGIE
361HUN ALAGYA
361ITA ELEGIA
361POL ELEGJA, SKARGA
361POR ELEGIA
361RUS ELEGIIA
361SPA ELEGÍA
361SWE ELEGI, KLAGOSANG

362AAA ELEMENT
362CZE PRVEK
362DAN ELEMENT
362DUT ELEMENT
362FRE ÉLÉMENT
362GER ELEMENT
362HUN ELEMI
362ITA ELEMENTO
362POL ELEMENT
362POR ELEMENTO
362RUS ELEMENT
362SPA ELEMENTO
362SWE ELEMENT

363AAA ELEVATE, TO
363CZE ZDVIHNOUTI
363DAN OPHØJE
363DUT VERHEVEN
363FRE ÉLEVER
363GER ERHABEN
363HUN EMELNI
363ITA ELEVARE
363POL PODNIEŚĆ
363POR ELEVAR
363RUS PODNIMAT'
363SPA ELEVAR
363SWE UPPHÖJA

364AAA ELEVEN
364CZE JEDENÁCT
364DAN ELLEVE
364DUT ELF
364FRE ONZE
364GER ELF
364HUN TIZENEGY
364ITA UNDICI
364POL JEDENAŚCIE
364POR ONZE
364RUS ODINNADTSAT'
364SPA ONCE
364SWE ELVA

365AAA ELSE
365CZE JINÝ
365DAN ELLERS
365DUT ANDERS
365FRE AUTRE
365GER SONST, WEITER
365HUN EGYÉB, VAGY
365ITA ALTRO, DI PIÙ
365POL JESZCZE, INNY
365POR OUTRO, MAIS
365RUS INOǏ
365SPA OTRO, QUALQUIER(A)
365SWE ELJEST

366AAA EMBELLISH, TO
366CZE OKRÁŠLITI
366DAN FORSKØNNE
366DUT VERZIEREN
366FRE EMBELLIR
366GER VERZIEREN
366HUN SZÉPÍTNI
366ITA ABBELLIRE, ABBELLARE
366POL UPIĘKSZAĆ
366POR EMBELEZAR
366RUS PRIUKRASHAT'
366SPA ADORNAR, EMBELLECER
366SWE FÖRSKÖNA

367AAA EMOTION
367CZE POHNUTÍ, VZRUŠENÍ
367DAN FØLELSE
367DUT ONTROERING
367FRE ÉMOTION
367GER EMPFINDUNG, RÜHRUNG
367HUN ÉRZÉS
367ITA EMOZIONE, CONCITAZIONE
367POL EMOCJA
367POR EMOÇÃO
367RUS EMOTSIIA
367SPA EMOCIÓN
367SWE RÖRELSE

368AAA EMPHASIS
368CZE DŮRAZ
368DAN EFTERTRYK
368DUT NADRUK
368FRE EMPHASE
368GER NACHDRUCK
368HUN NYOMATOSSÁG
368ITA ENFASI, ENFASO
368POL EMFAZA
368POR ÊNFASE
368RUS EMFAZA
368SPA ÉNFASIS
368SWE EFTERTRYCK

369AAA EMPHATIC
369CZE EMFATICKY, DŮRAZNÝ
369DAN EFTERTRYKKELIG
369DUT NADRUKKELIJK
369FRE EMPHATIQUE
369GER NACHDRÜCKLICH
369HUN NYOMATÉKKAL
369ITA ENFATICO
369POL EMFATYCZNY
369POR ENFÁTICO
369RUS EMFATICHESKIĬ
369SPA ENFÁTICO
369SWE EFTERTRYCKLIG

370AAA END
370CZE JEMNÝ, KONEC
370DAN ENDE
370DUT EINDE
370FRE FIN
370GER ENDE
370HUN VÉG
370ITA FINE
370POL KONIEC
370POR FINAL
370RUS KONETS
370SPA FIN
370SWE ÄNDE

371AAA ENERGY
371CZE ENERGIE
371DAN ENERGI
371DUT ENERGIE
371FRE ÉNERGIE
371GER ENERGIE
371HUN ERÉLY
371ITA ENERGIA
371POL ENERGIA
371POR ENERGIA
371RUS ENERGIIA
371SPA ENERGÍA
371SWE ENERGI

372AAA ENGLISH HORN
372CZE ANGLICKÝ ROH
372DAN ENGELSK HORN
372DUT ENGELSE HOORN
372FRE COR ANGLAIS
372GER ENGLISHES HORN
372HUN ANGOLKÜRT
372ITA CORNO INGLESE
372POL ANGIELSKI ROŻEK
372POR CORNE INGLÊS
372RUS ANGLIĬSKIĬ ROZHOK
372SPA CORNO INGLÉS
372SWE ENGELSKT HORN

373AAA ENJOYMENT
373CZE VKUS
373DAN ADSPREDELSE
373DUT SMAAK
373FRE GOÛT
373GER GESCHMACK
373HUN ÉLVEZET
373ITA GUSTO
373POL POSIADANIE
373POR GÔZO
373RUS VKUS
373SPA GUSTO
373SWE SMAK

374AAA ENOUGH
374CZE DOSTI
374DAN NOK
374DUT GENOEG
374FRE ASSEZ
374GER GENUG
374HUN ELÉG
374ITA BASTA
374POL DOSYĆ
374POR BASTANTE
374RUS DOSTATOCHNO
374SPA BASTANTE, BASTA
374SWE NOG

375AAA ENTRANCE
375CZE VSTUP, INTRÁDA
375DAN INDGANG
375DUT INTREDE
375FRE ENTRÉE
375GER EINTRITT, EINGANG
375HUN BELÉPÉS
375ITA ENTRADA, INGRESSO
375POL WSTĘP, WEJŚCIE
375POR ENTRADA
375RUS VSTUPLENIE
375SPA ENTRADA
375SWE ENTRATA

376AAA ENTHUSIASM
376CZE NADŠENÍ
376DAN BEGEJSTRING
376DUT GEESTDRIFT
376FRE ENTHOUSIASME
376GER ENTHUSIASMUS
376HUN LELKESEDÉS
376ITA ENTUSIASMO
376POL ENTUZJAZM
376POR ENTUSIASMO
376RUS ENTUZIAZM
376SPA ENTUSIASMO
376SWE ENTUSIASM

377AAA EPISODE
377CZE EPIZODA, MEZIVĚTA
377DAN EPISODE
377DUT EPISODE, TUSSENZIN
377FRE ÉPISODE
377GER EPISODE, ZWISCHENSATZ
377HUN EPIZÓD
377ITA EPISODIO
377POL EPIZOD
377POR EPISÓDIO
377RUS EPIZOD
377SPA EPISODIO
377SWE EPISOD

378AAA EQUABLE
378CZE STEJNOMĚRNÝ
378DAN JAEVN
378DUT GELIJK
378FRE EGÁLE
378GER GLEICHMÄSSIG
378HUN EGYENLETES
378ITA EQUABILE
378POL JEDNOSTAJNY
378POR IGUAL
378RUS RAVNOMERNYĬ
378SPA IGUAL, ECUABLE
378SWE JÄMN

379AAA EQUAL
379CZE STEJNÝ, ROVNÝ
379DAN LIGE
379DUT GELIJK
379FRE EGÁL
379GER GLEICH
379HUN EGYENLŐ
379ITA EGUALE, EQUABILE
379POL RÓWNY
379POR IGUAL
379RUS ROVNYĬ, RAVNYĬ
379SPA IGUAL
379SWE LIKA

380AAA EROTIC
380CZE EROTICKÝ, MILOSTNÝ
380DAN EROTISK
380DUT EROTISCH
380FRE ÉROTIQUE
380GER EROTISCH
380HUN SZERELMI
380ITA EROTICO
380POL EROTYCZNY
380POR ERÓTICO
380RUS EROTICHESKIĬ
380SPA ERÓTICO
380SWE EROTISK

381AAA EUPHONIUM
381CZE EUFONIO
381DAN SAXHORN
381DUT EUPHONIUM
381FRE SAXHORN BASSE
381GER FLÜGELHORN
381HUN EUFONIUM
381ITA FLICORNO
381POL EUFONIUM
381POR BOMBARDINO
381RUS FLIUGEL' HORN
381SPA EUFONO
381SWE SAXHORN

382AAA EUPHONY
382CZE LIBOZVUČNOST
382DAN VELKLANG
382DUT WELLUIDENDHEID
382FRE EUPHONIE
382GER EUPHONIE, WOHLKLANG
382HUN HANGKELLEM
382ITA EUFONIA
382POL EUFONJA
382POR EUFÓNIA
382RUS EVFONIIA
382SPA EUFONÍA
382SWE VÄLLJUD

383AAA EURHYTHMY(-ICS)
383CZE RYTHMOVÝ SOULAD
383DAN RYTMISK GYMNASTIK
383DUT RITMISCHE GYMNASTIEK
383FRE EURYTHMIE
383GER RHYTHMISCHE GYMNASTIK
383HUN EURITMIA
383ITA EURITMIA
383POL EURYTMIA
383POR EURRITMIA
383RUS EVRITMIA
383SPA EURITMIA
383SWE RYTMISK DANS

384AAA EVEN
384CZE VYROVNANÝ
384DAN EFFEN, LIG(E)
384DUT EENVOUDIG
384FRE EGALE, UNI
384GER EBEN, EGAL
384HUN EGYSZERŰEN
384ITA SPIANATO, EGUALE
384POL RÓWNY
384POR IGUAL
384RUS ROVNO
384SPA IGUAL
384SWE ENKELT, LIKA

385AAA EVENING
385CZE VEČERNÍ ZÁBAVA
385DAN AFTEN
385DUT AVOND
385FRE SOIR
385GER ABEND
385HUN ESTE
385ITA SERA, SERATA
385POL WIECZÓR
385POR VESPERTINO
385RUS VECHER
385SPA VESPERTINA
385SWE AFTON

386AAA EVER
386CZE VŽDY
386DAN ALTID
386DUT ALTIJD, STEEDS
386FRE TOUJOURS
386GER IMMER
386HUN MINDIG
386ITA SEMPRE
386POL ZAWSZE
386POR SEMPRE
386RUS VSEGDA
386SPA SIEMPRE
386SWE ALLTID

387AAA EXACT
387CZE PŘESNÝ, EXAKTNÍ
387DAN EKSAKT
387DUT EXACT
387FRE EXACTE
387GER EXAKT, GENAU
387HUN PONTOS
387ITA ESATTA
387POL ŚCISŁY
387POR EXATO
387RUS TOCHNYĬ
387SPA EXACTO
387SWE NOGGRANN

388AAA EXAGGERATE, TO
388CZE PŘEHÁNĚTI
388DAN OVERDRIVE
388DUT OVERDRIJVEN
388FRE EXAGÉRER
388GER ÜBERTREIBEN
388HUN TÚLOZNI
388ITA ESAGERARE
388POL PRZESADZAĆ
388POR EXAGERAR
388RUS PREUVELICHIVAT'
388SPA EXAGERAR
388SWE ÖVERDRIVA

389AAA EXALT, TO
389CZE ROZNÍTITI
389DAN OPHØJE
389DUT VERHEFFEN
389FRE EXALTER
389GER ERHEBEN
389HUN FÖLEMELNI
389ITA ESALTARE
389POL WYWYŻSZAĆ
389POR EXALTAR
389RUS VOZVYSHAT'
389SPA EXALTAR
389SWE UPPHÖJA

390AAA EXALTATION
390CZE VYNÁŠENI
390DAN OPHØJELSE
390DUT VERHEFFING, OPWINDING
390FRE EXALTATION
390GER ERHEBUNG
390HUN MAGASZTALÁS
390ITA ESALTAZIONE
390POL WYWYŻSZENIE
390POR EXALTAÇÃO
390RUS VOZVYSHENIE
390SPA EXALTACIÓN
390SWE UPPHÖJELSE

391AAA EXCITE, TO
391CZE PODRÁŽDITI
391DAN OPHIDSE
391DUT PRIKKELEN
391FRE EXCITER
391GER ERREGEN
391HUN IZGATNI
391ITA ECCITARE
391POL PODNIECAĆ
391POR EXCITAR
391RUS VOZBUZHDAT'
391SPA EXCITAR
391SWE RETA

392AAA EXECUTE, TO
392CZE PROVÉSTI
392DAN SPILLE
392DUT UITVOEREN
392FRE EXÉCUTER
392GER SPIELEN
392HUN JÁTSZANI, ZENÉLNI
392ITA ESEGUIRE
392POL SPEŁNIENIE
392POR EXECUTAR
392RUS IGRAT', ISTOLNIT'
392SPA EJECUTAR
392SWE SPELA

393AAA EXERCISE
393CZE CVIČENÍ
393DAN PRAKSIS, UDØVELSE
393DUT OEFENING
393FRE EXERCICE
393GER ÜBUNG
393HUN GYAKORLAT
393ITA ESERCIZIO
393POL ĆWICZENIE
393POR EXERCÍCIO
393RUS EKZERSISY
393SPA EJERSISIO
393SWE UTÖVANDE

394AAA EXHALE, TO
394CZE VYPRCHATI
394DAN UDDUNSTE
394DUT UITADEMEN
394FRE EXHALER
394GER AUSDÜNSTEN
394HUN KILEHELNI
394ITA ESALARE
394POL WYŻIEWAĆ, WYDAWAĆ
394POR EXALAR
394RUS VYDYKHAT'
394SPA EXHALAR
394SWE UTDUNSTA

395AAA EXIT
395CZE VÝCVIK
395DAN UDGANG
395DUT UITGANG
395FRE SORTIE
395GER ABGANG
395HUN LELÉPÉS
395ITA USCITA
395POL WYJŚCIE
395POR SAÍDA
395RUS VYKHOD
395SPA SALIDA
395SWE UTGÅNG

396AAA EXPAND, TO
396CZE ROZEPNOUTI SE
396DAN UDBREDE
396DUT UITBREIDEN
396FRE DILATER
396GER AUSSPANNEN
396HUN KIFESZÍTENI
396ITA ESPANDERSI
396POL ROZPRĘŻAĆ
396POR EXPANDIR
396RUS RASPROSTRANIAT'
396SPA EXPANDIR
396SWE UTBREDA

397AAA EXPECT, TO
397CZE ČEKATI
397DAN VENTE
397DUT VERWACHTEN
397FRE ATTENDRE
397GER ERWARTEN
397HUN VÁRNI
397ITA ASPETTARE
397POL OCZEKIWAĆ
397POR EXPECTAR
397RUS OZHIDAT'
397SPA ESPERAR
397SWE VÄNTA

398AAA EXPIRE, TO
398CZE VYDECHNOUTI
398DAN UDÅNDE
398DUT UITADEMEN
398FRE EXPIRER
398GER ERLÖSCHEN
398HUN KILEHELNI
398ITA SPIRARE
398POL WYDYCHAĆ
398POR EXPIRAR
398RUS VYDYKHAT'
398SPA EXPIRAR
398SWE UTANDA

399AAA EXPOSITION
399CZE EXPOSICE
399DAN EKSPOSITION
399DUT EXPOSITIE
399FRE EXPOSITION
399GER ERKLÄRUNG
399HUN EXPOZÍCIÓ
399ITA ESPOSIZIONE
399POL EKSPOZYCJA
399POR EXPOSIÇÃO
399RUS EKSPOZITSIIA
399SPA EXPOSICIÓN
399SWE EXPOSITION

400AAA EXPRESSION
400CZE VÝRAZ
400DAN UDTRYK
400DUT UITDRUK
400FRE EXPRESSION
400GER AUSDRUCK
400HUN ELŐADÁSI JELEK
400ITA ESPRESSIONE
400POL WYRAŻANIE
400POR EXPRESSÃO
400RUS EKSPRESSIIA
400SPA EXPRESIÓN
400SWE UTTRYCK

401AAA EXTENSION
401CZE ROZSAH
401DAN UDSTRAEKNING
401DUT EXTENSIE
401FRE ETENSION
401GER ERWEITUNG
401HUN HANGTERJEDELEM
401ITA ESTENSIONE
401POL ROZCIĄGANIE
401POR EXTENSÃO
401RUS RASHIRENIE
401SPA EXTENSIÓN
401SWE UTSTRÄCKANDE

402AAA EXTRAVAGANT
402CZE EXTRAVAGANTNÍ
402DAN BESYNDERLIG
402DUT BUITENSPORIG
402FRE EXTRAVAGANT
402GER EXTRAVAGANT, LUSTIG
402HUN KÜLÖNCKÖDÖEN
402ITA STRAVAGANTE
402POL NADMIERNY
402POR EXTRAVAGENTE
402RUS EKSTRAVAGANTNYĬ
402SPA EXTRAÑO
402SWE BESYNNERLIG

403AAA EXTREME
403CZE EXTRÉM
403DAN YDERST
403DUT UITERSTE
403FRE EXTRÊME
403GER ÄUSSERESTE, HÖCHST
403HUN SZÉLSÖSÉGES
403ITA ESTREMO, SOMMO
403POL SKRAJNY
403POR EXTREMO
403RUS KRAĬNIĬ
403SPA EXTREMO, SUMA
403SWE YTTERST

404AAA EXUBERANT
404CZE BUJNÝ
404DAN YPPIG
404DUT UITBUNDIG
404FRE EXUBÉRANT
404GER ÜPPIG
404HUN BÖSÉGES
404ITA ESUBERANTE
404POL BUJNY
404POR EXUBERANTE
404RUS BUĬNYĬ, OBIL'NYĬ
404SPA EXUBERANTE
404SWE YPPIG

405AAA EXULT, TO
405CZE JÁSATI
405DAN JUBLE
405DUT JUBELEN, JUICHEN
405FRE EXULTER
405GER FROHLOCKEN
405HUN UJJONGANI
405ITA ESULTARE
405POL RADOWAĆ SIĘ
405POR EXULTAR
405RUS RADOVAT'SĬA
405SPA TRIUNFAR
405SWE JUBLA

406AAA FACILE
406CZE SNADNÝ
406DAN FACIL
406DUT GEMAKKELIJK
406FRE FACILE
406GER LEICHT
406HUN KÖNNYEN
406ITA FACILE
406POL ŁATWY
406POR FÁCIL
406RUS LEGKIĬ
406SPA FÁCIL
406SWE LÄTT

407AAA FALL, TO
407CZE PADATI
407DAN FALDE
407DUT VALLEN
407FRE S'BAISSER, TOMBER
407GER FALLEN
407HUN ESNI
407ITA CADERE
407POL PADAĆ
407POR CAIR
407RUS PADAT'
407SPA CAER
407SWE FALLA

408AAA FALSE
408CZE FALEŠNY
408DAN FALSK
408DUT VALS
408FRE FAUX, FAUSSE
408GER FALSCH
408HUN HAMIS
408ITA FALSA, FALSO
408POL FAŁSZYWY
408POR FALSO
408RUS FAL'SHIVYĬ
408SPA FALSO
408SWE FALSK

409AAA FAMILIAR
409CZE DŮVĚRNÝ
409DAN FAMILIAER
409DUT GEMEENZAAM
409FRE FAMILIER
409GER GEWÖHNLICH, FAMILIÄR
409HUN CSALÁDIAS
409ITA FAMILIARE
409POL FAMILIJNY
409POR FAMILIAR
409RUS FAMIL'IARNYĬ
409S7A FAMILIAR
409SWE FAMILJÄR

410AAA FANFARE
410CZE FANFÁRA
410DAN FANFARE
410DUT FANFARE
410FRE FANFARE
410GER FANFARE, BLECHMUSIK
410HUN FANFÁR
410ITA FANFARA
410POL FANFARA
410POR FANFARRA
410RUS FANFARA
410SPA FANFARRIA
410SWE FANFAR

411AAA FANTASY
411CZE FANTASIE
411DAN FANTASI
411DUT FANTASIE
411FRE FANTAISIE
411GER PHANTASIE, FANTASIE
411HUN FANTÁZIA
411ITA FANTASIA
411POL FANTAZJA
411POR FANTASIA
411RUS FANTAZIIA
411SPA FANTASÍA
411SWE FANTASI

412AAA FARCE
412CZE FRAŠKA
412DAN FARCE
412DUT KLUCHT
412FRE FARCE
412GER GAUKELSPIEL
412HUN ZENÉS BOHÓZAT
412ITA FARSA
412POL FARSA
412POR FARSA
412RUS FARSH
412SPA FARSA
412SWE FARS

413AAA FAREWELL
413CZE ROZLOUČENÍ
413DAN FARVEL
413DUT VAARWEL
413FRE ADIEU
413GER LEBEWOHL
413HUN ISTENHOZZÁD
413ITA ADDIO
413POL ŻEGNAJ(CIE)
413POR ADEUS
413RUS PROSHCHAĬ, RAZLUKA
413SPA ADIÓS
413SWE FARVÄL

414AAA FAST
414CZE PEVNÝ, TVRDÝ
414DAN FAST
414DUT SNEL
414FRE RAPIDE
414GER SCHNELL
414HUN GYORS
414ITA RAPIDO
414POL SZYBSZE, PEWNIE
414POR APRESSADO
414RUS POSPESHNYĬ, BYSTRO
414SPA APRISA, RÁPIDO
414SWE FAST, HASTIGT

415AAA FEAR
415CZE STRACH
415DAN FRYGT
415DUT BESCHROOMD
415FRE CRAINTE
415GER FURCHT
415HUN FÉLELEM
415ITA TIMORE, PAURA
415POL STRACH
415POR MĚDO
415RUS STRAKH
415SPA MIEDO
415SWE FRUKTAN

416AAA FEAST
416CZE SLAVNOST
416DAN FEST
416DUT FEEST
416FRE FÊTE
416GER FEST, FEIER
416HUN ÜNNEP
416ITA FESTA
416POL ŚWIĘTO
416POR FESTA
416RUS PRAZDNIK, VECEL'E
416SPA FIESTA
416SWE FEST

417AAA FEELING
417CZE CÍTENIE
417DAN FØLELSE
417DUT GEVOEL
417FRE ÊTRE SENSIBLE
417GER EMPFINDUNG
417HUN ÉRZÉS
417ITA SENTIMENTO
417POL CZUCIE
417POR SENTIDO
417RUS CHUVSTVO
417SPA SENTIDO
417SWE KÄNSEL, KÄNSLIGHET

418AAA FELT
418CZE PLST
418DAN FILT
418DUT VILT
418FRE FEUTRE
418GER FILZ
418HUN NEMEZ
418ITA FELTRO
418POL PILŚŃ
418POR FÉLTRO
418RUS FETR
418SPA FIELTRO
418SWE FILT

419AAA FEMININE
419CZE ŽENSKÝ
419DAN FEMININ
419DUT VROUWELIJK
419FRE FÉMININ
419GER WEIBLICH
419HUN NÖI(ES)
419ITA FEMMININO
419POL KOBIECY
419POR FEMININO
419RUS ZHENSKIĬ
419SPA FEMENINO
419SWE FEMININ

420AAA FEROCIOUS
420CZE DIVOKÝ
420DAN VILDT
420DUT WILD
420FRE FÉROCE
420GER WILD
420HUN VAD
420ITA FEROCE
420POL DZIKO
420POR FEROZ
420RUS DIKIĬ
420SPA FEROZ
420SWE VILT

421AAA FERVENT
421CZE VROUCÍ
421DAN BRAENDENDE
421DUT VURIG
421FRE FERVENT
421GER GLÜHEND
421HUN BUZGÓ
421ITA FERV(I)ENTE
421POL GORĄCY
421POR FERVENTE
421RUS GORIACHIĬ
421SPA FERVIENTE
421SWE BRINNANDE

422AAA FESTIVE
422CZE SLAVNOSTNÍ; VESELÝ
422DAN FESTLIGT
422DUT FEESTELIJK
422FRE DE FÊTE, SOLENNEL
422GER FESTLICH, FEIERLICH
422HUN ÜNNEPÉLYESEN
422ITA FESTIVO
422POL WESOŁO
422POR FESTIVO
422RUS VESELYĬ
422SPA FESTIVO
422SWE FESTLIGT

423AAA FIBER
423CZE VLÁKNO
423DAN FIBER
423DUT FIBER, VEZEL
423FRE FIBRE
423GER FIBER, FASER
423HUN ROST, SZÁLAG
423ITA FIBRA
423POL WŁÓKNO
423POR FIBRA
423RUS VOLOKNO
423SPA FIBRA
423SWE FIBER

424AAA FIDDLE
424CZE SKRIPKY
424DAN VROVL
424DUT FIEDEL
424FRE CRINCRIN, VIOLON
424GER FI(E)DEL
424HUN FIDULA
424ITA VIOLINO
424POL SKRZYPKI
424POR RABECA
424RUS SKRIPKA
424SPA VIOLÍN
424SWE FIOL

425AAA FIERCE
425CZE DIVOKÝ
425DAN VILD
425DUT WILD
425FRE FAROUCHE
425GER WILD
425HUN DURVÁN
425ITA FEROCE
425POL DZIKO
425POR FERO
425RUS SVIREPYĬ
425SPA FEROZ, FIERO
425SWE VILT

426AAA FIFE
426CZE PÍŠŤ'ALA, FLÉTNIČKA
426DAN PIBE
426DUT DWARSFLUITJE
426FRE FIFRE
426GER QUERPFEIFE
426HUN FIFFARO
426ITA PIFFERO
426POL PISZCZAŁKA
426POR PÍFANO, PÍFARO
426RUS NEBOL'SHAIA
426SPA PÍFANO, PÍFARO
426SWE FLÖJT

427AAA FIGURE
427CZE FIGURA
427DAN FIGUR
427DUT FIGUUR
427FRE FIGURE
427GER FIGUR
427HUN ALAK
427ITA FIGURA
427POL FIGURA
427POR FIGURA
427RUS FIGURA
427SPA FIGURA
427SWE FIGUR

428AAA FIGURED BASS
428CZE ZAVAZNÝ BAS
428DAN BECIFRET BAS
428DUT GENERALBAS
428FRE BASSE CHIFFRÉE
428GER GENERALBASSSCHRIFT
428HUN SZÁMOZOTT BASSZUS
428ITA BASSO CON NUMERI
428POL FIGURALNY
428POR BAIXO CIFRADO
428RUS SHIFROVANNYĬ BAS
428SPA BAJO CIFRADO
428SWE BESIFFRAD BAS

429AAA FIGURE, TO
429CZE ZOBRAZITI
429DAN FIGURERE
429DUT FIGURENEN
429FRE FIGURER
429GER FIGURIEREN
429HUN ALAKÍTNI
429ITA FIGURARE
429POL FIGUROWAĆ
429POR FIGURAR
429RUS FIGURIROVAT'
429SPA FIGURAR
429SWE FIGURERA

430AAA FINAL
430CZE FINÁLE
430DAN SLUTNINGSSTYKKE
430DUT SLOTDEEL
430FRE FINAL
430GER FINALE, ENDSTÜCK
430HUN FINÁLÉ
430ITA FINALE
430POL FINAŁ
430POR FINAL
430RUS FINAL
430SPA FINAL
430SWE SLUTSATS

431AAA FINGER, TO
431CZE POLOŽITI PRSTY
431DAN FINGERERE
431DUT MET VINGERZETTING VAN
431FRE DOIGTER
431GER FINGERSATZ ANGEBEN
431HUN UJJALNI
431ITA DITEGGIARE
431POL DOTYKAĆ PALCAMIE
431POR DEDILHAR
431RUS UKAZYVAT' APPLIKATURU
431SPA DIGITAR
431SWE FINGRA

432AAA FINGERBOARD
432CZE HMATNIK
432DAN APPLIKATUR, KLAVIATUR
432DUT DE TOETS
432FRE TOUCHE, CLAVIER
432GER FINGERBRETT, TASTATUR
432HUN FOGÓLAP
432ITA TASTIERA, TASTATURA
432POL KLAWIATUR
432POR TECLADO
432RUS KLAVIATURA
432SPA TECLADO
432SWE KLAVIATUR

433AAA FINGERING
433CZE PROSTOKLAD
433DAN FINGERSAETNING
433DUT VINGERZETTING
433FRE DOIGTÉ
433GER APPLIKATUR
433HUN UJJREND
433ITA DITEGGIO
433POL U KLAD PALCOW
433POR DEDILHAÇÃO
433RUS RASSTANOVKA PAL'TSEV
433SPA DIGITACIÓN
433SWE FINGERSÄTTNING

434AAA FIRE
434CZE OHEŇ
434DAN FYRIGT
434DUT VUUR
434FRE FEU
434GER FEUER
434HUN TŰZ
434ITA FUOCO
434POL OGNIEN
434POR FOGO
434RUS OGON'
434SPA FUEGO
434SWE ELD

435AAA FIRM
435CZE PEVNÝ
435DAN FAST
435DUT VAST
435FRE FERME, SOLIDE
435GER FEST
435HUN ERÖS
435ITA FERMO
435POL PEWNY
435POR FIRMA
435RUS KREPKIĬ
435SPA FIRME
435SWE FAST

436AAA FIRST
436CZE ZAPRVÉ
436DAN FØRST
436DUT EERST
436FRE PREMIER(E)
436GER ERST(E)
436HUN ELSŐ
436ITA PRIMO
436POL PIERWSZY
436POR PRIMEIRO
436RUS PERVYĬ
436SPA PRIMERO
436SWE FÖRSTA

437AAA FIVE
437CZE PĚT
437DAN FEM
437DUT VIJF
437FRE CINQ
437GER FÜNF
437HUN ÖT
437ITA CINQUE
437POL PIĘĆ
437POR CINCO
437RUS PIAT'
437SPA CINCO-
437SWE FEM

438AAA FLACCID
438CZE MDLÝ, OCHABLÝ
438DAN SLAP
438DUT MAT, SLAP
438FRE FAIBLE
438GER SCHWACH
438HUN GYENGE
438ITA FIACCO, FLACCIDO
438POL SFLACZAŁY
438POR FLÁCIDO
438RUS SLABYĬ
438SPA FLÁCCIDO
438SWE SLAPP

439AAA FLAGEOLET
439CZE FLAŽOLET
439DAN FLAGEOLET
439DUT KLEINE BLOKFLUIT
439FRE FLAGEOLET
439GER FLAGEOLETT, FLASCHINET
439HUN FLAGEOLETT, ÜVEHANG
439ITA FLAGIOLETTO
439POL FLAŻOLET, PISZCZAŁKA
439POR FLAJOLÉ
439RUS FLAZHOLET
439SPA CARAMILLO, FLAJERLET
439SWE SPETSFLÖJT

440AAA FLAT
440CZE BÉ
440DAN TEGNET B
440DUT VERLAAGD
440FRE BÉMOL
440GER BEMOL
440HUN LAPOSÁG
440ITA BEMOLLE
440POL BEMOL
440POR BEMOL
440RUS BEMOL'
440SPA BEMOL
440SWE BEMOL

441AAA FLAT, TO
441CZE OPATŘITI ZNAMÉNKEM BÉ
441DAN SAETTE B FOR
441DUT VERLAGEN
441FRE BEMOLISER
441GER HERUNTERSTIMMEN
441HUN LAPOSÍTNI
441ITA BEMOLIZZARE, BEMOLLARE
441POL OBNIZAC O PÓL TONU
441POR BEMOLAR
441RUS STAVIT' BEMOL
441SPA ABEMOLAR, BEMOLIZAR
441SWE SÄNKA

442AAA FLEXIBLE
442CZE OHEBNÝ
442DAN BØJELIG
442DUT BUIGZAAM
442FRE SOUPLE
442GER BIEGSAM, GESCHMEIDIG
442HUN HAJLÉKONYAN
442ITA FLESSIBILE
442POL USTĘPLIWY
442POR FLEXÍVEL
442RUS GIBKIĬ
442SPA FLEXIBLE
442SWE BÖJLIG

443AAA FLORID
443CZE KVĚTNATÝ
443DAN BLOMSTRET
443DUT VERSIERINGEN
443FRE FLEURI, ORNÉ
443GER VERZIERT
443HUN VIRÁGOS
443ITA FIORISCENTE, FIORITO
443POL KWITNĄCY
443POR FLOREADO
443RUS TSVETUSHCHIĬ
443SPA FLOREADO, FLORIDA
443SWE BLOMSTERPRYDD

444AAA FLOURISH
444CZE FIORITURA
444DAN TROMPETSKRALD
444DUT VERSIERINGEN
444FRE FIORITURE
444GER VERZIERUNG
444HUN VIRÁNY
444ITA FIORITURA, ABBELLITURA
444POL OZDOBNIKI
444POR FLOREIO
444RUS PROTSVETANIE
444SPA FLOREO
444SWE FIORITUR

445AAA FLOWING
445CZE PLYNNÉ
445DAN HASTIGT
445DUT VLOEIEND
445FRE FLUIDE, EN COULANT
445GER FLIESEND
445HUN FOLYÓ
445ITA SCORRENDO
445POL PŁYNNY
445POR CORRENTE
445RUS PLAVNYĬ
445SPA CORRIENDO, CON FLUIDEZ
445SWE FLYTANDE

446AAA FLUGELHORN
446CZE KŘIDLOVKA
446DAN TROMBONE, BAZUN
446DUT VLEUGELHOORN
446FRE BUGLE
446GER FLÜGELHORN
446HUN SZOPRÁN SZAXKÜRT
446ITA FLICORNO
446POL FLIGELHORN
446POR FLISCORNE
446RUS FLIUGEL' HORN
446SPA F(L)ISCORNO
446SWE FLYGELHORN

447AAA FLUTE
447CZE FLÉTNA
447DAN FLØJTE
447DUT FLUIT
447FRE FLÛTE
447GER FLÖTE
447HUN FUVOLA
447ITA FLAUTO
447POL FLET
447POR FLAUTA
447RUS FLEĬTA
447SPA FLAUTA
447SWE FLÖJT

448AAA FLYING
448CZE PRCHAVÝ
448DAN FLYVEN(DE)
448DUT VLUCHTIG, VLIEGEND
448FRE VOLANT, FUYANT
448GER BESCHWINGT, FLÜCHTIG
448HUN REPÜLŐ
448ITA VOLANTE
448POL LATAJĄCY, LOTNY
448POR VOLATA
448RUS RULADA
448SPA DESFLORANDO LAS NOTAS
448SWE FLYGNING

449AAA FOLLOW, TO
449CZE NÁSLEDOVATI
449DAN FØLGE
449DUT VOLGEN
449FRE SUIVRE
449GER FOLGEN
449HUN KÖVETNI
449ITA SEGUIRE
449POL IŚĆ
449POR SEGUIR
449RUS SLEDOVAT'
449SPA SEGUIR
449SWE FÖLJA

450AAA FOOT
450CZE STOPA
450DAN FOD
450DUT VOET
450FRE PIED
450GER FUSS
450HUN LÁB
450ITA PIEDE
450POL STOPA
450POR PÉ
450RUS STUPNIA
453SPA PIE
450SWE FOT

451AAA FOR
451CZE PRO, ABY
451DAN FOR
451DUT VOOR
451FRE POUR, PAR
451GER FÜR
451HUN HELYETT
451ITA PER
451POL DLA
451POR POR
451RUS DLIA
451SPA POR, PARA
451SWE FÖR

452AAA FORCE
452CZE UŽIJ SÍLA
452DAN KRAFT
452DUT KRACHT
452FRE FORCE
452GER KRAFT
452HUN ERÖ
452ITA SFORZA
452POL SIŁA
452POR FÔRÇA
452RUS SILA
452SPA FUERZA, ESFUERZO
452SWE KRAFT

453AAA FORM
453CZE FORMA
453DAN FORM
453DUT VORM
453FRE FORM
453GER FORM, FÜHRUNG
453HUN FORMÁK
453ITA FORMA
453POL FORMA
453POR FORMA
453RUS FORMA
453SPA FORMA
453SWE FORM

454AAA FOUNDATION
454CZE ZÁKLAD
454DAN GRUNDLAEGGELSE
454DUT GRONDSLAG
454FRE FONDEMENT
454GER GRUNDLAGE
454HUN ALAP
454ITA FONDAMENTO
454POL FUNDAMENT
454POR FUNDAÇÃC
454RUS FUNDAMENT
454SPA FUNDACIÓN
454SWE GRUNDANDE

455AAA FOUR
455CZE ČTYŘI
455DAN FIRE
455DUT VIER
455FRE QUATRE
455GER VIER
455HUN NÉGY
455ITA QUATTRO
455POL CZTERY
455POR QUATRO
455RUS CHETYRE
455SPA CUATRO
455SWE FYRA

456AAA FRANTIC
456CZE FRENETICKY, ROZČILENÝ
456DAN RASENDE
456DUT RAZEND
456FRE FRÉNÉTIQUE
456GER RASEND
456HUN ÖRJÖNGÖ
456ITA FRENETICO
456POL ROZSZALAŁY
456POR FRENÉTICO
456RUS BEZUMNYĬ, NEISTOVYĬ
456SPA FRENÉTICO
456SWE RASANDE

457AAA FREE
457CZE NENUCENÝ, SVOBODNÝ
457DAN FRI
457DUT VRIJ
457FRE LIBRE
457GER FREI, UNGEZWUNGEN
457HUN SZABAD
457ITA LIBERO, SCIOLTO
457POL WOLNY
457POR LIVRE
457RUS SVOBODNYĬ
457SPA LIBRE
457SWE FRITT

458AAA FRENZY
458CZE TŘEŠTĚNÍ, ŠÍLENÍ
458DAN GALSKAB
458DUT WAANZIN
458FRE FRÉNÉSIE
458GER WAHNSINN
458HUN ŐRÜLET
458ITA DELIRIO
458POL W ŚCIEKŁOŚĆ, SZAŁ
458POR FRENESI
458RUS BESHENSTVO, NEISTOVSTO
458SPA FRENESÍ
458SWE RASERI

459AAA FREQUENCY
459CZE FREKVENCE
459DAN FREKVENS
459DUT FREQUENTIE
459FRE FRÉQUENCE
459GER FREQUENZ
459HUN GYAKORISÁG
459ITA FREQUENZA
459POL CZĘSTOŚĆ
459POR FREQÜÊNCIA
459RUS CHASTOTA
428SPA FRECUENCÍA
459SWE FREKVENS

460AAA FRESH
460CZE SVĚŽÍ, ČERSTVÝ
460DAN FRISKT
460DUT FRIS
460FRE FRAIS
460GER FRISCH
460HUN FRISSEN
460ITA FRESCO
460POL ŚWIEŻY
460POR FRESCO
460RUS SVEZHIĬ
460SPA FRESCO
460SWE FRISK

461AAA FRET(S)
461CZE PALCOVÁ POLOHA
461DAN TVAERBAAND
461DUT GREEPTOETS
461FRE TOUCHE, TOUCHETTE
461GER GRIFFLEISTE, BUNDE
461HUN ÉRINTŐK
461ITA CAPOTASTO, TÁSTO
461POL KLAWISZ
461POR TRASTO
461RUS KLAVISHA, KOBYLKA
461SPA TRASTE
461SWE TANGENT

462AAA FROG
462CZE ŽABKA
462DAN FROSCH
462DUT TALON,SLEUFJE
462FRE TALON, HAUSSE
462GER FROSCH, BOGENSTANGE
462HUN KÁPA
462ITA TACO, BIETTA
462POL KOLOK
462POR PESTANA
462RUS NATĬAT, KOLOK
462SPA TALÓN
462SWE FROSK

463AAA FROM
463CZE Z, OD
463DAN FRA, AF
463DUT VANAF
463FRE DE
463GER VON, VOM
463HUN ELŐTT
463ITA DA
463POL OD
463POR DE
463RUS OT
463SPA DE(L)
463SWE FRÅN

464AAA FUGUE
464CZE FUGA
464DAN FUGA
464DUT FUGA
464FRE FUGUE
464GER FUGE
464HUN FÚGA
464ITA FUGA
464POL FUGA
464POR FUGA
464RUS FUGA
464SPA FUGA
464SWE FUGA

465AAA FULL
465CZE PLNÝ, VŠICHNI
465DAN FULD
465DUT VOL
465FRE PLEIN, PARFAITE
465GER VOLL(KOMMENE)
465HUN TELJES
465ITA PIENO, TUTTI
465POL PEŁNY, WSZYSCY
465POR PLENO
465RUS POLNYĬ
465SPA LLENO
465SWE FULL

466AAA FUNCTION
466CZE FUNKCE
466DAN FUNKTION
466DUT FUNKTIE
466FRE FONCTION
466GER FUNKTION
466HUN FUNKCIÓ
466ITA FUNZIONE
466POL FUNKCJA
466POR FUNÇÃO
466RUS FUNKTSIIA
466SPA FUNCIÓN
466SWE FUNKTION

467AAA FUNDAMENTAL
467CZE ZÁKLAD
467DAN FUNDAMENTAL
467DUT GRONDNOOT
467FRE FONDAMENTAL
467GER FUNDAMENTAL
467HUN ALAPHANG
467ITA FONDAMENTO
467POL FUNDAMENT
467POR FUNDAMENTO
467RUS OSNOVNOE PRAVILO
467SPA FUNDAMENTO
467SWE GRUNDLÄGGA

468AAA FUNEREAL
468CZE POHŘEBNÍ
468DAN SØRGELIG
468DUT BEGRAFENIS
468FRE FUNÈBRE, TREURIG
468GER BEGRABNISMÄSSIG
468HUN TEMETÉSI
468ITA FUNEBRE, FUNERALE
468POL ŻAŁOBNIE
468POR FÚNEBRE, FUNERAL
468RUS POKHORONNOE BIURO
468SPA FÚNEBRE
468SWE BEGRAVNINGS

469AAA FURY
469CZE ZUŘIVOST, FÚRIE
469DAN FURIE
469DUT WOEDE
469FRE FURIE
469GER FURIE, WUT
469HUN DÜH
469ITA FURIA, FURORE
469POL FURIA, WŚCIEKŁOŚĆ
469POR FÚRIA
469RUS FURIIA
469SPA FURIA
469SWE FURIE

470AAA GALLANT
470CZE GALANTNÍ
470DAN GAL'AN
470DUT GALANT
470FRE GALANT
470GER GALANT, VORNEHM
470HUN UDVARIÁS
470ITA GALANTE
470POL GALANT
470POR GALANTE
470RUS GALANTNYĬ
470SPA GALANTE
470SWE GALANTA

471AAA GALOP
471CZE KVAPÍK
471DAN GALOP
471DUT GALOP(PADE)
471FRE GALOP
471GER GALOPP, HOPSER
471HUN GALOPP
471ITA GALOPPO
471POL GALOP(ADA)
471POR GALOPE
471RUS GALOP
471SPA GALOP
471SWE GALOPP

472AAA GAMUT
472CZE ŠKÁLA, STUPNICE
472DAN SKALA
472DUT TOONLADDER
472FRE GAMME
472GER TONLEITER
472HUN HANGLÉTRA
472ITA GAMMA
472POL GAMA
472POR GAMA, ESCALA
472RUS GAMMA
472SPA GAMA, ESCALA
472SWE SKALA

473AAA GAVOTTE
473CZE GAVOTA
473DAN GAVOTTE
473DUT GAVOTTE
473FRE GAVOTTE
473GER GAVOTTE
473HUN GAVOTTE
473ITA GAVOTTA
473POL GAWOT
473POR GAVOTA
473RUS GAVOT
473SPA GAVOTA
473SWE GAVOTT

474AAA GAY
474CZE VESELÝ
474DAN GLAD
474DUT VROLIJK
474FRE GAI
474GER FRÖHLICH, LUSTIG
474HUN JÓKEDVŰEN
474ITA GAIO, GAJO, GIOIOSO
474POL WESOŁO, ŻYWO
474POR ALEGRE
474RUS VESELYĬ
474SPA GAYO, ALEGRE
474SWE GLATT

475AAA GENERAL
475CZE OBECNÝ, GENERÁLNÍ
475DAN GENERAL
475DUT ALGEMENE
475FRE GÉNÉRAL
475GER ALLGEMEIN, GENERAL
475HUN GENERÁL
475ITA GENERALE
475POL GENERALNY
475POR GERAL
475RUS OBSHCHIĬ
475SPA GENERAL
475SWE GENERAL

476AAA GENERATOR
476CZE TVŮRČÍ
476DAN GENERATOR
476DUT VOORTBRENGEN
476FRE GÉNÉRATEUR
476GER GRUNDTON
476HUN FEJLESZTÓ
476ITA GENERATORE
476POL GENERATOR
476POR GERADOR
476RUS GENERATOR
476SPA GENERADOR
476SWE GENERATOR

477AAA GENIUS
477CZE GÉNIUS
477DAN GENIUS
477DUT GENIUS
477FRE GÉNIE
477GER GENIE
477HUN ŐRZELLEM
477ITA GENIO
477POL GENIUS
477POR GÊNIO
477RUS GENIĬ
477SPA GENIO
477SWE GENIUS

478AAA GENTLE
478CZE ROZTOMILOST
478DAN GENTIL
478DUT ZACHT
478FRE GENTIL, DOUX
478GER ANMUTIG, ARTIG
478HUN KEDVESEN
478ITA GENTILE
478POL SZLACHECKI
478POR GENTIL(ICO)
478RUS PRIĬATNYĬ
478SPA GENTIL
478SWE ÄLSKVÄRT

479AAA GIVE, TO
479CZE DÁTI
479DAN GIVE
479DUT GEVEN
479FRE DONNER
479GER GEBEN
479HUN MEGADNI
449ITA DARE
479POL DAWAĆ
479POR DAR
479RUS DAVAT'
479SPA DAR
479SWE GIVA

480AAA GLIDE, TO
470CZE KLOUZATI
480DAN GLIDE
480DUT GLIJDEN
480FRE GLISSER
480GER GLEITEN
480HUN CSÚSZNI
480ITA SDRUCCIOLARE, GLISSARE
480POL ŚLIZGAĆ SIĘ
480POR DESLIZAR
480RUS SKOL' ZIT'
480SPA GLISAR, RESBALAR
480SWE GLIDA

481AAA GLOOMY
481CZE TRCHLIVÝ, CHMURNÝ
481DAN MØRK
481DUT DONKER
481FRE OBSCURE, SOMBRE
481GER DÜSTER, TRÜB(E)
481HUN KOMORAN
481ITA OSCURO, CUPO
481POL MROCZNY
481POR TENEBROSO
481RUS TĖMNYĬ, MRACHNYĬ
481SPA TENEBROSO, SORDO
481SWE MÖRK

482AAA GLOTTIS
482CZE GLOTTIS
482DAN STEMMERIDSEN
482DUT STEMSPLEET
482FRE GLOTTE
482GER STIMMRITZE
482HUN HANGRÉS
482ITA GLOTTIDE
482POL GLOŚNIA
482POR GLOTE
482RUS GOLOSOVAĬA SHCHEL'
482SPA GLOTIS
482SWE RÖSTSPRINGA

483AAA GONG
483CZE GONG, BICÍ NÁSTROJ
483DAN GONGONG
483DUT GONG, TAMTAM
483FRE GONG, TAM-TAM
483GER TAM-TAM, GONG
483HUN KORONG-ALAKÚ
483ITA TAM-TAM
483POL GONG
483POR GONGO
483RUS GONG
483SPA TAM-TAM, GONG
483SWE GONGGONG

484AAA GOOD
484CZE DOBRÝ, TĚŽKÁ
484DAN GODT
484DUT GOED
484FRE BIEN, BON
484GER GUT
484HUN JÓ
484ITA BEN, BUONO
484POL DOBRZE
484POR BOM
484RUS DOBRYĬ
484SPA BIEN, BUEN(O)
484SWE BRA, VÄL

485AAA GRACE
485CZE PŮRAB, PŘÍZEŇ
485DAN YNDERFULDT, FORIRING
485DUT GRATIE
485FRE GRÂCE
485GER GRAZIE, ANMUTH
485HUN DÍSZÍTÉS
485ITA GRAZIA, GARBO
485POL GRACJA
485POR GRAÇA
485RUS GRATSIĬA
485SPA GRACIA, GARBO
485SWE BEHAG

486AAA GRACE NOTE
486CZE HUDEBNÍ OZDOBA
486DAN PYNTENODER
486DUT VÓÓRSLAG
486FRE NOTE SUPERFLUE
486GER VORSCHLAG
486HUN DÍSZÍTŐHANG
486ITA NOTA SUBJECTA
486POL PRZEDNUTKA KŔOTKA
486POR APOJATURA
486RUS FIORITURA
486SPA NOTA SUPERFLUA
486SWE FŐRSLAG

487AAA GRADUAL
487CZE GRADUÁL
487DAN GRADUALE
487DUT GRADUALE
487FRE GRADUEL
487GER GRADUALE
487HUN GRADUÁL
487ITA GRADUALE
487POL GRADUALE
487POR GRADUAL
487RUS GRADUAL
487SPA GRADUAL
487SWE GRADUALPSALM

488AAA GRADUAL(LY)
488CZE STUPŇOVITÝ, POSTUPNÝ
488DAN GRADVIS
488DUT GRADUAAL
488FRE GRADUEL
488GER ALLMÄHLICH, GRADUALE
488HUN FOKOZATOS
488ITA POCO A POCO
488POL STOPNIOWY
488POR GRADUAL
488RUS POSTĖPENNYĬ
488SPA GRADUAL
488SWE SMANINGOM

489AAA	GRAND	493AAA	GRIEF
489CZE	VELKÝ	493CZE	BOLEST
489DAN	STOR	493DAN	SMERTE, SORG
489DUT	GROOT	493DUT	DROEFHEID, VERDRIET
489FRE	GRAND(E)	493FRE	DOULEUR
489GER	GROSS, PRACHTVOLL	493GER	TRÜBE, SCHMERZ
489HUN	NAGY	493HUN	FÁJDALOM
489ITA	GRANDE	493ITA	DOLORE
489POL	WIELKI	493POL	ZMARTWIENIE
489POR	GRANDE	493POR	DOR
489RUS	GRANDIOZNYÏ	493RUS	GORE
489SPA	GRAND(E)	493SPA	DOLOR
489SWE	STOR	493SWE	SORG
490AAA	GRAND PIANO	494AAA	GROTESQUE
490CZE	KŘÍDLOVÉ KLAVÍR	494CZE	GROTESKNÍ
490DAN	FLYGEL	494DAN	GROTESK
490DUT	VLEUGEL	494DUT	GROTESKE
490FRE	PIANO À QUEUE	494FRE	GROTESQUE
490GER	FLÜGEL	494GER	GROTESK
490HUN	ZONGORA	494HUN	FANTASZTIKUSAN
490ITA	PIANOFORTE A CODA	494ITA	GROTTESCO
490POL	FORTEPIAN KONCERTOWY	494POL	DZIWACZNIE
490POR	PIANO DE CAUDA	494POR	GROTESCO
490RUS	ROÏAL'	494RUS	GROTESK
490SPA	PIANO DE COLA	494SPA	GROTESCO
490SWE	FLYGEL(FORTEPIANO)	494SWE	GROTESK
491AAA	GRAVE	495AAA	GROUND
491CZE	VÁŽNY, TĚŽKÝ	495CZE	ZÁKLAD, DNO
491DAN	TUNGT	495DAN	GRUND
491DUT	ERNSTIG, ZWAAR	495DUT	GROND
491FRE	GRAVE	495FRE	FOND
491GER	ERNSTHAFT, SCHWER	495GER	GRUND
491HUN	SÚLYOS	495HUN	ALAP
491ITA	GRAVE	495ITA	FONDO
491POL	POWAŻNIE, CIĘŻKO	495POL	GRUNT
491POR	GRAVE	495POR	FONDO
491RUS	VAZHNYÏ	495RUS	GRUNT
491SPA	GRAVE	495SPA	FONDO
491SWE	TUNGT	495SWE	GRUND
492AAA	GREAT	496AAA	GROUND BASS
492CZE	VELKÝ	496CZE	ZÁKLADNÍ BAS
492DAN	GROS	496DAN	GRUNDBAS
492DUT	GROOT	496DUT	GRONDTOON
492FRE	GROS(SE)	496FRE	BASSE CONTRAINTE
492GER	GROSS	496GER	GRUNDBASS
492HUN	NAGY	496HUN	ALSÓ BASZUS
492ITA	GROSSO	496ITA	BASSO OSTINATO
492POL	WIELKI, DUŻY	496POL	INACZEJ BAS UPORCZYWY
492POR	GRANDE	496POR	BAIXO OSTINADO
492RUS	VELIKIÏ	496RUS	BASSO OSTINATO
492SPA	GRUESO, GRAN(DE)	496SPA	BAJO OSTINADO
492SWE	STOR	496SWE	UPPREPAT BASMOTIV

497AAA GROUP	501AAA GUIDE
497CZE SKUPINKA	501CZE VŮDCE
497DAN DOBBELTSLAG	501DAN FØRER
497DUT DUBBELSLAG	501DUT GIDS
497FRE GROUPE	501FRE GUIDE
497GER DOPPELSCHLAG	501GER GUIDE, FÜHRER
497HUN CSOPORT	501HUN VEZETŐ
497ITA GRUPPETTO	501ITA GUIDA
497POL OBIEGNIK	501POL PRZEWODNIK
497POR GRUPETO	501POR GUIA
497RUS GRUPPETTO	501RUS GID
497SPA GRUPO, GLOPETE	501SPA GUÍA
497SWE DUBBEL TAKT	501SWE FÖRARE, GID
498AAA GROW, TO	502AAA GUITAR
498CZE RŮSTI	502CZE KYTARA
498DAN VOKSE	502DAN GUITAR
498DUT WASSEN	502DUT GITAAR
498FRE CROÎTRE	502FRE GUITARE
498GER WACHSEN	502GER GUITAR(RE)
498HUN NŐNI	502HUN GITÁR
498ITA CRESCERE	502ITA CHITARRA
498POL ROŚĆ	502POL GITARA
498POR CRESCER	502POR VIOLÃO
498RUS RASTI	502RUS GITARA
498SPA CRECER, AUMENTAR	502SPA GUITARRA
498SWE VÄXA	502SWE GITARR
499AAA GRUESOME	503AAA GUT
499CZE DĚSIVÝ, HROZNÝ	503CZE STŘEVOVÁ STRUNA
499DAN GRUFULDT, GYSELIG	503DAN TARM
499DUT DODEN, IJSELIJK	503DUT ARM
499FRE MACABRE	503FRE BOYAU
499GER GRAUSIG	503GER DARMSAITE
499HUN ISZONYÚ	503HUN BÉLHÚR
499ITA SPAVENTEVOLE	503ITA MINUGIA
499POL OKROPNY	503POL KISZKA
499POR MEDONHO, HORRÍVEL	503POR CORDA DE TRIPA
499RUS UZHASNYĬ	503RUS KISHKA
499SPA ESPANTOSO, HORRIBLE	503SPA CUERDA DE VIHUELA
499SWE OHYGGLIG, HEMSK	503SWE TARMAR
500AAA GRUFF	504AAA GYPSY
500CZE DRSNÝ, HRUBÝ	504CZE CIKÁN
500DAN GROV	504DAN SIGØJNER
500DUT GROF	504DUT ZIGEUNER
500FRE BOURRU	504FRE TZIGANE
500GER SCHROFF, MÜRRISCH	504GER ZIGEUNER
500HUN NYERS	504HUN CIGÁNYDAL
500ITA ROZZO	504ITA ZINGARO
500POL CIERPKI, SZORSTKI	504POL CYGAN
500POR GROSSEIRO, ÁSPERO	504POR CIGANO, GITANO
500RUS GRUBYĬ	504RUS TSYGAN
500SPA GROSERO, ÁSPERO	504SPA GITANO
500SWE GROV	504SWE ZIGENARE

505AAA HAIR   509AAA HAMMER, TO
505CZE VLAS, ŽÍŇ   509CZE BUŠITI
505DAN HÅR   509DAN HAMRE
505DUT HAAR   509DUT HAMEREN
505FRE CRINS   509FRE MARTELER
505GER HARRE   509GER HÄMMERN
505HUN HAJ   509HUN KALAPÁLNI
505ITA CRIN(E), PELO   509ITA MARTELLARE
505POL WŁOS   509POL MŁOTEM
505POR PÊLO   509POR MARTELAR
505RUS VOLOS   509RUS UDARIAT' MOLOTOM
505SPA PELO   509SPA MARTILLAR
505SWE HÅR   509SWE HAMRA

506AAA HALF   510AAA HAND
506CZE PROSTŘEDEK, POLOVICE   510CZE RUKA
506DAN HALV   510DAN HÅND
506DUT HALF   510DUT HAND
506FRE MOITIÉ, DEMI-   510FRE MAIN
506GER HALB, HÄLFTE   510GER HAND
506HUN FÉL   510HUN KÉZ
506ITA MEZZO, SEMI-   510ITA MANO
506POL POŁOWĘ   510POL RĘKA
506POR MEIO   510POR MÃO
506RUS POLOVINA   510RUS RUKA
506SPA MEDIO   510SPA MANO
506SWE HALVA, HÄLFT   510SWE HAND

507AAA HALL   511AAA HARD
507CZE SÁL   511CZE TVRDÝ
507DAN HAL   511DAN HÅRD
507DUT HAL   511DUT HARD
507FRE SALLE DES FÊTES   511FRE DUR
507GER HALLE, AULA   511GER HART
507HUN CSARNOK   511HUN KEMENY
507ITA SALA, AULA   511ITA DURO
507POL HALL   511POL TWARDY
507POR SALÃO   511POR DURO
507RUS ZAL   511RUS TVËRDYÏ
507SPA SALA   511SPA DURO
507SWE HALL, SALON   511SWE HÅRD

508AAA HALLELUJA   512AAA HARMONICA
508CZE ALELUJA   512CZE SKLENĚNÁ HARMONIKA
508DAN HALLELUJAH   512DAN GLASHARMONIKA
508DUT HALLELUJAH   512DUT MONDHARMONICA
508FRE ALLÉLUIA   512FRE ACCORDÉON
508GER HALLELUJA   512GER HARMONIKA
508HUN HALLELUJA   512HUN HARMONIKA
508ITA ALLELUIA   512ITA ARMONICA
508POL ALLELUJA   512POL HARMONJKA
508POR ALELUIA   512POR HARMÓNICA
508RUS ALLELUIÏA   512RUS HARMONIKA
508SPA ALELUYA   512SPA ARMÓNICA
508SWE HALLELUJA   512SWE MUNHARMONIKA

513AAA HARMONICS   517AAA HARP
513CZE SPODNÍ TÓNY   517CZE HARFA
513DAN RESONANSTONE   517DAN HARPE
513DUT HARMONICI   517DUT HARPE
513FRE HARMONIQUES   517FRE HARPE
513GER FLAGEOLETTÖNE   517GER HARFE
513HUN RÉZZHANGOK   517HUN HÁRFA
513ITA ARMONICI   517ITA ARPA
513POL ALIKOWTY   517POL HARFA
513POR ARMONICOS   517POR HARPA
513RUS HARMONIIA   517RUA ARFA
513SPA ARMONICOS   517SPA ARPA
513SWE NATURTONER   517SWE HARPA

514AAA HARMONIUM   518AAA HARSH
514CZE HARMONIUM   518CZE PŘIKRÝ, DRSNÝ
514DAN HARMONIUM   518DAN HÅRD
514DUT HARMONIUM   518DUT HARD
514FRE HARMONIUM   518FRE RUDE, ÂPRE
514GER HARMONIUM   518GER RAUH, HART
514HUN HARMÓNIUM   518HUN NYERSEN
514ITA ARMONIUM   518ITA ASPRO
514POL HARMONIJM   518POL SZORSTKI
514POR HARMÔNIO   528POR ÁSPERO
514RUS HARMONIUM   518RUS TERPKIĬ
514SPA HARMONIUM   518SPA ÁSPERO
514SWE KAMMARORGEL, HARMONIUM   518SWE HÅRD

515AAA HARMONIZE, TO   519AAA HARPSICHORD
515CZE HARMONISOVATI   519CZE KLAVÍCEMBALO
515DAN HARMONISERE   519DAN CEMBALO, CLAVICHORD
515DUT HARMONIEREN   519DUT KLAVECIMBEL
515FRE HARMONISER   519FRE CLAVECIN
515GER HARMONIEREN   519GER KLAVIZIMBAL, ZIMBEL
515HUN ÖSSZHANGZANI   519HUN CLAVICEMBALO
515ITA ARMONIZZARE   519ITA CLAVICEMBALO, ARPICORDO
515POL HARMONIZOWAĆ   519POL KLAWICYMBAŁ, KLAWESYN
515POR HARMONIZAR   519POR CLAVECINO, CRAVO
515RUS HARMONIROVAT'   519RUS KLAVIKORDY
515SPA ARMONIZAR   519SPA CLAVICORDIO, ARPICORDIO
515SWE HARMONIERA   519SWE KLAVICYMBAL

516AAA HARMONY   520AAA HASTE
516CZE HARMONIE   520CZE SPĚCH, CHVAT
516DAN HARMONI   520DAN HAST
516DUT HARMONIE   520DUT HAAST
516FRE HARMONIE   520FRE HÂTE
516GER HARMONIE   520GER HAST
516HUN ÖSSZHANG   520HUN SIETSÉG
516ITA ARMONIA   520ITA FRETTA
516POL HARMONJA   520POL POŚPIECH
516POR HARMONIA   520POR PRESA
516RUS HARMONIIA   520RUS SPESHKA
516SPA ARMONÍA   520SPA PRISA
516SWE HARMONI   520SWE HAST

521AAA HAUGHTY
521CZE NAKVAŠENÉ
521DAN HØGRØD, HOVMODIG
521DUT HOOGMOEDIG
521FRE EMPORTÉ, FIER
521GER HOCHMÜTIG, TROTZIG
521HUN FÖNNELGÖ
521ITA ALTEZZOSO, FIERO
521POL PYSZNY
521POR SOBERBO
521RUS NADMENNYÏ
521SPA ARREBATADO
521SWE HÖG

522AAA HEAD
522CZE HLAVA
522DAN HOVED
522DUT HOOFD
522FRE TÊTE
522GER KOPF
522HUN FÖ, FEJ
522ITA CAPO
522POL GŁOWA
522POR CABEÇA
522RUS GOLOVA
522SPA CABEZA
522SWE HUVUD

523AAA HEAR, TO
523CZE POSLOUCHATI
523DAN HØRE
523DUT HOREN
523FRE OUÏR, ENTENDRE
523GER HÖREN
523HUN HALLANI
523ITA UDIRE, ASCOLTARE
523POL SŁYSZEĆ
523POR OUVIR
523RUS CLYSHAT'
523SPA OÍR
523SWE HÖRA

524AAA HEARTFELT
524CZE SRDEČNÝ
524DAN INDERLIG, AERLIG
524DUT DIEPGEVOELD
524FRE DU COEUR, SINCÈRE
524GER INNIG
524HUN SZÍVBÖL
524ITA DI CUORE, SINCERO
524POL SERDECZNY
524POR SINCERO
524RUS ISKRENNIÏ
524SPA SINCERO
524SWE DJUPT KÄND

525AAA HEAT
525CZE TEPLO
525DAN VARME
525DUT WARMTE
525FRE CHALEUR, ARDEUR
525GER WÄRME
525HUN MELEGSEG
525ITA CALORE
525POL CIEPŁO
525POR CALOR
525RUS TEPLO
525SPA CALOR
525SWE VÄRME

526AAA HEAVY
526CZE TĚŽKÝ
526DAN VAEGTIGT, TUNGT
526DUT GEWICHTIG, ZWARR
526FRE PESANT, LOURD
526GER GEWICHTIG, SCHWER
526HUN SÚLYOSAN
526ITA PESANTE
526POL CIEŻKO
526POR PESADO
526RUS TIAZHÉLYÏ
526SPA PESADO
526SWE TUNGT, SVÅR

527AAA HELD
527CZE DRŽENÉ
527DAN FORHØJELSESTEGN
527DUT AANGEHOUDEN
527FRE TENU, SOSTENU
527GER AUSGEHALTEND
527HUN TARTOTT
527ITA TENUTO, SOSTENUTO
527POL WYTRZYMAĆ
527POR SUSTENTIDO
527RUS POVYSHENNYÏ
527SPA SOSTENIENDO
527SWE UTHÅLLET

528AAA HELICON
528CZE HELIKON
528DAN HELIKON
528DUT HELIKON
528FRE HÉLICON
528GER HELIKON
528HUN HELIKON
528ITA ELICON
528POL HELIKON
528POR HÉLICON
528RUS HELIKON
528SPA ELICÓN
528SWE HELIKON

529AAA HERE
529CZE ZDE, TU
529DAN HER
529DUT HIER
529FRE ICI
529GER HIER
529HUN ITT
529ITA QUI
529POL TU
529POR AQUI
529RUS TUT
529SPA AQUÍ
529SWE HÄR

530AAA HEROIC
530CZE HRDINSKÝ
530DAN HEROISK
530DUT HELDHAFTIG
530FRE HÉROÏQUE
530GER HEROISH, HELDENMÄSSIG
530HUN HŐSIESEN
530ITA EROICO
530POL PO BOHATERSKU
530POR HERÓICO
530RUS HEROICHESKIŸ
530SPA HEROICO
530SWE HEROISKT

531AAA HESITATING
531CZE NEROZHODNUTÝ
531DAN TØVEN
531DUT AARZELEND
531FRE IRRÉSOLU
531GER SCHWANKEND
531HUN HABOZÓ
531ITA IRRESOLUTO
531POL NIEREZOLUTNY
531POR IRRESOLUTO
531RUS NERESHITEL'NYŸ
531SPA IRRESOLUTO
531SWE TVEKANDE

532AAA HIGH
532CZE VYSOKÝ
532DAN HØJ
532DUT HOOG
532FRE HAUT
532GER HOCH
532HUN MAGAS
532ITA ALTO
532POL WYSOKI
532POR ALTO
532RUS VYSOKIŸ
532SPA ALTO
532SWE HÖG

533AAA HISS, TO
533CZE HVÍZDATI
533DAN HVISLE
533DUT SISSEN
533FRE SIFFLER
533GER ZISCHEN
533HUN PISSZEGNI
533ITA FISCHIARE
533POL SYKNAĆ
533POR SILVAR
533RUS SHIPET
533SPA SILBAR, SISEAR
533SWE VISSLA

534AAA HOLD, TO
534CZE DRŽETI
534DAN HOLDE
534DUT HOUDEN
534FRE TENIR
534GER AUSHALTEN
534HUN TARTANI
534ITA TENERE, RITENERE
534POL WYTRZYMAĆ
534POR SUSTENTAR
534RUS DERZHAT'
534SPA SOSTENER
534SWE HÅLLA

535AAA HOMOPHONY
535CZE HOMOFONIE
535DAN SAMKLANG
535DUT HOMOPHOON
535FRE HOMOPHONIE
535GER HOMOPHONIE
535HUN HOMOFÓNIA
535ITA OMOFONIA
535POL HOMOFONJA
535POR HOMOFONIA
535RUS HOMOFONIŸA
535SPA HOMOFONÍA
535SWE HOMOFON

536AAA HORN
536CZE ROH
536DAN HORN
536DUT HOORN
536FRE COR
536GER HORN
536HUN KÜRT
536ITA CORNO
536POL RÓG
536POR CORNO
536RUS ROG
536SPA CUERNO
536SWE HORN

537AAA HUM, TO
537CZE BRUČETI
537DAN NYNNEN
537DUT BROMMEN
537FRE FREDONNER
537GER TRÄLLERN, SUMMEN
537HUN DONGANI
537ITA CANTACCHIARE, GARRIRE
537POL BRZĘCZEĆ
537POR CANTAROLAR, ZUMBIR
537RUS NAPEVAT'
537SPA CANTURRIAR, TARAREAR
537SWE MUMLA

538AAA HUMBLE
538CZE POKORNÝ
538DAN YDMYG
538DUT NEDERIG
538FRE HUMBLE
538GER DEMÜTIG
538HUN ALÁZATOS
538ITA UMILE
538POL POKORNY
538POR HUMILDE
538RUS POKORNYĬ
538SPA HUMILDE
538SWE ÖDMJUK

539AAA HUMOR
539CZE HUMOR
539DAN HUMØR
539DUT HUMEUR
539FRE HUMEUR
539GER HUMOR, LAUNE
539HUN HUMOR
539ITA UMORE
539POL HUMOR
539POR HUMOR
539RUS IUMOR
539SPA HUMOR
539SWE HUMOR

540AAA HUNT
540CZE HONBA, LOV
540DAN JAGT
540DUT JACHT
540FRE CHASSE
540GER JAGD
540HUN VADÁSZÁS
540ITA CACCIA
540POL POLOWANIE
540POR CAÇA
540RUS OKHOTA
570SPA CAZA
540SWE JAKT

541AAA HURDY-GURDY
541CZE STRUNOVÝ KOLOVRÁTEK
541DAN LIREKASSE
541DUT DRAAILIER
541FRE VIELLE
541GER DREHLEIER, DREHORGEL
541HUN FORGÓLANT
541ITA GHIRONDA
541POL KATARYNKA
541POR REALEJO, VIELA
541RUS SHARMANKA
541SPA ORGANILLO
541SWE BÄRBAR ORGEL

542AAA HURRY, TO
542CZE USPÍŠITI
542DAN SKYNDE PA, HASTE
542DUT HAASTEN
542FRE HÂTER, PRESSER
542GER BESCHLEUNIGEN, BEEILEN
542HUN GYORSÓGATNI
542ITA AFFRETTARE
542POL ŚPIESZYĆ SIĘ
542POR APRESSAR
542RUS TOROPIT'
542SPA APRESURAR, ACELERAR
542SWE SKYNDA

543AAA HYMN
543CZE CHVALOZPĚV, HYMNA
543DAN HYMNE
543DUT LOFLIED
543FRE HYMNE
543GER LOBGESANG, HYMNE
543HUN HIMNUSZ
543ITA INNO
543POL HYMNY
543POR HINO
543RUS HIMN
543SPA HIMNO
543SWE HYMN

544AAA IDYL
544CZE IDYLA
544DAN IDYL
544DUT IDYLLE, HERDERSLIED
544FRE IDYLLE
544GER IDYLL(E)
544HUN IDILL, PÁSZTORI
544ITA IDILLIO
544POL IDYLLA
544POR IDÍLIO
544RUS IDILLIIA
544SPA IDILIO
544SWE IDYLL

545AAA IF
545CZE JESTLIŽE
545DAN HVIS
545DUT ALS, INDIEN
545FRE SI
545GER WENN
545HUN HA
545ITA SE
545POL JEŻELI
545POR SE
545RUS ESLI
545SPA SI
545SWE OM

546AAA IMITATE, TO
546CZE NAPODOBOVATI
546DAN EFTERLIGNE
546DUT NAVOLGEN
546FRE IMITER
546GER NACHAHMEN
546HUN UTÁNOZNI
546ITA IMITARE
546POL IMITOWAĆ
546POR IMITAR
546RUS IMITIROVAT'
546SPA IMITAR
546SWE EFTERLIKNA

547AAA IMITATION
547CZE IMITACE
547DAN EFTERLIGNING
547DUT NABOOTSEND, IMITATIE
547FRE IMITATION
547GER NACHAHMUNG
547HUN UTÁNZÁS
547ITA IMITAZIONE
547POL IMITACJA
547POR IMITAÇÃO
547RUS IMITATSIIA
547SPA IMITACIÓN
547SWE EFTERBILDNING

548AAA IMMEDIATE
548CZE BEZPROSTŘEDNÍ
548DAN ØJEBLIKKELIG
548DUT ONMIDDELLIJK
548FRE IMMÉDIAT
548GER UNMITTELBAR
548HUN KÖZVETLEN
548ITA IMMEDIATO
548POL BEZPOSREDNI
548POR IMEDIATO
548RUS NEMEDLENNYĬ
548SPA INMEDIATO
548SWE OMEDELBAR

549AAA IMPATIENT
549CZE NETRPĚLIVÝ
549DAN UTAALMODIG
549DUT ONGEDULDIG
549FRE IMPATIENT
549GER UNGEDULDIG
549HUN TÜRELMETLENUL
549ITA IMPAZIENTE
549POL NIECIERPLIWY
549POR IMPATIENTE
549RUS NETERPVLIVYĬ
549SPA IMPACIENTE
549SWE OTÅLIG

550AAA IMPERFECT
550CZE NEDOKONALÝ, IMPERFEKTNI
550DAN UFULDKOMMEN
550DUT ONVOLMAAKT
550FRE IMPARFAIT(E)
550GER UNVOLLKOMMEN
550HUN TÖKÉLETLEN
550ITA IMPERFETTO
550POL NIEDOKONANY
550POR IMPERFEITO
550RUS NESOVERSHENNYĬ
550SPA IMPERFECTO
550SWE OFULLKOMLIG

551AAA IMPETUOUS
551CZE BOUŘLIVÝ
551DAN STORMENDE
551DUT ONSTUIMIG
551FRE IMPÉTUEUX
551GER STÜRMISCH
551HUN HEVESEN
551ITA IMPETUOSO, IMPETO
551POL GWAŁTOWNIE
551POR IMPETUOSO
551RUS STREMITEL'NYĬ
551SPA IMPETUOSO
551SWE HÄFTIG

552AAA IMPROVISE, TO
552CZE IMPROVIZOVATI
552DAN IMPROVISERE
552DUT IMPROVISEREN
552FRE IMPROVISER
552GER IMPROVISIEREN
552HUN KÖLTENI
552ITA IMPROVVISARE
552POL IMPROWIZOWAĆ
552POR IMPROVISAR
552RUS IMPROVIZIROVAT'
552SPA IMPROVISAR
552SWE IMPROVISERA

553AAA IMPROVIZATION
553CZE IMPROVISACE
553DAN IMPROVISATION
553DUT IMPROVISATIE
553FRE IMPROVISATION
553GER IMPROVISIEREN
553HUN IMPROVIZACIO
553ITA IMPROVVISAZIONE
553POL IMPROWIZACJA
553POR IMPROVISAÇÃO
553RUS IMPROVIZATSIIA
553SPA IMPROVISACIÓN
553SWE IMPROVISATION

554AAA IN
554CZE V(E)
554DAN INDE
554DUT IN
554FRE EN, DANS
554GER IN, IM
554HUN -BAN, -BEN
554ITA IN
554POL WE
554POR EM
554RUS V
554SPA EN
554SWE UTI

555AAA INCISIVE
555CZE ŘEZAVÝ, OSTRÝ
555DAN SKAERENDE
555DUT SNIJDEND
555FRE INCISIF
555GER SCHNEIDEND
555HUN BEMETSZŐ
555ITA INCISIVO
555POL OSTRY
555POR INCISIVO
555RUS OSTRYĬ, REZUSHCHIĬ
555SPA INCISIVO
555SWE SKÄRANDE

556AAA INCREASE, TO
556CZE RŮSTI
556DAN VOKSE
556DUT AANGROEIEN
556FRE CROÎTRE
556GER ANWACHSEN, ZUNEHMEN
556HUN NÖVEKEDNI
556ITA CRESCERE
556POL WZRASTAĆ
556POR CRESCER, AUMENTAR
556RUS RASSHIRIAT'
556SPA ACRECENTAR, ACRECER
556SWE ÖKA

557AAA INDICATE, TO
557CZE ONAZNAČITI
557DAN ANGIVE
557DUT AANWIJZEN
557FRE INDIQUER
557GER HINWEISEN
557HUN MUTATNI
557ITA INDICARE
557POL WSKAZYWAĆ
557POR INDICAR
557RUS UKAZYVAT'
557SPA INDICAR
557SWE ANGE

558AAA INFERIOR
558CZE DOLNÍ, SPODNÍ
558DAN LAVERE
558DUT MINDER
558FRE INFÉRIEUR
558GER UNTERGEORDNET
558HUN ALÁBBVALÓ
558ITA INFERIORE
558POL DOLNY
558POR INFERIOR
558RUS NIZSHIĬ
558SPA INFERIOR
558SWE LÄGRE

559AAA INFINITE
559CZE NEKONEČNÝ
559DAN UENDELIG
559DUT ONEINDIG
559FRE INFINI
559GER UNENDLICH
559HUN VÉG NÉLKÜL
559ITA INFINITO
559POL NIESKOŃCZONY
559POR INFINITO
559RUS BESKONECHNYĬ
559SPA INFINITO
559SWE OÄNDLIG

560AAA INFLECTION
560CZE FLEXE, OHYB
560DAN BØJNING
560DUT BUIGING
560FRE INFLEXION
560GER BIEGSAMKEIT
560HUN HAJLAS
560ITA INFLESSIONE
560POL FLEKSJA
560POR INFLEXÃO
560RUS MODULIATSIIA
560SPA INFLEXIÓN
560SWE BÖJANDE

561AAA INHALE, TO
561CZE VDECHOVATI
561DAN INHALERE
561DUT INHALEREN
561FRE INHALER
561GER EINATMEN
561HUN BESZÍNI
561ITA INALARE
561POL WDYCHIWAĆ
561POR INALAR
561RUS VLYKHAT'
561SPA INHALAR
561SWE INANDAS

562AAA INNOCENT
562CZE NEVINNÝ
562DAN USKYLDIGT
562DUT ONSCHULDIG
562FRE INNOCENT
562GER UNSCHULDIG
562HUN ÁRTATLANUL
562ITA INNOCENTE
562POL NIEWINNIE
562POR INOCENTE
562RUS NEVINNYĬ
562SPA INOCENTE
562SWE OSKYLDIG

563AAA INSENSIBLE
563CZE NEZNATELNÝ
563DAN UNMAERKELIG
563DUT ONMERKBAAR
563FRE INSENSIBLE
563GER UNMERKLICH
563HUN ÉRZETLEN
563ITA INSENSIBILE
563POL NIEZNACNY
563POR INSENSIVEL
563RUS NEZAMETNYĬ
563SPA INSENSIBLE
563SWE OMÄRKLIG

564AAA INSPIRATION
564CZE INSPIRACE, VDECHNUTÍ
564DAN INDAANDING
564DUT INSPIRATIE
564FRE INSPIRATION
564GER BEGEISTERUNG
564HUN LELKESEDÉS
564ITA INSPIRAZIONE
564POL INSPIRACJA
564POR INSPIRAÇÃO
564RUS VDOKHNOVENIE
564SPA INSPIRACIÓN
564SWE INANDNING

565AAA INSTEAD
565CZE MÍSTO
565DAN ISTEDET
565DUT IN PLAATS
565FRE AU LIEU DE
565GER ANSTATT
565HUN HELYETT
565ITA IN LUOGO
565POL ZAMIAST
565POR EM LUGAR
565RUS VMESTO
565SPA EN LUGAR
565SWE I STÄLLET

566AAA INSTRUMENT
566CZE NÁSTROJ
566DAN INSTRUMENT
566DUT INSTRUMENT
566FRE INSTRUMENT
566GER INSTRUMENT
566HUN HANGSZER
566ITA STRUMENTO
566POL INSTRUMENT
566POR INSTRUMENTO
566RUS INSTRUMENT
566SPA INSTRUMENTO
566SWE INSTRUMENT

567AAA INSTRUMENTATE, TO
567CZE INSTRUMENTOVATI
567DAN INSTRUMENTERE
567DUT INSTRUMENTEREN
567FRE INSTRUMENTER
567GER INSTRUMENTIEREN
567HUN HANGSZERELNI
567ITA STROMENTARE
567POL INSTRUMENTOWAĆ
567POR INSTRUMENTAR
567RUS INSTRUMENTOVAT'
567SPA INSTRUMENTAR
567SWE INSTRUMENTERA

568AAA INSTRUMENTATION
568CZE INSTRUMENTACE
568DAN INSTRUMENTERING
568DUT INSTRUMENTATIE
568FRE INSTRUMENTATION
568GER INSTRUMENTIERUNG
568HUN HANGSZERELÉS
568ITA INSTRUMENTAZIONE
568POL INSTRUMENTACJA
568POR INSTRUMENTAÇÃO
568RUS INSTRUMENTOVKA
568SPA INSTRUMENTACIÓN
568SWE INSTRUMENTERING

569AAA INTENSE
569CZE PRONIKAVÝ
569DAN INTENS
569DUT HEVIG
569FRE INTENSE
569GER HEFTIG, INTENSIV
569HUN FESZÜLT, HATÉKONY
569ITA INTENSO
569POL INTENSYWNY
569POR INTENSO
569RUS INTENSIVNYÍ
569SPA INTENSO
569SWE INTENSIV

570AAA INTER-
570CZE MEZI-
570DAN MELLEM-
570DUT TUSSEN-
570FRE INTER-
570GER ZWISCHEN-
570HUN INTER-
570ITA INTER-
570POL INTER-
570POR INTER-
570RUS MEZH-
570SPA INTER-
570SWE INTER-

571AAA INTERFERENCE
571CZE INTERFERENCE
571DAN INTERFERENS
571DUT INTERFERENTIE
571FRE INTERFÉRENCE
571GER INTERFERENZ
571HUN KÖZBEJÖVÉS
571ITA INFRAMMETTENZA
571POL INTERFERENCJA
571POR INTERFERÊNCIA
571RUS INTERFERENTSIÍA
571SPA INTERFERENCIA
571SWE INTERFERENS

572AAA INTERLUDE
572CZE MEZIHRA
572DAN MELLEMSPIL
572DUT TUSSENSPEL
572FRE INTERLUDE
572GER ZWISCHENSPIEL
572HUN INTERLUDIUM
572ITA INTERLUDIO
572POL PRZEGRYAKA
572POR INTERLÚDIO
572RUS ANTRAKT
572SPA INTERLUDIO
572SWE MELLANSPEL

573AAA INTERMEDIATE
573CZE MEZIPOLOHA
573DAN MELLEMLIGGENDE
573DUT BEMIDDELEN
573FRE INTERMÉDIARE
573GER DAZWISCHEN LIEGEND
573HUN AKÖZÖTT
573ITA INTERMEDIO
573POL POŚREDNI
573POR INTERMÉDIO
573RUS INTERMEDIÍA
573SPA INTERMEDIO
573SWE MELLANLIGGANDE

574AAA INTERMEZZO
574CZE MEZIAKT
574DAN MELLEMAKTSMUSIK
574DUT INTERMEZZO
574FRE INTERMÈDE, ENTR'ACTE
574GER ZWISCHENAKT
574HUN KÖZJÁTÉK
574ITA INTERMEZZO
574POL INTERMEDIUM
574POR INTERMEZZO
574RUS INTERMETSTSO
574SPA INTERMEDIO, ENTREACTO
574SWE MELLANSPEL, INTERMEZZO

575AAA INTERPRET, TO
575CZE PROVÉSTI
575DAN FORTOLKE
575DUT UITLEGGEN
575FRE INTERPRÉTER
575GER DARSTELLEN
575HUN INTERPRETÁLNI
575ITA INTERPRETARE
575POL INTERPRETOWAĆ
575POR INTERPRETAR
575RUS INTERPRETIROVAT'
575SPA INTERPRETAR
575SWE UTTOLKA

576AAA INTERRUPT, TO
576CZE PŘERUŠITI
576DAN AFBRYDE
576DUT ONDERBREKEN
576FRE INTERROMPRE
576GER UNTERBRECHEN
576HUN MEGSZAKASZTANI
576ITA INTERROMPERE
576POL PRZERYWAĆ
576POR INTERROMPER
576RUS PRERYVAT'
576SPA INTERRUMPIR
576SWE AVBRYTA

577AAA INTERVAL
577CZE INTERVAL
577DAN INTERVAL, AFSTANDS
577DUT INTERVAL, AFSTAND
577FRE INTERVALLE
577GER INTERVALL, TONABSTAND
577HUN HANGKÖZÖK
577ITA INTERVALLO
577POL INTERWAL (E)
577POR INTERVALO
577RUS INTERVAL
577SPA INTERVALO
577SWE INTERVALL

578AAA INTIMATE
578CZE INTIMNÍ, DŮVĚRNÝ
578DAN FORTROLIG, INDERST
578DUT INNIG
578FRE INTIME
578GER INNIG
578HUN BENSŐSÉGESEN
578ITA INTIMO
578POL INTYMNY
578POR ÍNTIMO
578RUS INTIMNYĬ
578SPA ÍNTIMO
578SWE FÖRTROLIG

579AAA INTONATION
579CZE INTONACE
579DAN INTONERING
579DUT INTONATIE
579FRE INTONATION
579GER TONANSATZ
579HUN HANGOZTATÁS
579ITA INTONAZIONE
579POL INTONACJA
579POR ENTONAÇÃO
579RUS INTONATSIĬA
579SPA ENTONACIÓN
579SWE INTONATION

580AAA INTONE, TO
580CZE INTONOVATI
580DAN INTONERE
580DUT INTONEREN
580FRE ENTONNER
580GER INTONIEREN
580HUN INTONÁLNI
580ITA INTONARE
580POL INTONOWAĆ
580POR ENTOAR
580RUS INTONIROVAT'
580SPA ENTONAR
580SWE INTONERA

581AAA INTREPID
581CZE NEOHROŽENÝ
581DAN UFORFAERDET
581DUT ONVERSCHROKKEN
581FRE INTRÉPIDE
581GER UNERSCHROCKEN
581HUN RENDÍTHETETLEN
581ITA INTREPIDO
581POL NIEUSTRASZONY
581POR INTRÉPIDO
581RUS NEUSTRASHIMYĬ
581SPA INTRÉPIDO
581SWE OFÖRSKRÄCKT

582AAA INTRODUCTION
582CZE INTRODUKCE, ÚVOD
582DAN INTRODUKTION
582DUT VOORSPEL
582FRE INTRODUCTION
582GER VORSPIEL, EINGANG
582HUN BEVEZETÉS
582ITA INTRODUZIONE
582POL WSTĘP
582POR INTRODUÇÃO
582RUS INTRODUKTSIĬA
582SPA INTRODUCCIÓN
582SWE INTRODUKTION

583AAA INTROIT
583CZE INTROITUS
583DAN INTROITUS
583DUT INTROITUS
583FRE INTROÏT
583GER INTROITUS
583HUN INTROITUS
583ITA INTROITO
583POL INTROIT
583POR INTROITO
583RUS NACHALO
583SPA INTROITO
583SWE INTROITUS

584AAA IN TUNE
584CZE INTONOVANÝ
584DAN FIN
584DUT ZUIVER GESTEMD
584FRE D'ACCORD
584GER GUTGESTIMMT
584HUN HANGULATOS
584ITA INTONATO, IN ACCORDO
584POL NASTROJONY
584POR AFINADO
584RUS NASTROENNYĬ
584SPA AFINADO
584SWE STÄMD

585AAA INVENTION
585CZE INVENCE, NÁPAD
585DAN INVENTION
585DUT INVENTIO
585FRE INVENTION
585GER INVENTION
585HUN INVENCIÓ
585ITA INVÉNZIONE
585POL INWENJA
585POR INVENÇÃO
585RUS INVENTSIÎA
585SPA INVENCIÓN
585SWE INVENTION

586AAA INVERSION
586CZE INVERZE, OBRÁCENÍ
586DAN INVERION, OMSTILLING
586DUT INVERSIE, OMKERING
586FRE INVERSION
586GER UMKEHRUNG
586HUN MEGFORDÍTÁS
586ITA INVERSIONE, ROVESCIO
586POL INWERSJA
586POR INVERSÃO
586RUS INVERSIÎA
586SPA INVERSIÓN
586SWE INVERSION, OMKASTNING

587AAA INVERT, TO
587CZE PREVRÁTITI
587DAN OMSTILLE
587DUT OMKEREN
587FRE RENVERSER
587GER UMKEHREN
587HUN MEGFORDÍTANI
587ITA INVERTIRE, ROVESCIARE
587POL INWERTOWAČ
587POR INVERTER
587RUS PEREVĚRTYVAT'
587SPA INVERTIR
587SWE INVERTERA

588AAA IONIAN
588CZE JONICKÝ
588DAN JONISK
588DUT JONISCH
588FRE IONIEN
588GER IONISCH
588HUN IÓN
588ITA IONIO
588POL JOŃSKA
588POR JÓNIO
588RUS IONICHESKIÍ
588SPA JÓNICO
588SWE JONISK

589AAA IRE
589CZE HNĚV
589DAN VREDE
589DUT TOORN
589FRE COLÈRE
589GER ZORN
589HUN HARAG
589ITA IRA
589POL GNIEW
589POR IRA
589RUS GNEV
589SPA IRA
589SWE VREDE

590AAA IRONY
590CZE IRONIE
590DAN IRONI
590DUT IRONIE
590FRE IRONIE
590GER IRONIE
590HUN GÚNYOR
590ITA IRONIA
590POL IRONIA
590POR IRONIA
590RUS IRONIÎA
590SPA IRONÍA
590SWE IRONI

591AAA ISO-
591CZE IZO-, STEJNO-
591DAN ISO-
591DUT ISO-
591FRE ISO-
591GER ISO-
591HUN IZO-
591ITA ISO-
591POL IZO-
591POR ISO-
591RUS IZO-
591SPA ISO-
591SWE ISO-

592AAA IT
592CAE ONO
592DAN DET
592DUT HET, HIJ, ZIJ
592FRE LE L', LA
592GER DER, DIE, DAS
592HUN AZ, EZ
592ITA LO
592POL ONO
592POR ÊLE
592RUS ON
592SPA EL, LA, LO
592SWE DET

593AAA IVORY
593CZE SLONOVINA
593DAN ELFENBEN
593DUT IVOOR
593FRE IVOIRE
593GER ELFENBEIN
593HUN ELEFÁNTCSONT
593ITA AVORIO
593POL KOŚĆ SŁONIOWA
593POR MARFIM
593RUS SLONOVAIA KOST'
593SPA MARFIL
593SWE ELFENBEN

594AAA JANISSARY
594CZE JANIČIAR
584DAN JANITSCHAR
594DUT JANITSCHAR
594FRE JANISSAIRE
594GER JANITSCHAR
594HUN JANICSÁR
594ITA GIANNIZZERO
594POL JANCZAR(SKA)
594POR JANÍCARO, JANÍZARO
594RUS IANYCHAR
594SPA GENÍZARO
594SWE JANITSCHAR

595AAA JAZZ
595CZE DŽEZ
595DAN JAZZ
595DUT JAZZ
595FRE JAZZ
595GER JAZZ
595HUN DZEESZ
595ITA JAZZ
595POL DŻEZ
595POR JAZZ
595RUS DZHAZ
595SPA JAZZ
595SWE ZAZZ

596AAA JEW'S HARP
596CZE BRNKAČKA ÚSTNÍ
596DAN MUNDHARPE
596DUT MONDHARP
596FRE GUIMBARDE
596GER BRUMMEISEN, MAULTROMMEL
596HUN DOROMB
596ITA SCACCIAPENSIERI, TROMBA
596POL DRUMLA
596POR BERIMBAU
596RUS VARGAN
596SPA GÜIMBARDA
596SWE MUNGIGA

597AAA JIG
597CZE DŽIGA, ZIGA
597DAN GIGA, JIG
597DUT JIG
597FRE GIGUE
597GER GIGUE
597HUN JIGG
597ITA GIGA
597POL JIG
597POR JIGA
597RUS DZHIGA
597SPA GIGA, JIGA
597SWE JIGG

598AAA JINGLE, TO
598CZE CINKATI
598DAN RINGLE, KLINGEN
598DUT RINKELEN
598FRE TINTER
598GER KLINGELN
598HUN CSILINGELVE
598ITA TINTINNARE
598POL BRZĘKAĆ
598POR TILINTAR
598RUS ZVENET'
598SPA TILINTEAR
598SWE KLINGA

599AAA JOCULAR
599CZE HRAVÝ
599DAN MUNTER
599DUT SCHERTSEND
599FRE BADIN, JOYEUX
599GER SCHÄKERHAFT, SPASSHAFT
599HUN TRÉFÁSAN
599ITA GIOCOSO
599POL WESOŁO, RADOŚNIE
599POR JOCOSO
599RUS VESELYĬ
599SPA JOCOSO
599SWE MUNTER

600AAA JOKE, JEST, TO
600CZE ŽERTOVZTI
600DAN SPØGE
600DUT SCHERTSEN
600FRE BADINER
600GER SCHERZEN
600HUN TRÉFÁLNI
600ITA SCHERZARE
600POL ŻARTOWAĆ
600POR BRINCAR
600RUS SHUTIT'
600SPA JUGUETEAR
600SWE SKÄMTA

601AAA JOVIAL
601CZE ZOVIÁLNÍ, BODRÝ
601DAN JOVIAL
601DUT VROLIJK
601FRE JOVIAL
601GER JOVIAL, LUSTIG
601HUN JÓKEDVŰ
601ITA GIOVIALE
601POL JOWIALNY
601POR JOVIAL
601RUS VESELYĬ
601SPA JOVIAL
601SWE JOVIALISK

602AAA JOY
602CZE RADOST
602DAN GLAEDE
602DUT VREUGDE
602FRE JOIE
602GER FREUNDE, HEITER
602HUN DERŰ
602ITA GIOIA, GAUDIO
692POL RADOŚĆ
602POR REGOZIJO
602RUS RADOST'
602SPA GOZO
602SWE GLÄDJE

603AAA JUBILANT
603CZE JÁSAVÝ
603DAN JUBLENDE
603DUT JUBELEND
603FRE JUBILANT
603GER JUBELND
603HUN ÖRÖMUJJONGVA
603ITA GIUBILANTE, GIUBILOSO
603POL ROZRADOWANY
603POR JUBILOSO
603RUS LIKUIŪSHCHIĬ
603SPA JUBILOSO, JUBILO
603SWE JUBLANDE

604AAA JUBILEE
604CZE JUBILEUM
604DAN JUBILAEUM
604DUT JUBILEUM, JUBEL
604FRE JUBILÉ
604GER JUBILÄUM
604HUN VIGALOM ÜNNEP
604ITA GIUBILEO
604POL JUBILACJE, JUBILEUSZ
604POR JUBILEU, JUBILAÇÃO
604RUS IŪBILEĬ
604SPA JUBILEO
604SWE JUBILEUM, JUBEL

605AAA JUST
605CZE SPRÁVNÝ
605DAN RIGTIGT
605DUT JUIST
605FRE JUSTE
605GER RIGHTIG
605HUN KELLŐ
605ITA GIUSTO
605POL DOKLADNIE
605POR JUSTO
605RUS SPRAVEDLIVYĬ
605SPA JUSTO
605SWE RIKTIGT

606AAA JUXTAPOSITION
606CZE PROTIPOLOŽENÍ
606DAN SIDESTILLING
606DUT NAASTANDERPLAATSING
606FRE JUXTAPOSITION
606GER NEBENEINANDERSTELLUNG
606HUN EGYMASUTÁNISÁG
606ITA GIUSTAPPOSIZIONE
606POL ZESTAWIENIE
606POR JUSTAPOSIÇÃO
606RUS SOPOSTAVLENIE
606SPA YUXTAPOSITIÓN
606SWE JUXTAPOSITION

607AAA KETTLEDRUM
607CZE KOTEL
607DAN PAUKE
607DUT PAUKE, KETELTROM
607FRE TIMBALE
607GER KESSELPAUKE, PAUKE
607HUN ÜSTDOB
607ITA TIMPANO, TABALLO
607POL KOTŁOW
607POR TIMBALE, TÍMPANO
607RUS TSIMBALY
607SPA TIMBAL
607SWE PUKA

608AAA KEY
608CZE ZPŰSOB, TÓNINA
608DAN TONEART
608DUT TOONAARD
608FRE MODE
608GER TONART
608HUN HANGNEM
608ITA MODO
608POL TONACJA
608POR MODO
608RUS SPOSOB, LAD
608SPA MODO
608SWE TONART

609AAA KEY(INSTRUMENT)
609CZE KLAVESA, KLAPKA
609DAN TASTE
609DUT TOETS, SLEUTEL
609FRE TOUCHE, CLÉ
609GER TASTE, KLAPPE
609HUN KULCS
609ITA CHIAVE, TASTO
609POL KLUCZ
609POR TECLA
609RUS KLIUCH
609SPA TECLA
609SWE TANGENT

610AAA KEYBOARD
610CZE KLÁVESNICE
610DAN KLAVIATUR
610DUT TOETSENBORD
610FRE CLAVIER, TOUCHE
610GER KLAVIATUR, TASTATUR
610HUN BILLENTYŰZET
610ITA TASTIERA, TASTATURA
610POL KLAWIATURA
610POR TECLADO
610RUS KLAVIATURA
610SPA TACLADO
610SWE KLAVIATUR

611AAA KEYNOTE
611CZE ZÁKLADNÍ TON
611DAN GRUNDTONE
611DUT GRONDTOON
611FRE TONIQUE
611GER TONIKA
611HUN ALAPHANG
611ITA TONICA
611POL NUTA KLUCZOWA
611POR TOM
611RUS TONAL'NOST'
611SPA NOTA TÓNICA
611SWE GRUNDTON

612AAA KNEE
612CZE KOLENO
612DAN KNAE
612DUT KNIE
612FRE GENOU
612GER KNIE
612HUN TÉRD
612ITA GINOCCHIO
612POL KOLANO
612POR JOELHO
612RUS KOLENO
612SPA RODILLA
612SWE KNA

613AAA LABIAL
613CZE LABIÁLNÍ, VETNÝ
613DAN LABIAL
613DUT LIBIAAL
613FRE LABIAL
613GER LABIAL
613HUN AJAK
613ITA LABIALE
613POL WARGOWY
613POR LABIAL
613RUS LABIAL'NYĬ
613SPA LABIAL
613SWE LABIAL

614AAA LAMENT, TO
614CZE NAŘÍKATI
614DAN JAMRE
614DUT KLAGEN, JAMMEREN
614FRE LAMENTER
614GER BEKLAGEN
614HUN PANASZOLNI
614ITA LAMENTARE
614POL LAMENTOWAĆ
614POR LAMENTAR
614RUS ZHALOVAT'SIA
614SPA LAMENTAR
614SWE KLAGA, JÄMRA SIG

615AAA LAMENTATION
615CZE NÁŘEK
615DAN KLAGENDE, VEMODIGT
615DUT WEEKLACHT
615FRE LAMENTATION
615GER KLAGEN
615HUN PANASZOSAN
615ITA LAMENTAZIONE
615POL LAMENTACJA, ZALOSNIE
615POR LAMENTAÇÃO
615RUS ZHALOBA, SETOVANIE
615SPA LAMENTACIÓN
615SWE VELKAGEN

616AAA LANGUAGE
616CZE JAZYK
616DAN SPROG
616DUT SPRAAK
616FRE LANGUE
616GER SPRACHE
616HUN NYELV
616ITA LINGUA
616POL JĘZYK
616POR LINGUA
616RUS IAZYK
616SPA LENGUA
616SWE SPRÅK

617AAA LANGUID
617CZE OCHABLÝ
617DAN MAT
617DUT SMACHTEND
617FRE LANGUISSANT
617GER SCHMACHTEND, MATT
617HUN BÁGYACT
617ITA LANGUIDO
617POL OMDLEWAJĄCO
617POR LÁNGUIDO
617RUS SLABYĬ
617SPA LÁNGUIDO
617SWE MATT

618AAA LARGE
618CZE VELKÝ
618DAN STOR
618DUT GROOT
618FRE GRAND, GROS
618GER GROSS
618HUN BŐSÉGES
618ITA GROSSO
618POL WIELKI, DUZY
618POR GRANDE
618RUS BOL'SHOĬ
618SPA GRANDE, GRUESO
618SWE STOR

619AAA LARYNX
619CZE HRTAN
619DAN STRUBEHOVED
619DUT STROTTENHOOFD
619FRE LARYNX
619GER KEHLKOPF
619HUN GÉG
619ITA LARINGE
619POL KRTAŃ
619POR LARINGE
619RUS GORTAN'
619S7A LARINGE
619SWE STRUPHUVUD

620AAA LAST
620CZE POSLEDNÍ
620DAN SIDST
620DUT LAATST
620FRE ULTIME, DERNIER
620GER LETZT
620HUN UTOLSÓ
620ITA ULTIMO
620POL OSTATNI
620POR ÚLTIMO
620RUS POSLEDNIĬ
620SPA ÚLTIMO
620SWE SIST

621AAA LATE
621CZE POZDĚ, POMALÝ
621DAN SENT
621DUT LANGZAAM
621FRE TARD(IF)
621GER LANGSOM, SPÄT
621HUN KÉSLELTETVE
621ITA TARDO
621POL PÓŹNY
621POR TARDIO
621RUS POZNIĬ
621SPA TARDÍO
621SWE SEN

622AAA LAUD
622CZE CHVÁLA
622DAN LOVPRISNING
622DUT LOFZANG
622FRE HYMNE
622GER LOBGESANG
622HUN LANT
622ITA LAUDA
622POL POCHWALA
622POR LAUDA
622RUS SHVALA
622SPA LAUDE
622SWE LOVSÅNG

623AAA LAUGH, TO
623CZE SMÁTI SE
623DAN LE
623DUT LACHEN
623FRE RIRE
623GER LACHEN
623HUN NEVETNI
623ITA RIDERE
623POL ŚMIAĆ SIĘ
623POR RIR
623RUS SMEĬAT'SĬA
623SPA REIR
623SWE LE

624AAA LAY
624CZE PÍSEŃ
624DAN SANG
624DUT LIED
624FRE LAI
624GER LIED, GESANG
624HUN LAI
624ITA CANZONE
624POL PIEŚŃ
624POR CANTIGA
624RUS PESNĬA
624SPA LAY, LAI
624SWE SÅNG

625AAA LEADER
625CZE VŮDCÍ
625DAN LEDER, DIRIGENT
625DUT AANVOERDER, DIRIGENT
625FRE CHEF D ATTAQUE
625GER INTENDANT, CHORFÜHRER
625HUN VEZETŐ, ANGLIÁBAN
625ITA DIRITTORE
625POL DYRYGENT
625POR CHEFE, DIRECTOR
625RUS DIRIZHÉR
625SPA CABEZA DE COROS
625SWE LEDARE

626AAA LEADING TONE
626CZE CITLIVÝ
626DAN LEDERTONE
626DUT LEITOON
626FRE NOTE SENSIBLE
626GER LEIT,TON
626HUN VEZETŐHANG
626ITA SENSIBILE
626POL CZULE, DOTYKALNIE
626POR SENSÍVEL
626RUS VVODNYI TON
626SPA NOTA SENSIBLE
626SWE LEDARNOT

627AAA LEAD, TO
627CZE RÍDITI, VEDENÍ HLASŮ
627DAN DIRIGERE, FØRE
627DUT DIRIGEREN
627FRE MENER, CONDUIRE
627GER FÜHREN
627HUN VESETNI
627ITA MENARE, CONDURRE
627POL PROWADZIĆ
627POR SER CONDUZIDO
627RUS DIRIZHIROVAT'
627SPA CONDUCIR
627SWE DIRIGERA, FÖRA

628AAA LEANING TONE
628CZE PŘÍRAZ, OPORA
628DAN FORBEREDT
628DUT VOORSLAG
628FRE APOGGIATURE
628GER VORSCHLAG
628HUN ELŐKE
628ITA APPOGGIATURA
628POL PODPIS
628POR APOYADURA
628RUS APODZHATURA
628SPA APOYATURA, APOYADOR
628SWE FORSLAG

629AAA LEFT
629CZE LEVÝ
629DAN VENSTRE
629DUT LINKS
629FRE GAUCHE
629GER LINK(E)
629HUN BAL
629ITA SINISTRA
629POL LEWY
629POR ESQUERDA
629RUS LEVYI
629SPA SINIESTRA, IZQUIERDA
629SWE VÄNSTER

630AAA LEGEND
630CZE LEGENDA
630DAN LEGENDE
630DUT LEGENDE
630FRE LÉGENDE
630GER LEGENDE
630HUN LEGENDA
630ITA LEGGENDA
630POL LEGENDA
630POR LEGENDA, LENDA
630RUS LEGENDA
630SPA LEGENDA, LEYENDA
630SWE LEGEND

631AAA LEGER LINE(S)
631CZE OSNOVA LINKOVÀ
631DAN HJAELPELINIE
631DUT HULPLIJN
631FRE LIGNE AJOUTÉE
631GER NOTENLINIE
631HUN SEGÉDVONAL
631ITA RIGA AGGIUNTA
631POL LINIA DODANA
631POR LINHAS SUPLEMENTARES
631RUS DOBAVOCHNYI LINEIKA
631SPA LINEA ADICIONAL
631SWE HJÄLPLINJE

632AAA LENGTH
632CZE DÉLKA
632DAN LAENGDE
632DUT LENGTE
632FRE LONGUEUR
632GER LÄNGE
632HUN TARTAM
632ITA LUNGHEZZA
632POL DLUGOSĆ
632POR DURAÇÃO
632RUS DLINA
632SPA DURACIÓN
632SWE LÄNGD

633AAA LENGTHEN, TO
633CZE PRODLOUŽITI
633DAN FORLAENGE
633DUT VERLENGEN
633FRE ALLONGER
633GER VERLÄNGERN
633HUN SZÉLESEN
633ITA ALLUNGARE
633POL PRZYDŁUŻAĆ
633POR ALONGAR
633RUS UDLINIAT'
633SPA ALARGAR
633SWE FORLÄNGA

634AAA LESS
634CZE MÉNĚ
634DAN MINDRE
634DUT MINDER
634FRE MOINS
634GER MINDER, WENIGER
634HUN KISEBB
634ITA MENO
634POL MNIEJ
634POR MENOS
634RUS MENEE
634SPA MENOS
634SWE MINDRE

635AAA LESSON
635CZE LEKCE
635DAN LEKTIE, LAESNING
635DUT LEZEN
635FRE LEÇON
635GER LEKTION, AUFGABE
635HUN LECZKE
635ITA LEZIONE
635POL LEKCJA
635POR LIÇÃO
635RUS UROK
635SPA LECCIÓN
635SWE LEKTION, LÄXA

636AAA LETTER
636CZE LITERA
636DAN BOGSTAV
636DUT LETTER
636FRE LETTRE
636GER BUCHSTABE, LETTER
636HUN BETÜ
636ITA LETTERA
636POL LITERA
636POR LETRA
636RUS LITERA
636SPA LETRA
636SWE BOKSTAV

637AAA LICENSE
637CZE LICENCE, ODCHYLKA
637DAN LICENS
637DUT VRIJHEID
637FRE LICENCE
637GER LIZENZ, FREIHEIT
637HUN SZABADSÁG
637ITA LICENZA
637POL LICENJA, POZWOLENIE
637POR LICENÇA
637RUS LITSENZIIA
637SPA LICENCIA
637SWE LICENS

638AAA LID
638CZE VÍKO
638DAN LAAG, DAEKE
638DUT DEKSEL, LID
638FRE COUVERCLE
638GER DECKEL, HUT
638HUN FEDEL
638ITA COPERCHIO
638POL WIEKO
638POR TAMPA
638RUS VEKO
638SPA TAPA
638SWE LOCK

639AAA LIGATURE
639CZE LIGATURA
639DAN LIGATUR
639DUT LIGATUUR, LIGATURA
639FRE LIGAITURE, LIAISON
639GER LIGATUR, BINDBOGEN
639HUN LIGATURA, KÖTÉS
639ITA LEGATURA
639POL LIGATURA
639POR LIGADURA
639RUS LIGATURA
639SPA LIGADURA
639SWE LIGATUR, LEGATOBÅGE

640AAA LIGHT
640CZE LEHKÝ
640DAN LET, UTVUNGET
640DUT LICHT
643FRE LÉGER, DÉLIÉ
640GER LEICHT
640HUN KÖNNYÜ
640ITA LEGGIERO, SLEGATO
640POL LEKKO
640POR LIGEIRO
640RUS LËGKII
640SPA LIGERO
640SWE LÄTT

641AAA LIKE
641CZE PODOBNÝ
641DAN LIGESOM
641DUT HOE, ZOALS, GELIJK
641FRE COMME, SEMBLABLE
641GER WIE, ÄHNLICH
641HUN HASONLÓAN
641ITA COME, SIMILE
641POL JAK, PODOBNY
641POR SOMO, SEMELHANTE
641RUS KAK, PODOBNYĬ
641SPA COMO
641SWE LIKSOM

642AAA LIMP, TO
642CZE KULHATI
642DAN HALTE
642DUT HINKEN
642FRE BOITER
642GER HINKEN
642HUN SÁNTIKÁLNI
642ITA ZOPPICCARE
642POL KULEĆ
642POR COXEAR
642RUS KHROMAT'
642SPA COJEAR
642SWE HALTA

643AAA LINE
643CZE LINKA
643DAN LINIE
643DUT LIJN, NOTENLIJN
643FRE LIGNE
643GER LINIE, NOTENLINIE
643HUN VONAL
643ITA RIGA
643POL LINIA
643POR LINHA
643RUS LINIĬA
643SPA LÍNEA
643SWE LINA

644AAA LINEAR
644CZE LINEÁRNÍ
644DAN LINEAER
644DUT LINEAIR
644FRE LINÉAIRE
644GER LINEAR
644HUN VONALOS
644ITA LINEARE
644POL LINEARNY
644POR LINEAR
644RUS LINEĬNYĬ
644SPA LINEAL
644SWE LINEAR

645AAA LIP
645CZE RET, PYSK
645DAN LAEBE
645DUT LIP
645FRE LÈVRE
645GER LIPPE
645HUN AJAK
645ITA LABBRO
645POL WARGA
645POR LÁBIO
645RUS GUBA
645SPA LABIO
645SWE LÄPP

646AAA LISTEN, TO
646CZE POSLOUCHATI
646DAN LYTTE
646DUT LUISTEREN
646FRE ÉCOUTER
646GER ZUHÖREN
646HUN HALLGATNI
646ITA ASCOLTARE
646POL SŁUCHAĆ
646POR ESCUTAR
646RUS SLUCHAT'
646SPA ESCUCHAR
646SWE LYSSNA

647AAA LITANY
647CZE LITANIE
647DAN LITANI
647DUT LITANIE
647FRE LITANIE
647GER LITANEI
647HUN LITÁNIA
647ITA LITANIA, LITANIE
647POL LITANJA
647POR LITANIA
647RUS LITANIĬA
647SPA LETANÍA
647SWE LITANIA

648AAA LITTLE, SOMEWHAT
648CZE MALÝ, MÁLO
648DAN LIDT, LILLE
648DUT KLEIN, WENIG
648FRE PEU, PETIT
648GER ETWAS, WENIG, KLEIN
648HUN KIS
648ITA POCO, PICCOLO
648POL MAŁY, TROCHE
648POR POUCO
648RUS MALEN'KIĬ
648SPA POCO, PEQUEÑO
648SWE LITEN

649AAA LITURGY
649CZE LITURGIE
649DAN LITURGI
649DUT LITURGIE
649FRE LITURGIE
649GER LITURGIE
649HUN LITURGIKA
649ITA LITURGIA
649POL LITURGJA
649POR LITURGIA
649RUS LITURGIIA
649SPA LITURGIA
649SWE LITURGI

650AAA LIVELY
650CZE ŽIVÝ
650DAN LIVLIG
650DUT LEVENDIG
650FRE PLEIN DE VIE
650GER LEBENDIG, LEBHAFT
650HUN ÉLÉNK
650ITA ANIMATO
650POL ŻYWY
650POR ANIMADO
650RUS ZHIVOI
650SPA ANIMATO
650SWE LIVLIG

651AAA LONG
651CZE DLOUHÝ
651DAN LANG
651DUT LANG
651FRE LONG(UE)
651GER LANG
651HUN HOSSZAN
651ITA LUNGO
651POL DŁUGA
651POR LONGO
651RUS DOLGO, LARGO
651SPA LONGA, LARGO
651SWE LÅNG

652AAA LOOSE
652CZE VOLNÝ, NENUCENÝ
652DAN LØS
652DUT LOS
652FRE DÉGAGÉ, DÉLIÉ
652GER LOS, UNGEBUNDEN
652HUN FELODOTT
652ITA SCOILTO
652POL ZRĘCZNIE, SWOBODNIE
652POR SÓLTA
652RUS SVOBODNYI
652SPA LIBRE, FLOJO
652SWE LÖS

653AAA LOUD
653CZE SILNÝ, HLASITÉ
653DAN HØJ
653DUT STERK, LUID
653FRE BRUYANT, FORT(E)
653GER LAUT
653HUN HANGOS
653ITA FORTE, ALTO
653POL SILNIE
653POR FORTE, ALTO
653RUS FORTE, GROMKII
653SPA FUERTE, RUIDOSO
653SWE HÖG

654AAA LOVE
654CZE LÁSKA
654DAN KAERLEGHED
654DUT LIEFDA
654FRE AMOUR
654GER LIEBE
654HUN SZERETET
654ITA AMORE
654POL MIŁOSĆ
654POR AMOR
654RUS LIUBOV'
654SPA AMOR
654SWE KÄRLEK

655AAA LOVELY
655CZE KRÁSNY
655DAN SKØN
655DUT BEMINNELIJK
655FRE BEAU
655GER LIEBLICH
655HUN KELLEMES
655ITA BELLO
655POL ŚLICZNY
655POR BELO
655RUS KRASIVYI
655SPA BELLO
655SWE LJUVLIG

656AAA LOW
656CZE NÍZKÝ
656DAN LAV
656DUT LAAG
656FRE BAS
656GER TIEF, LEISE
656HUN ALACSONY
656ITA GRAVE, PIANO
656POL NISKI
656POR BAIXO
656RUS NIZHKII
656SPA BAJO, PIANO
656SWE LÅG

657AAA LOWER, TO
657CZE SNÍŽITI
657DAN GØRE LAV
657DUT VERLAGEN
657FRE ABAISSER, DESCENDER
657GER ERNIEDRIGEN
657HUN ALACSONYABB
657ITA ABBASSARE
657POL OBNIŽAĆ
657POR ABAIXAR
657RUS SNOSIT'
657SPA BAJAR
657SWE BLI LÅGRE

658AAA LUGUBRIOUS
658CZE TRUCHLIVÝ
658DAN SØRGELIG KLAGENDE
658DUT TREURIG
658FRE LUGUBRE
658GER TRAURIG, DÜSTER
658HUN GYÁSZOSAN
658ITA LUGUBRE
658POL PONURO
658POR LÚGUBRE
658RUS PECHAL'NYĬ
658SPA LÚGUBRE
658SWE SORGLIG

659AAA LULLABY
659CZE UKOLÉBAVKA
659DAN VUGGEVISE, VUGGESANG
659DUT WIEGELIED(JE)
659FRE BERCEUSE
659GER WIEGENLIED
659HUN BÖLCSŐDAL
659ITA NINNA NANNA
659POL KOLYSANKA
659POR ARROLO, ARRULHO
659RUS KOLYBEL'NAĬA
659SPA ARRULLO, NANA
659SWE VAGGVISA

660AAA LUTE
660CZE LOUTNA
660DAN LUT
660DUT LUIT
660FRE LUTH
660GER LAUTE
660HUN LANT
660ITA LIUTO
660POL LUTNIA
660POR LUTO, ALAÚDE
660RUS LIUTNIA
660SPA LAUD
660SWE LUTA

661AAA LYDIAN
661CZE LYDICKÝ
661DAN LYDISK
661DUT LYDISCH
661FRE LYDIEN
661FER LYDISCH
661HUN LID
661ITA LIDIO
661POL LIDYJSKI
661POR LIDIO
661RUS LIDIĬSKIĬ
661SPA LIDIO
661SWE LIDISK

662AAA LYRE
662CZE LYRA
662DAN LYRE
662DUT LIER
662FRE LYRE
662GER LEIER, LYRA
662HUN LANT
662ITA LIRA
662POL LIRA
662POR LIRA
662RUS LIRA
662SPA LIRA
662SWE LUT

663AAA LYRIC
663CZE LYRICKÝ
663DAN LYRISK
663DUT LYRISCH
663FRE LYRIQUE
663GER LYRISCH
663HUN LIRAI
663ITA LIRICA
663POL LIRYCZNY
663POR LIRICO
663RUS LIRICHESKIĬ
663SPA LÍRICO, LÍRICA
663SWE LYRISK

664AAA MACHINE
664CZE STROJ
664DAN MASKINE
664DUT MACHINE
664FRE MACHINE
664GER MASCHINE
664HUN GÉP
664ITA MACCHINA
664POL MASZYNA
664POR MÁQUINA
664RUS MASHINA
664SPA MÁQUINA
664SWE MASKIN

665AAA MADRIGAL
665CZE MADRIGAL
665DAN MADRIGAL
665DUT MADRIGAAL
665FRE MADRIGAL
665GER SCHÄFERGEDIGHT
665HUN MADRIGAL
665ITA MADRIGAŁE, MADRIAL(E)
665POL MADRYGAŁ
665POR MADRIGAL
665RUS MADRIGAL
665SPA MADRIGAL
665SWE MADRIGAL

666AAA MAGICAL
666CZE MAGICKÝ
666DAN MAGISK
666DUT MAGISCH
666FRE MAGIQUE
666GER MAGISCH
666HUN BŰVOS
666ITA MAGICO
666POL MAGICZNY
666POR MÁGICA
666RUS MAGICHESKIĬ
666SPA MÁGICO
666SWE MAGISK

667AAA MAJESTIC
667CZE MAJESTÁTNÍ
667DAN MAJESTAETISK
667DUT MAJESTUEUS
667GRE MAJESTUEUX
667GER MAJESTÄTISCH
667HUN FENSÉGESEN
667ITA MAESTOSO
667POL MAJESTATYCZNIE
667POR MAJESTOSO
667RUS BELICHESTVENNO
667SPA MAJESTUOSO
667SWE MAJESTÄTISK

668AAA MAJOR
668CZE VĚTŠÍ, DUROVÝ
668DAN DUR, MAJOR, STØRRE
668DUT DUR, MAJEUR
668FRE MAJEUR
668GER DUR(TONART)
668HUN DÚR, NAGY
668ITA MAGGIORE
668POL DOSŁOWNIE
668POR MAIOR
668RUS MASHORNYĬ
668SPA MAYOR
668SWE DUR, MAJOR

669AAA MAKE, TO
669CZE DĚLATI
669DAN GØRE
669DUT MAKEN
669FRE FAIRE
669GER MACHEN
669HUN TENNI
669ITA FARE
669POL UCZYNIĆ
669POR FAZER
669RUS DELAT'
669SPA HACER
669SWE GÖRA

670AAA MALE
670CZE MUŽSKÝ
670DAN MAND(L)IG
670DUT MANNELIJK
670FRE MÂLE
670GER MÄNNLICH
670HUN HÍM
670ITA MASCHIO, MASCHILE
670POL MĘSKI
670POR MACHO, MACHINHO
670RUS MUZHSKOĬ
670SPA MACHO
670SWE MANLIG

671AAA MANDOLIN
671CZE MANDOLÍNA
671DAN MANDOLIN
671DUT MANDOLINE
671FRE MANDOLINE
671GER MANDOLINE
671HUN MANDOLIN
671ITA MANDOLINO, MANDOLA
671POL MANDOLINA
671POR BANDOLIM
671RUS MANDOLINA
671SPA BANDOLIN
671SWE MANDOLIN

672AAA MANNER
672CZE ZPŮSOB
672DAN MAADE
672DUT MANIER
672FRE MANIÈRE, FAÇON
672GER MANIER, SPIELMANIEREN
672HUN MODOR
672ITA MANIERA
672POL MANIERA
672POR MANIERA
672RUS MANERA
672SPA MANERA, DE MODO
672SWE MANER

673AAA MANUAL
673CZE MANUAL
673DAN MANUAL
673DUT MANUAAL
673FRE MANUEL
673GER MANUAL
673HUN MANUÁL
673ITA MANUALE
673POL KLAWIATURA
673POR TECLADO DE ÓRGÃO
673RUS MANUAL
673SPA TECLADO DE ÓRGANO
673SWE MANUAL

674AAA MARCH
674CZE CHOD, POCHOD
674DAN MARSCH
674DUT MARS
674FRE MARCHE
674GER MARSCH
674HUN INDULÓ
674ITA MARCIA
674POL MARSZ, CHOD
674POR MARCHA
674RUS MARSH
674SPA MARCHA
674SWE MARSCH

675AAA MARK, TO
675CZE ZDŮRAŽŇOVATI
675DAN MAERKE, MARKERE
675DUT MERKEN
675FRE MARQUER
675GER MARKIEREN, HERVORHEBEN
675HUN JELELNI
675ITA MARCARE
675POL ZNAKOWAĆ
675POR MARCAR
675RUS STAVIT' ZNAK
675SPA MARCAR
675SWE MÄRKE

676AAA MASS
676CZE MŠE
676DAN MESSE
676DUT MIS
676FRE MESSE
676GER MESSE
676HUN MISE
676ITA MESSA
676POL MSZA
676POR MISSA
676RUS MESSA
676SPA MISA
676SWE MÄSSA

677AAA MASTER
677CZE MISTR
677DAN MESTER
677DUT MEESTER
677FRE MAÎTRE
677GER MEISTER
677HUN MESTER
677ITA MAESTRO
677POL MISTRZ
677POR MESTRE
677RUS MASTER
677SPA MAESTRO, JEFE
677SWE MÄSTER

678AAA MASTERSINGER
678CZE MISTR PĚVEC
678DAN MESTERSANGER
678DUT MEESTERZANGER
678FRE MAÎTRE CHANTEUR
678GER MEISTERSINGER
678HUN MENESTREL, KÖLTŐ
678ITA MAESTRI CANTORE
678POL MEISTERSINGERZY
678POR MESTRE-CANTORE
678RUS MEÏSTERZINGER
678SPA MAESTRO CANTOR
678SWE MÄSTERSÅNGARE

679AAA MAZURKA
679CZE MAZURKA
679DAN MAZURKA
679DUT MAZURKA
679FRE MAZURKA
679GER MAZURKA
679HUN MAZUREK
679ITA MAZURCA, MAZURKA
679POL MAZUR(EK)
679POR MAZURCA
679RUS MAZURKA
679SPA MAZURCA
679SWE MASURKA

680AAA MEANING
680CZE VÝZNAM, SMYSL
680DAN MENING, SANS
680DUT BETEKNIS
680FRE SIGNIFICATION
680GER BEDEUTUNG
680HUN JELENTÉS, JELENTŐSÉG
680ITA SIGNIFICATO, SENSO
680POL ZNACZENIE
680POR SENTIDO
680RUS SMYSL, ZNACHENIE
680SPA SENTIDO
680SWE MENING

681AAA MEASURE
681CZE TAKT, MÍRA
681DAN TAKT
681DUT MAAT, TAKT
681FRE MESURE
681GER TAKT
681HUN TACTUS, ÜTEM
681ITA MISURA
681POL TAKT
681POR MEDIDA
681RUS TAKT
681SPA MEDIDA, COMPAS
681SWE TAKT

682AAA MEASURE, TO
682CZE MĚŘITI
682DAN MALE
682DUT METEN
682FRE MESURER
682GER ABMESSEN
682HUN MÉRNI
682ITA MISURARE
682POL ZMIERZYĆ
682POR MEDIR
682RUS MERIT'
682SPA MEDIR, ACOMPASAR
682SWE MÄTA

683AAA MEDIANT
683CZE MEDIANTA
683DAN TERTS
683DUT MEDIANT
683FRE MÉDIANTE
683GER MEDIANTE, MITTELS
683HUN SEGÉLYÉSVEL
683ITA MEDIANTE
683POL MEDJANTA
683POR MEDIANTE
683RUS MEDIANTA
683SPA TERCERA
683SWE MEDIANT, TERC

684AAA MEDIUM
684CZE PROSTŘEDEK
684DAN MEDIUM
684DUT HALF
684FRE MILIEU, MOYENNE
684GER MITTEL, MITTLERE
684HUN KÖZÉP
684ITA MEZZO
684POL O POŁOWE
684POR MÉDIO
684RUS VLOLOVINU
684SPA MEDIO
684SWE MEDIUM

685AAA MEDLEY
685CZE SLÁTANINA, POPURI
685DAN PORPOURRI
685DUT POTPOURRI
685FRE POT POURRI, PASTISCHE
685GER VERMISCHUMG, GEMENGSEL
685HUN EGYVELEG
685ITA PASTICCIO, MESSANZA
685POL MIESZANINA
685POR POT-POURRI, FANTASIA
685RUS POPURRY
685SPA MEZCOLANZA, CENTÓN
685SWE POTPURRI

686AAA MEEK
686CZE JEMNÝ
686DAN YDMYG, BLID
686DUT ZACHTMOEDIG
686FRE MANSUET
686GER SANFTMÜTIG
686HUN SZELID
686ITA MANSUETO
686POL ŁAGODNY
686POR MANSO
686RUS MIAGKIĬ
686SPA MANSO, SUAVE
686SWE ÖDMJUK

687AAA MELANCHOLY
687CZE ZÁDUMČIVOST
687DAN MELANKOLISK
687DUT MELANCHOLIEK
687FRE MÉLANCOLIE
687GER MELANCHOLISCH
687HUN MÉLABÚS
687ITA MELANCOLICO
687POL MELANCOLIJNY
687POR MELANCÓLICO
687RUS MELANKHOLICHNYĬ
687SPA MELANCÓLICO
687SWE MELANKOLISK

688AAA MELO-
688CZE MELO-
688DAN MELO-
688DUT MELO-
688FRE MELO-
688GER MELO-
688HUN MELO-
688ITA MELO-
688POL MELO-
688POR MELO-
688RUS MELO-
688SPA MELO-
688SWE MELO-

689AAA MELODY
689CZE MELODIE
689DAN MELODI
689DUT MELODIE
689FRE MELODIE
689GER MELODIE
689HUN MELÓDIA, DALLAM
689ITA MELODIA
689POL MELODJA
689POR MELODIA
689RUS MELODIIA
689SPA MELODÍA
689SWE MELODI

690AAA MEMBRANE
690CZE BLÁNA
690DAN MEMBRAN
690DUT MEMBRAN
690FRE MEMBRANE
690GER MEMBRAN(E)
690HUN MEMBRÁN, HÁRTYA
690ITA MEMBRANA
690POL MEMBRANA
690POR MEMBRANA
690RUS MEMBRANA
690SPA MEMBRANA
690SWE MEMBRAN

691AAA MEMOIRS
691CZE VLASTNÍ
691DAN MEMOIRER
691DUT MEMOIRES
691FRE MÉMOIRES
691GER MEMOIREN
691HUN EMLÉKEZE TESSÉGEK
691ITA MEMORIE
691POL PAMIĘTNIKI
691POR MEMÓRIAS
691RUS MEMUARY
691SPA MEMORIAS
691SWE MEMOARER

692AAA MENACE
692CZE HROZBA
692DAN TRUSEL, TRUEN
692DUT BEDREIGING
692FRE MENACE
692GER DROHUNG
692HUN FENYEGETÉS
692ITA MINACCIA
692POL GROŹBA
692POR AMEAÇA
692RUS UGROZA
692SPA AMENAZA
692SWE HOTELSE

693AAA MENSURATION
693CZE MĚRENI
693DAN MÅLING
693DUT MENSURAALGEZANG
693FRE MESURAGE
693GER ABMESSEN
693HUN MÉRÉS
693ITA MISURAZIONE
693POL MIERZENIE
693POR MENSURA
693RUS IZMERENIE
693SPA MENSURA
693SWE MÄTNING

694AAA MERRY
694CZE VESELÝ
694DAN MUNTER
694DUT VROLIJK
694FRE ECLAT, JOYEUX
694GER AUFGERÄUMT
694HUN VIDÁMAN
694ITA DI GALA
694POL WESOŁY
694POR RISONHO
694RUS VESÉLYĬ
694SPA GALANO
694SWE MUNTER

695AAA METAL
695CZE MOSAZ
695DAN METAL
695DUT METAAL
695FRE METAL
695GER METALL
695HUN FÉM
695ITA OTTONE, METALLO
695POL METAL
695POR METAL
695RUS METALL
695SPA METAL
695SWE METALL

696AAA METER
696CZE METRUM
696DAN METER
696DUT METRIEK
696FRE MÈTRE
696GER METER
696HUN METER
696ITA METRO
696POL METR
696POR METRO
696RUS METR
696SPA METRO
696SWE MÄTARE

697AAA METHOD
697CZE METHODA
697DAN METODE
697DUT METHODE
697FRE METHODE
697GER METHODE
697HUN MÓD
697ITA METODO
697POL METODA
697POR MÉTODO
697RUS METOD
697SPA MÉTODO
697SWE METOD

698AAA METRICAL
698CZE METRICKÝ
698DAN METRISK
698DUT METRISCH
698FRE MÉTRIQUE
698GER METRISCHE
698HUN VERSMERETES
698ITA METRICO
698POL METRYCZNY
698POR MÉTRICO
698RUS METROVYĬ
698SPA MÉTRICO
698SWE METRISK

699AAA METRONOME
699CZE METRONOM
699DAN METRONOM
699DUT METRONOOM
699FRE MÉTRONOME
699GER METRONOM, TATKMESSER
699HUN METRONOM
699ITA METRONOMO
699POL METRONOM
699POR METRÓNOMO
699RUS METRONOM
699SPA METRÓNOMO
699SWE METRONOM

700AAA MICRO-
700CZE MIKRO-
700DAN MIKRO-
700DUT MICRO-
700FRE MICRO-
700GER MIKRO-
700HUN MIKRO-
700ITA MICRO-
700POL MIKRO-
700POR MICRO-
700RUS MIKRO-
700SPA MICRO-
700SWE MIKRO-

701AAA MIDDLE
701CZE STŘEDNÍ
701DAN MIDTE
701DUT MIDDLEBAAR
701FRE MOYEN
701GER MITTE(L)
701HUN KÖZÉN
701ITA MEZZO, MEDIO
701POL ŚREDNI
701POR MEIO
701RUS SREDNIĬ
701SPA MEDIO
701SWE MEDEL

702AAA MILITARY
702CZE VOJENSKÝ
702DAN MILITAER
702DUT MILITAIR
702FRE MILITAIRE
702GER MILITÄRISCH
702HUN KATONAI
702ITA MILITARE
702POL MILITARNY
702POR MILITAR
702RUS VOENNYĬ
702SPA MILITAR
702SWE MILITÄR(ISK)

703AAA MINIATURE
703CZE MINIATURA
703DAN MINIATUR
703DUT MINIATUUR
703FRE MINIATURE
703GER MINIATUR
703HUN KISFESTES
703ITA MINIATURA
703POL MINIATURE
703POR MINIATURA
703RUS MINIATIURA
703SPA MINIATURA
703SWE MINIATYR

704AAA MINIM
704CZE PŮLOVÁ NOTA
704DAN HALVTAKTS NODE
704DUT HALVE NOOT
704FRE MINIME, BLANCHE
704GER MINIME, HALBE NOTE
704HUN FÉL HJEGY
704ITA MINIMA
704POL PÓŁNUTA
704POR MINIMA
704RUS POLOVINNA NOTA
704SPA MÍNIMA, BLANCA
704SWE HALVNOT

705AAA MINIMUM
705CZE VELMI MALÝ
705DAN MINIMUM
705DUT MINIMUM
705FRE MINIMUM
705GER MINIMUM
705HUN MINIMÁLIS
705ITA MINIMO
705POL MINIMUM
705POR MÍNIMO
705RUS MINIMUM
705SPA MÍNIMO
705SWE MINIMUM

706AAA MINNESINGER
706CZE TRUBADÚR
706DAN MINNESANGER
706DUT TROVEORS
706FRE TROUVÈRE, TROUBADOUR
706GER MINNESÄNGER
706HUN SZAZAD
706ITA TROVATORE
706POL MINNESÄNGER
706POR TROVADOR
706RUS MINNEZINGER
706SPA TROBADOR
706SWE MINNESÅNGARE

707AAA MINOR
707CZE MOLL, MENŠÍ
707DAN MOL(L), MINDRE
707DUT MOL, MINEUR
707FRE BÉMOL
707GER MOLL
707HUN MINORE, KISEBB
707ITA MINORE
707POL MNIEJSZY
707POR MENOR
707RUS MOL, MINORNYÍ
707SPA MENOR
707SWE MOLL

708AAA MINSTREL
708CZE POTULNÝ ZPĚVÁK
708DAN SKJALD
708DUT MINSTREEL
708FRE MÉNESTREL
708GER MINSTREL, SÄNGER
708HUN MÉNESTREL
708ITA MENESTRELLO
708POL MINSTREL, TRUBADUR
708POR MENESTREL
708RUS MENESTREL
708SPA MINISTRIL, TROBADOR
708SWE SKALD, SÅNGARE

709AAA MINUET
709CZE MENUET
709DAN MENUET(MELODI)
709DUT MENUET
709FRE MENUET
709GER MENUETT
709HUN MENÜETT
709ITA MINUETIO, MENUETTO
709POL MENUET
709POT MINUETE
709RUS MENUET
709SPA MINUETE, MINUÉ
709SWE MENUETT

710AAA MISSAL
710CZE MISÁL
710DAN MISSAL, MESSEBOG
710DUT MISBOEK
710FRE MISSEL
710GER MISSAL, MESSBUCH
710HUN MISEMONDÓ KÖNYV
710ITA MESSAL
710POL MSZAŁ
710POR MISSAL
710RUS TREBNIK
710SPA MISAL
710SWE MÄSSBOK

711AAA MIXTURE
711CZE MIXTURA
711DAN BLANDING
711DUT MENGELING
711FRE MÉLANGE
711GER MIXTURE, MISCHUNG
711HUN KEVERÉK
711ITA MISTURA, RIPIENO
711POL MIKSTURA
711POR MISTURA
711RUS MELANZH, SMES'
711SPA MIXTURA, MEZCLA
711SWE BLANDNING

712AAA MOAN, TO
712CZE STÉNATI
712DAN KLAGE
712DUT KLAGEN
712FRE GÉMIR
712GER KLAGEN, STÖHNEN
712HUN NYÖGNI
712ITA GEMERE
712POL JĘKNAĆ
712POR GEMER, DOLENTAR
712RUS STONAT'
712SPA DOLENTAR
712SWE KLAGA

713AAA MODAL
713CZE TÓNINOVÝ
713DAN MODAL
713DUT MODAAL
713FRE MODAL
713GER MODAL
713HUN MODALE
713ITA MODALE
713POL MODALNY
713POR MODAL
713RUS MODAL'NYĬ
713SPA MODAL
713SWE MODAL

714AAA MODALITY
714CZE POHYBLIVOST
714DAN MODALITET
714DUT MODALITEIT
714FRE MODALITÉ
714GER MODALITÄT
714HUN MODOZAT
714ITA MODALITÀ
714POL MODALNOŚĆ
714POR MODALIDADE
714RUS MODAL'NOST'
714SPA MODALIDAD
714SWE MODALITET

715AAA MODE
715CZE ZPŮSOB, TÓNINA
715DAN TONEART
715DUT TOONSOORT
715FRE MODE
715GER TONART
715HUN MÓD
715ITA MODO
715POL SPOSOB
715POR MODO
715RUS MODA
715SPA MODO
715SWE TONART

716AAA MODEL
716CZE VZOR
716DAN MODEL
716DUT MODEL
716FRE MODÈLE
716GER MODELL
716HUN MINTA
716ITA MODELLO
716POL MODEL
716POR MODELO
716RUS MODEL'
716SPA MODELO
716SWE MODELL

717AAA MODERATE
717CZE UMÍRNĚNÝ
717DAN MAADEHOLDENT
717DUT MATIG
717FRE MODÉRÉ
717GER MÄSSIG
717HUN MÉRSÉKELTEN
717ITA MODERATO
717POL UMIARKOWANIE
717POR MODERADO
717RUS UMERENNYĬ
717SPA MODERADO
717SWE MÅTTLIG

718AAA MODERN
718CZE MODERNÍ
728DAN MODERNE
718DUT MODERN
718FRE MODERNE
718GER MODERN
718HUN KORSZERŰ
718ITA MODERNO
718POL NOWOŻYTNY
718POR MODERNO
718RUS SOVREMENNYĬ
718SPA MODERNO
718SWE MODERN, NYMODIG

719AAA MODIFY, TO
719CZE POZMENITI
719DAN MODIFICERE
719DUT TOONSCHAKEREN
718FRE MODIFIER
719GER MODIFIZIEREN
719HUN MÓDOSÍTANI
719ITA MODIFICARE
719POL MODYFIKOWAĆ
719POR MODIFICAR
719RUS MODIFITSIROVAT'
719SPA MODIFICAR
719SWE MODIFIERA

720AAA MODULATE, TO
720CZE MODULOVATI
720DAN MODULERE
720DUT MODULEREN
720FRE MODULER
720GER MODULIEREN, DURCHFÜHREN
720HUN HANGLEJTENI
720ITA MODULARE
720POL MODULOWAĆ
720POR MODULAR
720RUS MODULIROVAT'
720SPA MODULAR
720SWE MODULERA

721AAA MODULATION
721CZE MODULACE
721DAN MODULATION
721DUT MODULATIE
721FRE MODULATION
721GER DURCHFÜHRUNG
721HUN MODULÁCIÓ
721ITA MODULAZIONE
721POL MODULACJA
721POR MODULAÇÃO
721RUS MODULIATSIIA
721SPA MODULACIÓN
721SWE MODULATION

722AAA MOMENT
722CZE OKAMŽIK
722DAN ØJEBLIK
722DUT MOMENT
722FRE MOMENT
722GER AUGENBLICK
722HUN PILLANAT
722ITA MOMENTO
722POL MOMENT
722POR MOMENTO
722RUS MOMENT
722SPA MOMENTO
722SWE ÖGONBLICK

723AAA MONO-
723CZE MONO-
723DAN MONO-
723DUT EEN-
723FRE MONO-
723GER EIN-, MONO-
723HUN MONO-
723ITA MONO-
723POL MONO-
723POR MONO-
723RUS MONO-
723SPA MONO-
723SWE MONO-

724AAA MONODY
724CZE MONODIE
724DAN MONODI
724DUT MONODIE
724FRE MONODIE
724GER MONODIE
724HUN MONÓDIA
724ITA MONODIA
724POL MONODJA
724POR MONODIA
724RUS MONODIIA
724SPA MONODIA
724SWE MONODI

725AAA MONOTONE
725CZE JEDNOTVÁRNÝ
725DAN MONOTONI, ESTONIG
725DUT ÉÉNTOON
725FRE MONOTONE
725GER EINTÖNIGKEIT
725HUN EGYHANGÚ
725ITA MONOTONO
725POL MONOTONIA
725POR MONOTÓNICO
725RUS MONOTONNAIA
725SPA MONÓTONO
725SWE ENTONIG

726AAA MOOD
726CZE NÁLADA, HUMOR
726DAN LUNE, HUMØR
726DUT LUIM, HUMEUR
726FRE MODE, HUMEUR
726GER LAUNE
726HUN HUMOR
726ITA UMORE
726POL TONACJA, HUMOR
726POR HUMOR
726RUS LAD
726SPA HUMOR
726SWE LYNNE, HUMÖR

727AAA MORBID
727CZE MĚKKÝ, PODDAJNÝ
727DAN MORBID
727DUT ZIEKELIJK
727FRE MORBIDE
727GER KRANKHAFT
727HUN LÁGYAN
727ITA MORBIDO
727POL CHOROBLIWY
727POR MÓRBIDO
727RUS BOLEZNENNYĬ
727SPA MÓRBIDO
727SWE SJULKIG

728AAA MORDENT
728CZE MORDENT, HÁRAZ
728DAN MORDENT
728DUT BEISSER
728FRE MORDENT, MORDANT
728GER PRALLTRILLER, BEISSER
728HUN MORDENT, HARAPÓ
728ITA MORDENTE
728POL MORDENT
728POR MORDENTE
728RUS MORDENT
728SPA MORDENTE
728SWE MORDENT

729AAA MORE   733AAA MOUTH
729CZE VÍCE   733CZE ÚSTA
729DAN MERE   733DAN MUND
729DUT MEER   733DUT MOND
729FRE PLUS   733FRE BOUCHE
729GER MEHR   733GER MUND
729HUN TÖBB   733HUN SZAJ
729ITA PIÙ   733ITA BOCCA
729POL WIĘCEJ   733POL USTA
729POR MAIS   733POR BOCA
729RUS BOL' SHE   733RUS USTA
729SPA MÁS   733SPA BOCA
729SWE MER(A)   733SWE MUN

730AAA MOTET   734AAA MOUTHPIECE
730CZE MOTET   734CZE NASAZENÍ
730DAN MOTET   734DAN MUNDSTYKKE
730DUT MOTET   734DUT MONDSTUK, AANZET
730FRE MOTET   724FRE EMBOUCHURE, BOCAL
730GER MOTETTE   734GER MUNDSTÜCK, ANSATZ
730HUN MOTETTA   734HUN SZOPÓKA
730ITA MOTTET(T)O   734ITA IMBOCCATURA
730POL MOTET   734POL USTNIK
730POR MOTETE, MOTETO   734POR BOCAL
730RUS MOTET   734RUS MUNDSHTUK
730SPA MOTETE   734SPA BOQUILLA, EMBOCADURA
730SWE MOTETT   734SWE MUNSTYCKE

731AAA MOTIVE   735AAA MOVEMENT, MOTION
731CZE MOTIV   735CZE POHYB
731DAN MOTIV   735DAN BEVAEGELSE
731DUT MOTIEF   735DUT BEWEGING
731FRE MOTIF   735FRE MOUVEMENT
731GER MOTIV   735GER BEWEGUNG
731HUN MOTÍVUM   735HUN MOZGÁS
731ITA MOTIVO   735ITA MOTO
731POL MOTYW   735POL RUCH, ŻYWOŚĆ, CZĘŚĆ
731POR MOTIVO   735POR MOVIMENTO
731RUS MOTIV   735RUS RAZMER
731SPA MOTIVO   735SPA MOVIMENTO, MOVIDO
731SWE MOTIV   735SWE BEVAEGELSE, SATS

732AAA MOURNFUL   736AAA MUCH
732CZE STÉNANÍ   736CZE MNOHO, VELMI
732DAN BEKLAGELIG   736DAN MEGEN
732DUT TREURIG, DROEVIG   736DUT ZEER
732FRE TRISTE, LAMENTABLE   736FRE TRÈS, BEAUCOUP
732GER KLÄGLICH, KUMMERVOLL   736GER VIEL
732HUN GYÁSZOS   736HUN NAGYON
732ITA MESTO, LAMENTOSO   736ITA MOLTO
732POL ŻAŁOBNY   736POL BARDZO
732POR PESAROSO   736POR MUITO
732RUS ZHALKII   736RUS OCHEN', VES'MA, MNOGO
732SPA LAMENTABLE   736SPA MUCHO, MUY
732SWE SORGLIG   736SWE MYCKET

737AAA MULTI-
737CZE MNOHO-
737DAN MANGE-
737DUT VEEL-
737FRE MULTI-
737GER VIEL-
737HUN SOK-
737ITA MULTI-, MOLTI-
737POL WIELO-
737POR MULTI-
737RUS MNOGO-, MUL TI-
737SPA MULTI-
737SWE MÅNG

738AAA MULTIPLY, TO
738CZE MNOŽITI
738DAN MULTIPLICERE
738DUT VERMENIGVULDIGEN
738FRE MULTIPLIER
738GER MULTIPLIZIEREN
738HUN SZOROZNI
738ITA MOLTIPLICARE
738POL MNOŻYĆ
738POR MULTIPLICAR
738RUS MNOZHIT
738SPA MULTIPLICAR
738SWE MULTIPLICERA

739AAA MURMUR, TO
739CZE BRUCETI, BUBLATI
739DAN MUMLE, SUMME
739DUT MOMPELEN
739FRE MURMURER
739GER MURMELN
739HUN MORMOLNI
739ITA MORMORARE
739POL MRUCZEĆ
739POR MURMURAR
739RUS ZHURCHAT'
739SPA MURMURAR
739SWE MUMLA

740AAA MUSIC
740CZE HUDBA
740DAN MUSIK
740DUT MUZIEK
740FRE MUSIQUE
740GER MUSIK
740HUN ZENE
740ITA MUSICA
740POL MUZYKA
740POR MÚSICA
740RUA MUZYKA
740SPA MÚSICA
740SWE MUSIK

741AAA MUTATION
741CZE MUTACE
741DAN MUTATION
741DUT MUTATIE
741FRE MUTATION
741GER MUTIERUNG, MUTATION
741HUN VÁLTOZÁS
741ITA MUTAZIONE
741POL MUTACJA
741POR MUTAÇÃO
741RUS MUTATSIIA
741SPA MUTACIÓN
741SWE MUTATION

742AAA MUTE
742CZE DUSÍTKO
742DAN SORDIN
742DUT DEMPER
742FRE SOURDINE
742GER DÄMPFER, SORDINE
742HUN HANGTOMPÍTÓ
742ITA SORDINA
742POL TŁUMIK
742POR SURDINA
742RUS SURDINKA
742SPA SORDINA
742SWE SORDIN, DÄMMARE

743AAA MUTE, TO
743CZE DUSITI, TLUMITI
743DAN DAEMPE
743DUT DE SOURDINE OPZETTEN
743FRE METTRE UNE SOURDINE
743GER DÄMPFEN
743HUN ELFOJTANI
743ITA METTERE LA SORDINA
743POL TŁUMIC
743POR TOCAR NA SURDINA
743RUS NADEVAT' SURDINKY
743SPA APAGAR
743SWE DÄMMA

744AAA MYSTERY
744CZE MYSTÉRIUM
744DAN MYSTERIUM
744DUT MYSTERIE
744FRE MYSTÈRE
744GER GEHEIMNIS, MYSTERIEN
744HUN TITOK, REJTELEM
744ITA MISTERO
744POL TAJEMNICA
744POR MISTÉRIO
744RUS MISTERIIA
744SPA MISTERIO
744SWE MYSTERIUM

745AAA MYSTIC
745CZE BÁJNÝ, MYSTICKÝ
745DAN MYSTISK
745DUT MYSTIEK
745FRE MYSTIQUE
745GER MYSTISK
745HUN MISZTIKUS, TITOKZATOS
745ITA MISTICO
745POL MISTYCZNY
745POR MÍSTICO
745RUS MISTIK
745SPA MÍSTICO
745SWE MYSTISK

746AAA NARRATE, TO
746CZE VYPRAVOVATI
746DAN FORTAELLE
746DUT VERHALEN
746FRE NARRER
746GER ERZÄHLEN
746HUN ELBESZÉLNI
746ITA NARRARE
746POL OPOWIADAĆ
746POR NARRAR
746RUS RASSKAZYVAT'
746SPA NARRAR
746SWE FORTAELLE

747AAA NARROW
747CZE ÚZKÝ
747DAN STRAM
747DUT ENG
747FRE ÉTROIT
747GER ENG
747HUN SÜRGŐS, GYORSITOTT
747ITA STRETTO
747POL ŚCISŁY
747POR ESTREITO
747RUS UZKII
747SPA ESTRECHO
747SWE TRÅNG

748AAA NATURAL
748CZE ODRÁŽKA
748DAN OPLØSNINGSTEGN
748DUT HERSTELLINGSTEKEN
748FRE BÉCARRE
748GER AUFLÖSUNGSZEICHEN
748HUN TERMÉSZETES
748ITA BEQUADRO
748POL NATURALNE
748POR BÉQUADRO
748RUS BEKAR
748SPA BECUADRO
748SWE ÅTERSTÄLLINGSTECKEN

749AAA NEAPOLITAN
749CZE NEAPOLITÁNSKY
749DAN NEAPOLITANSK
749DUT NAPOLITAAN
749FRE NAPOLITAIN
749GER NEOPOLITANISCH
749HUN NÁPOLYI
749ITA NAPOLETANO
749POL NEAPOLITAŃSKI
749POR NAPOLITANO
749RUS NEAPOLITANSKII
749SPA NAPOLITANO
749SWE NEAPOLITAN

750AAA NEAR
750CZE BLÍZKO
750DAN NAER
750DUT NA
750FRE PRÈS DE, A COTÉ
750GER NÄHE, GEGEN
750HUN KÖZEL
750ITA VICINO
750POL BLISKO
750POR PERTO, VIZINHO
750RUS BLIZKII
750SPA CERCA, AL LADO
750SWE NÄRA

751AAA NEAT
751CZE ZŘETELNĚ
751DAN NETTO, REN
751DUT ZUIVER
751FRE NET, PROPRIETÉ
751GER NETT, KLAR
751HUN VILÁGOSAN
751ITA NETTO
751POL CZYSTO
751POR CLARO
751RUS CHISTO
751SPA NETO, LIMPIO
751SWE REN

752AAA NECK
752CZE KRK
752DAN GRIBEBRAET, HALS
752DUT HALS
752FRE MANCHE
752GER STIEL, HALS
752HUN NYAK
752ITA MANICO
752POL KARK
752POR GARGALO
752RUS GRIF
752SPA MANUBRIO, MASTIL
752SWE HALS

753AAA NEGLIGENT   757AAA NEUME(S)
753CAE NEDBALÝ   757CZE NEUMA
753DAN FORSØMMELIG, SKØDESLØS   757DAN NEUMA
753DUT ACHTELOOS   757DUT NEUME
753FRE NÉGLIGENT   757FRE NEUME
753GER NACHLÄSSIG   757GER NEUME(N)
753HUN HANYAG(UL)   757HUN NEUMÁK
753ITA NEGLIGENTE   757ITA NEUMA, NEUMI
753POL NIEDBAŁY   757POL NEUMY
753POR NEGLIGENTE   757POR NEUMA
753RUS NEBREZHNYĬ   757RUS NEVMA
753SPA NEGLIGENTE   757SPA NEUMA(S)
753SWE FORSUMLIG   757SWE NEUMER

754AAA NEIGHBOR   758AAA NEUTRAL
754CZE SOUSED, BLÍZKO   758CZE NEUTRÁLNÍ
754DAN NABO   758DAN NEUTRAL
754DUT NABUUR   758DUT NEUTRAAL
754FRE VOISIN   758FRE NEUTRE
754GER NÄHE   758GER NEUTRAL
754HUN KÖZELÉG   758HUN SEMLEGES
754ITA VICINO   758ITA NEUTRALE
754POL BLIŹNI, SĄSIAD   758POL NEUTRALNY
754POR VIZINHO   758POR NEUTRO
754RUS SOSED   758RUS NEĬTRAL'NYĬ
754SPA VECINO   758SPA NEUTRAL
754SWE NABO   758SWE NEUTRAL

755AAA NEO-   759AAA NEW
755CZE NEO-, NOVO-   759CZE NOVÝ
755DAN NEO-   759DAN NY
755DUT NEO-   759DUT NIEUW
755FRE NÉO-   759FRE NOUVEAU, NEUF, NEUVE
755GER NEO-, NEU-   759GER NEU
755HUN NYEL-   759HUN ÚJ
755ITA NEO-   759ITA NUOVO
755POL NEO-   759POL NOWY
755POR NEO-   759POR NOVO
755RUS NIO-   759RUS NOVYĬ
755SPA NEO-   759SPA NUEVO
755SWE NY-   759SWE NY

756AAA NERVOUS   760AAA NEXT
756CZE NERVOVÝ   760CZE NEJBLIŽŠÍ
756DAN NERVØS   760DAN NAESTE
756DUT NERVEUS   760DUT NAAST
756FRE NERVEUX   760FRE PROCHAIN
756GER NERVÖS, NERVIG   760GER NÄCHST
756HUN IDEGES   760HUN LEGKÖZELEBB
756ITA NERVOSO   760ITA PROSSIMO
756POL NERWOWY   760POL NAJBLIŻSZY
756POR NERVOSO   760POR SEGUINTE
756RUS NERVNYĬ   760RUS BLIZKIĬ
756SPA NERVIOSO, AGITADO   760SPA PROXIMO
756SWE NERVERNA   760SWE NÄST

761AAA NIMBLE
761CZE JAŘNY, SVIŽNÝ
761DAN SLANK, LET
761DUT OPGEWEKT
761FRE SVELTE, AGILE
761GER FREI, BEHENDE
761HUN KÖNNYÜ
761ITA SVELTO, AGILE
761POL ZWINNIE, LEKKO
761POR ÁGIL
761RUS LËGKIĬ
761SPA ESBELTO, ÁGIL
761SWE LÄTT

762AAA NINE
762CZE DEVĚT
762DAN NI
762DUT NEGEN
762FRE NEUF
762GER NEUN
762HUN KILENC
762ITA NOVE
762POL DZIEWIĘĆ
762POR NOVE
762RUS DEVIAT'
762SPA NUEVE
762SWE NIO

763AAA NO
763CZE NE
763DAN IKKE
763DUT NEEN, NIET
763FRE NON
763GER NICHT, KEIN
763HUN NEM
763ITA NO
763POL NIE
763POR NÃO
763RUS NET
763SPA NO
763SWE INGEN

764AAA NOBLE
764CZE UŠLECHTILÝ
764DAN AEDEL
764DUT EDEL
764FRE NOBLE
764GER EDEL
764HUN NEMESEN
764ITA NOBILE
764POL SZLACHETNIE
764POR NOBRE
764RUS BLAGORODNYĬ
764SPA NOBLE, ESPLENDIDA
764SWE ADLIG

765AAA NOCTURNE
765CZE NOKTURNO
765DAN NOCTURNE
765DUT NOCTURNE
765FRE NOCTURNE
765GER NOKTURNE, NACHTSTÜCK
765HUN NOKTYURN
765ITA NOTTURNO
765POL NOKTURN
765POR NOCTURNO
765RUS NOKTIURN
765SPA NOCTURNO
765SWE NOCTURNE

766AAA NODE
766CZE UZEL
766DAN KNUDE
766DUT KNOBBEL
766FRE NOEUD
766GER KNOTE
766HUN BÜTYÖK
766ITA NODO
766POL GUZ
766POR NODO
766RUS UZEL
766SPA NUDO
766SWE KNUT

767AAA NOISE
767CZE LOMOZ
767DAN LARM, STØJ
767DUT GELUID
767FRE BRUIT, RUMEUR
767GER LÄRM, RUMOR
767HUN LÁRMA
767ITA RUMORE
767POL HAŁAS
767POR RUIDO
767RUS SHUM
767SPA RUMOR, RUIDO
767SWE LJUD

768AAA NONET
768CZE NONET
768DAN NONET
768DUT NONET
768FRE NONETTE
768GER NONETT
768HUN NONETT
768ITA NONETTO
768POL NONETTO
768POR NONETO
768RUS NONET
768SPA NONETTO
768SWE NONETT

769AAA NOSE
769CZE NOS
769DAN NAESE
769DUT NEUS
769FRE NEZ
769GER NASE
769HUN ORR
769ITA NASO
769POL NOS
769POR NARIZ
769RUS NOS
769SPA NARIZ
769SWE NÄSA, NOS

770AAA NOTATION
770CZE NOTACE
770DAN NODESKRIFT
770DUT NOTERING
770FRE NOTATION
770GER NOTENSCHRIFT
770HUN HANGJEGYÍRÁS
770ITA NOTAZIONE
770POL NOTACJA
770POR NOTAÇÃO
770RUS NOTATSIIA
770SPA NOTACIÓN
770SWE BETECKNINGS SYSTEM

771AAA NOTE
771CZE NOTA
771DAN NOTE
771DUT NOOT
771FRE NOTE
771GER NOTE
771HUN HANGJEGY
771ITA NOTA
771POL NUTA
771POR NOTA
771RUS NOTA
771SPA NOTA
771SWE NOT

772AAA NUANCE
772CZE ODSTÍN, NUANCE
772DAN TONETRIN, NUANCE
772DUT NUANCE
772FRE NUANCE
772GER NUANCE, SCHATTIERUNG
772HUN ARNYALAT
772ITA CHIAROSCURO
772POL ODCIEŃ, NIUANS
772POR NUANCA
772RUS NIUANS
772SPA MATIZ
772SWE NYANS

773AAA NUMBER, TO
773CZE ČÍSLOVATI
773DAN NUMMERERE
773DUT NUMMEREN
773FRE NUMÉROTER
773GER ZÄHLEN
773HUN SZÁMLÁLNI
773ITA NUMERARE, CIFRARE
773POL LICZYĆ
773POR NUMERAR
773RUS NUMEROVAT'
773SPA NUMERAR
773SWE NUMRERA

774AAA NUPTIAL, WEDDING
774CZE SVATEBNÍ
774DAN BRYLLUP
774DUT NUZIALE
774FRE NUPTIAL
774GER HOCHZEITLICH
774HUN LAKODALMAS
774ITA NUZIALE
774POL ŚLUBNY
774POR NUPCIAL
774RUS SVADEBNYI
774SPA NUPCIAL
774SWE BRÖLLOPS

775AAA OBLIQUE
775CZE PŘÍČNY, STRANNÝ
775DAN INDIREKTE
775DUT SCHEEF
775FRE OBLIQUE
775GER SCHIEF
775HUN REZSÚTOS
775ITA OB(B)LIQUO
775POL UKOŚNY
775POR OBLÍQUO
775RUS KOSOI
775SPA OBLICUO
775SWE OBLIK

776AAA OBOE
776CZE HOBOJ
776DAN OBO
776DUT HOBO
776FRE HAUTBOIS
776GER OBOE, HOBOE
776HUN OBOA
776ITA OBOE
776POL OBÓJ
776POR OBOÉ
776RUS GOBOI
776SPA OBOE
776SWE OBOE

777AAA OBSERVE, TO   781AAA OCTET
777CZE ZACHOVÁVATI   781CZE OKTET
777DAN OBSERVERE   781DAN .OKTET
777DUT WAARNEMEN   781DUT OCTET
777FRE OBSERVER   781FRE OCTUOR, OCTETTE
777GER BEOBACHTEN   781GER OKTETT
777HUN MEGFIGYELNI   781HUN OKTETT
777ITA OSSERVARE   781ITA OTTETTO
777POL OBSERWOWAĆ   781POL OKTET
777POR OBSERVAR   781POR OCTETO
777RUS NABLIUDAT   781RUS OKTET
777SPA OBSERVAR   781SPA OCTETO
777SWE OBSERVERA   781SWE OKTET

778AAA OBSTINATE   782AAA ODE
778CZE TVRDOŠÍJNÝ, ZATVRZELÝ   732CZE ÓDA
778DAN HAARDNAKKET   782DAN ODE
778DUT OBSTINAAT, HARDNEKKIG   782DUT ODE
778FRE OBSTINÉ(E)   782FRE ODE
778GER HARTNÄCKIG   782GER ODE
778HUN SZÓSZERINT   782HUN ÓDA
778ITA OSTINATO   782ITA ODE
778POL UPORCZYWIE   782POL ODA
788POR OBSTINADO   782POR ODE
778RUS UPRIAMYI, UPORNYI   782RUS ODA
778SPA OBSTINADO   782SPA ODA
778SWE HÅRDNACKAD   782SWE ODE

779AAA OCARINA   783AAA OF
779CZE OKARINA   783CZE OD
779DAN OKARINA   783DAN AF
779DUT OCARINA   783DUT VAN
779FRE OCARINA   783FRE DE
779GER OKARINA   783GER VON, AUS
779HUN OKARINA   783HUN -É, -NAK, -NEK
779ITA OCARINA   783ITA DI
779POL OKARYNA   783POL OD
779POR OCARINA   783POR DE
779RUS OKARINA   783RUS OB
779SPA OCARINA   783SPA DE
779SWE OKARINA   783SWE AV

780AAA OCTAVE   784AAA OFF
780CZE OKTÁVA   784CZE OD
780DAN OKTAV   784DAN BORT, AF STED
780DUT OCTAFF   784DUT AF
780FRE OCTAVE   784FRE DE
780GER OKTAVE   784GER AB
780HUN OKTÁV   784HUN EL
780ITA OTTAVA   784ITA DA
780POL OKTAWA   784POL OD
780POR OITAVA   784POR DA, DE
780RUS OKTAVA   784RUS IZ, OT
780SPA OCTAVA   784SPA DE
780SWE OKTAV   784SWE BORT

785AAA OFFERTORY
785CZE OFFERTORIUM
785DAN OFFERTORIUM
785DUT OFFERTORIUM
785FRE OFFERTOIRE
785GER OFFERTORIUM, OPFER
785HUN OFFERTORIUM
785ITA OFFERTORIO
785POL OFERTORIUM
785POR OFERTÓRIO
785RUS DAROPRINOSHENIE
785SPA OFERTORIO
785SWE OFFERTORIUM

786AAA OLD
786CZE STARÝ
786DAN GAMMAL
786DUT OUD
786FRE VIEUX, ANCIEN
786GER ALT, ANTIK
786HUN ÖREG
786ITA VECCHIO, ANTICO
786POL STARY
786POR VELHO
786RUS STARYĬ
786SPA VIEJO
786SWE GAMMAL

787AAA ON
787CZE NA
787DAN PÅ
787DUT OP, AAN
787FRE SUR
787GER AUF, UBER
787HUN -ON, -EN, -ON
787ITA SU
787POL NA
787POR SÔBRE
787RUS NA
787SPA SOBRE
787SWE PÅ

788AAA ONE
788CZE JEDEN
788DAN EN
788DUT EEN
788FRE UN
788GER EIN(E)
788HUN EGY
788ITA UNO,
788POL JEDEN
788POR UM(A)
788RUS ODIN
788SPA UN
788SWE EN

789AAA ONLY
789CZE JEDINÝ, SÓLO, JENOM
789DAN ENESTE
789DUT ENIG
789FRE SEUL, SOLO
789GER ALLEIN, SOLO
789HUN EGYETLEN
789ITA SOLO
789POL JEDYNY
789POR ÚNICO
789RUS EDINSTVENNYĬ
789SPA ÚNICO, SOLO
789SWE ENSAM

790AAA OPEN
790CZE OTEVŘENÝ
790DAN ÅBEN
790DUT OPEN
790FRE OUVERT
790GER OFFEN
790HUN NYILT
790ITA APERTO
790POL OTWARTY
790POR ABERTO
790RUS OTKRYTYĬ
790SPA ABIERTO, VACÍO
790SWE ÖPPEN

791AAA OPERA
791CZE OPERA
791DAN OPERA
791DUT OPERA
791FRE OPÉRA
791GER OPER
791HUN ZENE-SZÍNMŰ
791ITA OPERA
791POL OPERA
791POR ÓPERA
791RUS OPERA
791SPA ÓPERA
791SWE OPERA

792AAA OPERA GLASS(ES)
792CZE DIVADELNÍ KUKÁTKO
792DAN TEATERKIKKERT
792DUT TONEELKIJKER
792FRE JUMELLE(S) DE TÉÂTRE
792GER OPERNGLAS
792HUN KUKUCS-ÜVEG
792ITA BINOCOLO DA TEATRO
792POL LORNETKA TEATRALNA
792POR BINÓCULO DE TEATRO
792RUS TEATRAL'NYĬ BINOKL'
792SPA GEMELOS DE TEATRO
792SWE TEATERKIKARE

793AAA OPHICLEIDE
793CZE OFIKLEJDA
793DAN OPHIKLEID
793DUT OPHICLEÏDE
793FRE OPHICLÉÏDE
793GER OPHIKLEÏD(E)
793HUN OFIKLEID
793ITA OF(F)ICLEIDE, OFLEIDE
793POL OFIKLEJDA
793POR OFICLIDE
793RUS OFIKLEID
793SPA OFIGLE, OFICLEIDO
793SWE OFIKLEID

794AAA OR
794CZE NEBO
794DAN ELLER
794DUT OF
794FRE OU
794GER ODER
794HUN VAGY
794ITA O
794POL ALBO, LUB
794POR OU
794RUS LIBO
794SPA O
794SWE ELLER

795AAA ORATORIO
795CZE ORATORIUM
795DAN ORATORIUM
795DUT ORATORIUM
795FRE ORATORIO
795GER ORATORIUM
795HUN IMATEREM
795ITA ORATORIO, AZIONE SACRA
795POL ORATORJUM
795POR ORATÓRIO
795RUS ORATORIIA
795SPA ORATORIO
795SWE ORATORIUM

796AAA ORCHESTRA
796CZE ORCHESTR
796DAN ORKESTER
796DUT ORKEST
796FRE ORCHESTRE
796GER ORCHESTER
796HUN ZENEKAR
796ITA ORCHESTRA
796POL ORKIESTRA
796POR ORQUESTRA
796RUS ORKESTR
796SPA ORQUESTA
796SWE ORKESTER

797AAA ORCHESTRATE, TO
797CZE ORKESTROVATI
797DAN INSTRUMENTERE
797DUT ORCHESTREREN
797FRE ORCHESTRER
797GER ORCHESTRIEREN
797HUN ORKESZTRÁLNI
797ITA ORCHESTRARE
797POL UKŁADAĆ NA ORKIESTRE
797POR ORQUESTRAR
797RUS ORKESTROVAT'
797SPA ORQUESTAR
797SWE ORKESTRERA

798AAA ORCHESTRATION
798CZE ORCHESTRACE
798DAN INSTRUMENTERING
798DUT ORKESTRATIE
798FRE ORCHESTRATION
798GER ORCHESTRIERUNG
798HUN ÉKESÍTÉS
798ITA ORCHESTRAZIONE
798POL ORKIESTRACJA
798POR ORQUESTRAÇÃO
798RUS ORKESTROVKA
798SPA INSTRUMENTACIÓN
798SWE INSTRUMENTERING

799AAA ORDER
799CZE ŘÁD, POŘÁDEK
799DAN ORDEN
799DUT ORDE
799FRE ORDRE
799GER ORDNUNG
799HUN REND
799ITA ORDINE
799POL PORZADEK
799POR ORDEM
799RUS PORIADOK
799SPA ORDEN
799SWE ORDEN

800AAA ORDINARY
800CZE OBYČEJNÝ
800DAN ORDINAERT
800DUT GEWOON
800FRE ORDINAIRE
800GER GEWÖHNLICH
800HUN SZOKOTT
800ITA ORDINARIO
800POL ZWYCZAJNY
800POR ORDINÁRIO
800RUS OBYCHNYI
800SPA ORDINARIO
800SWE ORDINARIE

801AAA ORGAN
801CZE VARHANY, ORGÁN
801DAN ORGEL
801DUT ORGEL
801FRE ORGUE
801GER ORGEL
801HUN ORGONA
801ITA ORGANO
801POL ORGANY
801POR ÓRGÃO
801RUS ORGAN
801SPA ÓRGANO
801SWE ORGAN, ORGEL

802AAA ORIGINAL
802CZE PŮRODNÍ
802DAN ORIGINAL
802DUT ORIGINEEL
802FRE ORIGINAL
802GER ORIGINAL, ORIGINELL
802HUN EREDETI
802ITA ORIGINALE
802POL ORYGINAŁ
802POR ORIGINAL
802RUS ORIGINAL'NYĬ
802SPA ORIGINAL
802SWE URSPRINGLIG

803AAA ORNAMENT(S)
803CZE OKRASA
803DAN ORNAMENTIK
803DUT VERSIERUNG
803FRE ORNEMENTS, AGRÉMENTS
803GER VERZIERUNG
803HUN ORNAMENSEK
803ITA ORNAMENTO, ABBELLIMENTI
803POL UPIĘKSŻENIE
803POR ORNAMENTO
803RUS ORNAMENT
803SPA ORNAMENTO, ADORNO
803SWE ORNAMENTERING

804AAA ORNAMENTATION
804CZE VÝZDOBENÍ
804DAN ORNAMENTERING
804DUT ORNAMENTIEK
804FRE ORNEMENTATION
804GER ORNAMENTIERUNG
804HUN EKESÍTÉS
804ITA ABBELLITURA, FIORITURA
804POL ORNAMENTACJE
804POR ORNAMENTAÇÃO
804RUS ORNAMENTATSIĬA
804SPA ORNAMENTACIÓN
804SWE DEKORERING

805AAA OSCILLATE, TO
805CZE OSCILOVATI
805DAN OSCILLERE
805DUT SLINGEREN
805FRE OSCILLER
805GER OSZILLIEREN, SCHWINGEN
805HUN REZGENI
805ITA OSCILLARE
805POL OSCYLOWAĆ
805POR OSCILAR
805RUS KACHAT'SĬA
805SPA OSCILAR
805SWE OSCILLERA

806AAA OTHER
806CAE JINÝ, JINÁ
806DAN ANDEN
806DUT ANDER
806FRE AUTRE
806GER ANDERE(R)
806HUN MÁS
806ITA ALTRA
806POL INNY
806POR OUTRO
806RUS INOĬ
806SPA OTRO, OTRA
806SWE ANNAN

807AAA OUT OF TUNE
807CZE ROZLADĚNÝ
807DAN FORSTEMT, FALSK
807DUT VALS
807FRE DÉSACCORDÉ, FAUX
807GER VERSTIMMT
807HUN LEHANGOLT
807ITA FUORI ACCORDO
807POL ROZSTROJONY
807POR DISAFINADO
807RUS RASSTROENNYĬ
807SPA DESAFINADO
807SWE FÖRSTÄMD

808AAA OVER
808CZE NAD
808DAN OVENFOR
808DUT OVER
808FRE SUR, (AU) DESSUS
808GER ÜBER, OBER, OBEN
808HUN FÖLÖTT
808ITA SOPRA
808POL NAD, WYŻEJ
808POR SOBRA
808RUS NAD
808SPA SOBRE
808SWE ÖVER

809AAA OVERTONE(S)
809CZE SPODNI TONY
809DAN NATURTONER, RESONSTONE
809DUT BOVENTOON
809FRE HARMONIQUE(S)
809GER OBERTÖNE
809HUN FELHANGOK
809ITA ARMONICI
809POL TON HARMONICZNY
809POR ALÍQUOTA
809RUS OBERTON
809SPA ARMONICOS
809SWE ALIKVOLTONE, ÓVERTON

810AAA OVERTURE
810CZE PŘEDEHRA, OTVOR
810DAN OUVERTURE
810DUT OUVERTURE
810FRE OUVERTURE
810GER ERÖFFNUNGSSTÜCK
810HUN NYITÁNY
810ITA OVERTURA, SINFONIA
810POL UWERTURA
810POR ABERTURA
810RUS UVERTIURA
810SPA ABERTURA, OBERTURA
810SWE UVERTYR

811AAA PACE
811CZE KROK
811DAN PACE
811DUT PAS
811FRE PAS
811GER SCHRITT
811HUN LÉPÉS
811ITA PASSO
811POL KROK
811POR PASSO
811RUS SHAG
811SPA PASO
811SWE STEG

812AAA PAIN
812CZE BOLEST
812DAN SMERTE
812DUT PIJN
812FRE DOULEUR
812GER PEIN, SCHMERZ
812HUN FÁJDALOM
812ITA DOLORE
812POL BÓL
812POR DOR
812RUS BOL'
812SPA DOLOR
812SWE SMÄRTA

813AAA PAIR
813CZE PÁR
813DAN PAR
813DUT PAAR
813FRE PAIRE
813GER PAAR
813HUN PÁR
813ITA PAIO
813POL PARA
813POR PAR
813RUS PARA
813SPA PAR(EJA)
813SWE PAR

814AAA PANTOMIME
814CZE NÉMOHRA
814DAN PANTOMIME
814DUT PANTOMIME
814FRE PANTOMIME
814GER PANTOMIME
814HUN NÉMAJÁTÉK
814ITA PANTOMIMA
814POL PANTOMIMA
814POR PANTOMIMA
814RUS PANTOMIMA
814SPA PANTOMIMA
814SWE PANTOMIM

815AAA PAPER
815CZE NOTOVÝ PAPÍR
815DAN PAPIR
815DUT PAPIER
815FRE PAPIER DE MUSIQUE
815GER PAPIER
815HUN PAPIROS
815ITA CARTA DA MUSICA
815POL PAPIER
815POR PAPEL
815RUS BUMAGA
815SPA PAPEL
815SWE PAPPER

816AAA PARALLEL
816CZE PARALELNÍ, ROVNOBEŽNÝ
816DAN PARALLEL
816DUT PARALLEL
816FRE PARALLÈLE
816GER PARALLEL
816HUN PARALLEL, PÁRHUZAMOS
816ITA PARALLELO
816POL PARALELE
816POR PARALELO
816RUS PARALLEL'NYĬ
816S7A PARALELO
816SWE PARALLELL

817AAA PARAPHRASE   821AAA PASSION
817CZE PARAFRÁZE   821CZE PAŠIJE
817DAN PARAFRASE   821DAN LIDENSKAB
817DUT PARAPHRASE   821DUT HARTSTOCHT
817FRE PARAPHRASE   821FRE PASSION
817GER PARAPHRASE   821GER LEIDENSCHAFT
817HUN PARAFRÁSIS   821HUN PASSIÓ
817ITA PARAFRASI   821ITA PASSIONE
817POL PARAFRAŻA   821POL PASJA
817POR PARÁFRASE   821POR PAIXÃO
817RUS PARAFRAZA   821RUS STRAST'
817SPA PARÁFRASIS   821SPA PASION
817SWE OMSKRIVNING   821SWE LIDELSE

818AAA PARODY   822AAA PASSIONATE
818CZE PARODIE   822CZE VÁŠNIVÝ
818DAN PARODI   822DAN LIDENSKABELIG
818DUT PARODIE   822DUT HARTSTOCHTELIJK
818FRE PARODIE   822FRE PASSIONNÉ
818GER PARODIE   822GER LEIDENSCHAFTLICH
818HUN PARODIA   822HUN SZENVEDÉLLYEL
818ITA PARODIA   822ITA APPASSIONATO
818POL PARODIA   822POL NAMIĘTNY
818POR PARODIA   822POR APAIXONADO
818RUS PARODIIA   822RUS STRASTNYÏ
818SPA PARODIA   822SPA APASIONADO
818SWE PARODI(ERA)   822SWE LIDELSEFULL

819AAA PART   823AAA PASTORAL
819CZE HLAS, ČÁST, DÍL   823CZE PASTORÁLNÍ
819DAN PART   823DAN PASTORAL
819DUT STEM, PARTIJ   823DUT PASTORALE, LANDELIJK
819FRE PART(IE)   823FRE PASTORALE
819GER STIMME, TEIL   823GER PASTORALE
819HUN SZÓLAM   823HUN PASZTORI
819ITA PARTE   823ITA PASTORALE
819POL PARTJA   823POL SIELANKOWO
819POR PARTE   823POR PASTORAL
819RUS PARTIIA   823RUS PASTORAL'NYÏ
819SPA PARTE, VOZ   823SPA PASTORAL
819SWE STÄMMA   823SWE PASTORAL

820AAA PASSAGE   824AAA PATHETIC
820CZE PASÁŽ, BĚH   824CZE PATETICKÝ
820DAN PASSAGE   824DAN PATETISK
820DUT PASSAGE   824DUT PATHETISCH
820FRE PASSAGE   824FRE PATHÉTIQUE
820GER DURCHGANG, PASSAGE   824GER PATHETISCH
820HUN PASSZÁZS   824HUN PÁTOSSZAL
820ITA PASSAGGIO   824ITA PATETICO
820POL PASAŻ   824POL WZRUSZAJACO
820POR PASSAGEM   824POR PATÉTICO
820RUS PASSAZH   824RUS PATETICHESKIÏ
820SPA PASAJE   824SPA PATÉTICO
820SWE PASSAGE   824SWE RÖRANDE

825AAA PATHOS
825CZE PATHOS
825DAN HØJHED
825DUT PATHOS
825FRE PATHOS
825GER PATHOS
825HUN HÉV
825ITA PAT(H)OS
825POL PATOS
825POR PATHOS
825RUS PAFOS
825SPA PATETISMO
825SWE PATOS

826AAA PATRIOTIC
826CZE VLASTENECKÝ
826DAN PATRIOTISK
826DUT PATRIOTISCH
826FRE PATRIOTIQUE
826GE9 PATRIOTISCH
826HUN HAZAFIÚI
826ITA PATRIOTTICO
826POL PATRIOTA
826POR PATRIÓTICO
826RUS PATRIOTICHESKIĬ
826SPA PATRIÓTICO
826SWE PATRIOTISK

827AAA PAVAN
827CZE PAVANA
827DAN PAVANE, PADOVANA
827DUT PAUWENDANS
827FRE PAVANE
827GER PADUANA, PFAUENTANZ
827HUN PADOVANA, PADUANA
827ITA PAVANA
827POL PAVANA
827POR PAVANA
827RUS PAVANA
827SPA PAVANA
827SWE PAVANE

828AAA PEACEFUL
828CZE KLIDNĚ, UKLIDNĚNĚ
828DAN FREDELIGT
828DUT VREDIG, VREEDZAAM
828FRE PACIFIQUE
828GER RUHIG, GELASSEN
828HUN NYUGODT
828ITA PACIFICO, PACATO
828POL SPOKOJNIE
828POR PACIFICO
828RUS SPOKOĬNYĬ
828SPA PACIFICO
828SWE FREDLIG, FRIDFULL

829AAA PEDAGOGY
829CZE PEDAGOGIKA
829DAN PAEDAGOGIK
829DUT PEDAGOGIE
829FRE PÉDAGOGIE
829GER PEDAGOGIE
829HUN NEVELÉSTAN
829ITA PEDAGOGIA
829POL PEDAGOGIA
829POR PEDAGOGIA
829RUS PEDAGOGIKA
829SPA PEDAGOGÍA
829SWE PEDAGOGIK

830AAA PEDAL
830CZE PEDÁL, PRODLEVA
830DAN PEDAL
830DUT PEDAAL
830FRE PÉDALE
830GER PEDAL
830HUN PEDAL
830ITA PEDALE
830POL PEDAŁ
830POR PEDAL
830RUS PEDAL'
830SPA PEDAL
830SWE PEDAL

831AAA PEDAL, TO
831CZE PEDALOVATI
831DAN BRUGE PEDALEN
831DUT HET PEDAAL
831FRE PÉDALER
831GER PEDALIEREN
831HUN PEDÁLOZNI
831ITA PEDALEGGIARE
831POL PEDAŁOWAĆ
831POR PEDALAR
831RUS RABOTAT' PEDALIAMI
831SPA PEDALEAR
831SWE ATT TRAMPA PEDALEN

832AAA PEG
832CZE KOLÍČEK
832DAN TOMMESKRUE
832DUT SCHROEF
832FRE CHEVILLE
832GER WIRBEL
832HUN KULCS
832ITA BISCHERO
832POL KOŁEK
832POR CRAVELHA
832RUS KOLOK
832SPA CLAVIJA
832SWE SKRUF

833AAA PENDULUM
833CZE KYVADLO
833DAN PENDUL
833DUT SLINGER
833FRE PENDULE
833GER PENDEL
833HUN INGA
833ITA PENDOLO
833POL WAHADŁO
833POR PÊNDULO
833RUS MAIATNIK
833SPA PÉNDULO
833SWE PENDEL

834AAA PENETRATE, TO
834CZE PRONIKNOUTI
834DAN GENNEMTRAENGE
834DUT DOORDRINGEN
834FRE PÉNÉTRER
834GER DURCHDRINGEN
834HUN ÁTHATNI
834ITA PENETRARE
834POL PRZENIKAĆ COŚ
834POR PENETRAR
834RUS PRONIKAT'
834SPA PENETRAR
834SWE GENOMTRÄNGA

835AAA PENSIVE
835CZE ZADUMANÝ
835DAN TANKEFULD
835DUT PEINZEND
835FRE PENSIF
835GER GEDANKENVOLL, GEDANKE
835HUN ELMÉLYEDVE
835ITA PENSIEROSO, PENSOSO
835POL ZADUMANY, ZAMYŚLONY
835POR PENSATIVO
835RUS ZADUMCHIVYÏ
835SPA PENSATIVO
835SWE TANKFULL

836AAA PENTA-
836CZE PĚTI-
836DAN PENTA-
836DUT VIJF-
836FRE PENTA-
836GER FUNF-
836HUN OT-
836ITA PENTA-
836POL PENTA-
836POR PENTA-
836RUS PIATI-
836SPA PENTA-
836SWE PENTA-

837AAA PERCUSSION
837CZE ÚDER
837DAN PERKUSSION
837DUT SLAGWERK
837FRE PERCUSSION
837GER SCHLAGWERK
837HUN CSAPÁS
837ITA PERCUSSIONE, PERCOSSA
837POL PERKUSYJNY
837POR PERCUSSÃO
837RUS UDAR
837SPA PERCUSIÓN
837SWE PERKUSSION

838AAA PERFECT
838CZE DOKONALÝ
838DAN FULDENDT
838DUT VOLMAAKT, VOLKOMEN
838FRE PARFAIT, JUSTE
838GER VOLLKOMMEN, RICHTIG
838HUN TISZTA
838ITA PERFETTO, GIUSTO
838POL DOSKONAŁY
838POR PERFEITO
838RUS PERFEKT
838SPA PERFECTO
838SWE FULLÄNDAD

839AAA PERFORM, TO
839CZE PROVÉSTI
839DAN FOREDRAGE
839DUT VOLVOEREN
839FRE EXÉCUTER, JOUER
839GER AUSFÜHREN, VORTRAGEN
839HUN ELŐADNI
839ITA ESEGUIRE
839POL SPEŁNIAĆ
839POR EJECUTAR
839RUS ISPOLNIT'
839SPA EJECUTAR
839SWE FÖREDRAGA

840AAA PERIOD
840CZE PERIODA
840DAN PERIODE
840DUT PERIODE
840FRE PÉRIODE
840GER PERIODE
840HUN PERIÓDUS
840ITA PERIODO
840POL PERIOD
840POR PERÍODO
840RUS PERIOD
840SPA PERÍODO
840SWE PERIOD

841AAA PERPETUAL
841CZE VĚČNÝ, USTAVIČNÝ
841DAN PERPETUUM
841DUT EEUWIGDUREND
841FRE PERPÉTUEL, A L'INFINI
841GER UNENDLICH
841HUN FOLYTONES, VÉGTELEN
841ITA PERPETUO
841POL WIECZNY
841POR PERPÉTUO
841RUS VECHNYĬ
841SPA PERPETUO
841SWE PERPETUUM

842AAA PHASE
842CZE FÁZE
842DAN FASE
842DUT FASE
842FRE PHASE
842GER PHASE
842HUN FÁZIS
842ITA FASE
842POL FAZA
842POR FASE
842RUS FAZA
842SPA FASE
842SWE FAS

843AAA PHILHARMONIC
843CZE FILHARMONICKÝ
843DAN FILHARMONISK
843DUT FILHARMONISCH
843FRE PHILHARMONIQUE
843GER PHILHARMONISCH
843HUN FILHARMONIKUS
843ITA FILARMONICO
843POL FILHARMONICZNY
843POR FILARMÔNICO
843RUS FILARMONICHESKIĬ
843SPA FILARMÓNICO
843SWE FILHARMONISK

844AAA PHONOGRAPH
844CZE FONOGRAF
844DAN FONOGRAF
844DUT PHONOGRAAF
844FRE PHONOGRAPHE
844GER PHONOGRAPH
844HUN GRAMOFON
844ITA FONOGRAFO
844POL FONOGRAF
844POR FONÓGRAFO
844RUS FONOGRAF
844SPA FONÓGRAFO
844SWE FONOGRAF

845AAA PHRASE
845CZE FRÁZE
845DAN FRASE
845DUT FRASE, FRASERING
845FRE PHRASE
845GER PHRASE, PHRASIERUNG
845HUN FRAZÍROZÁS, FRÁZIS
845ITA FRASE
845POL FRAZA
845POR FRASE
845RUS FRAZA
845SPA FRASE
845SWE FRAS, UTTRYCK

846AAA PHRASE, TO
846CZE FRÁZOVATI
846DAN FRASERE
846DUT FRASEREN
846FRE PHRASER
846GER PHRASIEREN
846HUN FRAZÍROZ
846ITA FRASEGGIARE
846POL FRAZOWAĆ
846POR FRASEAR
846RUS FRAZIROVAT'
846SPA FRASEAR
846SWE UTTRYCKA

847AAA PHRYGIAN
847CZE FRYGICKÝ
847DAN FRYGISK
847DUT PHRYGISCH
847FRE PHRYGIEN
847GER PHRIGISCH
847HUN FRÍG
847ITA FRIGIO
847POL FRYGIJSKI
847POR FRÍGIO
847RUS FRIGIĬSKIĬ
847SPA FRIGIO
847SWE FRYGISK

848AAA PIANO(FORTE)
848CZE PIANO
848DAN PIANO(FORTE)
848DUT PIANO(FORTE)
848FRE PIANO
848GER CLAVIER
848HUN ZONGORA
848ITA PIANOFORTE
848POL FORTEPIAN
848POR PIANO, FORTE-PIANO
848RUS FORTEPIANO
848SPA PIANO(FORTE)
848SWE PIANO

849AAA PICCOLO
849CZE PIKOLA
849DAN PIKKOLOFLØJTE
849DUT PICCOLOFLUIT
849FRE PICCOLO, OCTAVIN
849GER PICKELFLÖTE, OKTAFLÖTE
849HUN KISFUVOLA
849ITA PICCOLO, OTTAVINO
849POL PIKULINA
849POR PICOLLO
849RUS PIKKOLO
849SPA FLAUTIN
849SWE PICKOLAFLÖJT

850AAA PIECE
850CZE KUS, SKLADBA
850DAN STYKKE
850DUT STUK
850FRE PIÈCE, MORCEAU
850GER STÜCK
850HUN DARAB, ZENEDARAB
850ITA PEZZO
850POL SZTUKA
850POR PEÇA
850RUS P'ESA
850SPA PIEZA, TROZO
850SWE STYCKE

851AAA PIPE
851CZE PŘÍČNÁ PÍŠŤALA, PIŠTEC
851DAN PIPPE
851DUT PIJP, SCHALMEI
851FRE PIPEAU, CHALUMEAU
851GER PFEIFE, QUERPFEIFE
851HUN PIPA, SÍP
851ITA PIFFERO, SCIALUMO
851POL FUJARKA
851POR PIPA
851RUS SVIREL'
851SPA PIPA, PIPI(RI)TAÑA
851SWE PIPA

852AAA PISTON
852CZE PÍST
852DAN PISTON, VENTIL
852DUT VENTIEL
852FRE PISTON
852GER PISTON, VENTIL
852HUN PISZTON, NYOMO-VENTIL
852ITA PISTONE, VALVOLA
852POL PISTON
852POR PISTÃO
852RUS PISTON, KLAPAN
852SPA PISTÓN, LLAVE
852SWE VENTIL

853AAA PITCH
853CZE TÓN
853DAN TONHØJDE
853DUT TOONHOOGTE, DIAPASON
853FRE TON, DIAPASON
853GER TONHÖHE, KLANG
853HUN HANGMAGASSÁG
853ITA TONO
853POL WYSOKOŚĆ TONU
853POR TOM
853RUS DIAPAZON, VYSOTA TONA
853SPA DIAPASÓN
853SWE TONHÖJD

854AAA PITCH, TO
854CZE NALADITI
854DAN GIVE TONEN, ISTEMME
854DUT AANGEVEN TOON
854FRE ACCORDER
854GER ZUSAMMEN STIMMEN
854HUN HANGZAT
854ITA ACCORDARE
854POL NATROIĆ
854POR ENTOAR
854RUS DAVAT' OSNOVOI TON
854SPA AFINAR, ENTONAR
854SWE ANGE TONEN FÖR, STÄMMA

855AAA PITY
855CZE SOUCIT
855DAN MEDLIDENHED
855DUT MEDELIJDEN
855FRE PITIÉ
855GER MITLEID
855HUN KEGYELETTEL
855ITA PIETÀ
855POL LITOŚĆ
855POR PENA
855RUS ZHALOST'
855SPA PIEDAD
855SWE MEDLIDANDE

856AAA PLACID
856CZE KLIDNÝ
856DAN ROLIG(T)
956DUT RUSTIG
856FRE PLACIDE
856GER RUHIG
856HUN NYUGODTAN
856ITA PLACIDO
856POL SPOKOJNIE
856POR PLÁCIDO
856RUS SPOKOINYI
856SPA PLÁCIDO
856SWE MILD, STILLA

857AAA PLAGAL
857CZE PLAGÁLNÍ
857DAN PLAGALISK
857DUT PLAGAAL
857FRE PLAGAL
857GER PLAGAL
857HUN PLAGÁLIS
857ITA PLAGALE
857POL PLAGALNA
857POR PLAGAL
857RUS PLAGAL'NYĬ
857SPA PLAGAL
857SWE PLAGALA

858AAA PLAINSONG, PLAINCHANT
858CZE STARÝ CHORÁL
858DAN GREGORIANISK KIRKESANG
858DUT GREGORIAANS
858FRE PLAIN CHANT
858GER FESTER GESANG
858HUN MEGENEK
858ITA CANTO FERMO
858POL CANTUS PLANUS
858POR CANTO FIRME
858RUS TSERKOVNOE PENIE
858SPA CANTO FERMO
858SWE UNISON SÅNG

859AAA PLAINTIVE
859CZE LKAVÝ, ŽALOSTNÝ
859DAN KLAGENDE
859DUT KLAGEND
859FRE PLAINTIF
859GER KLÄGLICH
859HUN PANASZOSAN
859ITA LAMENTEVOLE
859POL ŁZAWO, ŻALOSNIE
859POR LASTIMOSO
859RUS ZHALOBNYĬ
859SPA DOLOROSO, LASTIMOSO
859SWE KLAGENDE

860AAA PLAY, TO
860CZE HRÁTI
860DAN SPILLE
860DUT SPELEN
860FRE JOUER, SONNER
860GER SPIELEN
860HUN ÉRINTENI, JÁTSZANI
860ITA TOCCARE, SONARE
860POL GRAĆ
860POR TOCAR
860RUS IGRAT'
860SPA TOCAR, SONAR, TAÑER
860SWE SPELA

861AAA PLEASING
861CZE LÍBIVÉ
861DAN BEHAG
861DUT BEHAAGELIJK
861FRE AGRÉABLE, AMIABILE
861GER GEFÄLLIG, LAUNIG
861HUN SZÍVES
861ITA GRADEVOLE, COMPIACEVOLE
861POL PRZYJEMNY
861POR AGRADÁVEL
861RUS PRIĬATNYĬ
861SPA AGRADABLE
861SWE BEHAGLIG

862AAA PLEASURE
862CZE RADOST
862DAN VITTEEGHED
862DUT PLEZIER
862FRE PLAISIR
862GER BELIEBEN, FREUDE
862HUN TETSZÉS
862ITA PIACERE
862POL DOWOLNIE, PRZYJEMNOŚĆ
862POR PRAZER
862RUS RADOST'
862SPA PLACER
862SWE VALBEHAG

863AAA PLECTRUM, QUILL
863CZE TRSÁTKO
863DAN PLEKTRUM
863DUT PLEKTRUM
863FRE PLECTRE
863GER PLECKTRUM, FEDERKIEL
863HUN PLEKTRUM
863ITA PLETTRO
863POL PLEKTRON
863POR PLECTRO
863RUS PLEKTR
863SPA PLECTRO
863SWE PLEKTRUM

864AAA PLUCK, TO
864CZE DRNKOT
864DAN TRYKKE, KLIMPRE
864DUT PLUKKEN, TOKKELEN
864FRE PINCER
864GER KNEIF(F)EN
864HUN MEGSCÍPNI
864ITA PIZZICARE
864POL SZARPAĆ
864POR PICAR
864RUS PUNKTIROVAT'
864SPA PISAR, PUNTEAR
864SWE KNÄPPA

865AAA POEM
865CZE BÁSEŇ
865DAN DIGT
865DUT GEDICHT
865FRE POÈME
865GER GEDICHT, DICHTUNG
865HUN KÖLTEMÉNY
865ITA POEMA
865POL POEMAT
865POR POEMA
865RUS POEMA
865SPA POEMA
865SWE POEM

866AAA POINT
866CZE BOD
866DAN PUNKT
866DUT PUNT
866FRE POINT(E)
866GER POINTE, PUNKT, SPITZE
866HUN PONT
866ITA PUNTO, PUNTA
866POL PUNKT
866POR PONTA
866RUS PUNKT
866SPA PUNTA
866SWE PUNKT

867AAA POLKA
867CZE POLKA
867DAN POLKA
867DUT POLKA
867FRE POLKA
867GER POLKA
867HUN POLKA
867ITA POLCA
867POL POLKA
867POR POLCA
867RUS POL'KA
867SPA POLCA
867SWE POLKA

868AAA POLONAISE
868CZE POLONÉZA
868DAN POLONAISE
868DUT POLONAISE
868FRE POLONAISE
868GER POLONAISE, POLONÄSE
868HUN POLONÉZ
868ITA POLACCA, POLONESE
868POL POLONEZ
868POR POLACO
868RUS POLONEZ
868SPA POLONESA
868SWE POLONÄS

869AAA POLY-
869CZE POLY-
869DAN POLY-
869DUT POLY-, POLI-
869FRE POLY-
869GER VIEL-
869HUN SOK-
869ITA POLI-
869POL POLI-
869POR POLI-
869RUS POLI-
869SPA POLI-
869SWE FLER-

870AAA POLYPHONY
870CZE POLYFONIE
870DAN POLYPHONI
870DUT MEERSTEMMIGHEID
870FRE POLIPHONIE
870GER POLYPHONIE
870HUN TÖBBSZÓLAMÚSÁG
870ITA POLOFONIA
870POL POLIFONJA
870POR POLÍFONO
870RUS POLIFONIIA
870SPA POLIFONÍA
870SWE POLYFONI

871AAA POMP
871CZE OKÁZALOST, POMPA
871DAN POMP
871DUT PRACHT
871FRE POMPE
871GER POMP
871HUN POMPA
871ITA POMPA
871POL POMPA
871POR POMPA
871RUS POMPA
871SPA POMPA
871SWE POMP

872AAA PONDEROUS
872CZE ROZVÁŽNÝ, ZÁVAŽNÝ
872DAN TUNG
872DUT GEWICHTIG
872FRE PONDÉRÉ
872GER GEWICHTVOLL, WUCHTIG
872HUN SÚLYOSAN
872ITA PONDEROSO
872POL CIĘŻKI
872POR PONDEROSO
872RUS TIAZHĚLYĬ
872SPA PONDEROSO
872SWE TUNG

873AAA POSITION
873CZE POLOHA
873DAN POSITION
873DUT POSITIE
873FRE POSITION
873GER LAGE, STELLUNG
873HUN FEKVÉS
873ITA POSIZIONE
873POL POŁOŻENIE, USTAWIENIE
873POR POSIÇÃO
873RUS POLOZHENIE
873SPA POSICIÓN
873SWE STÄLLNING

874AAA POSSIBLE
874CZE MOŽNÝ
874DAN MULIG
874DUT MOGELIJK
874FRE POSSIBLE
874GER MÖGLICH
874HUN LEHETŐLEG
874ITA POSSIBILE
874POL MOŻLIWY
874POR POSSÍVEL
874RUS VOZMOZHNYÏ
874SPA POSIBLE
874SWE MÖJLIG

875AAA POSTHUMOUS
875CZE POSMRTNÝ
875DAN POSTHUM
875DUT POSTUUM
875FRE POSTHUME
875GER NACHGEBOREN
875HUN POSTHUMUS
875ITA POSTUMO
875POL POSMIERTNY
875POR POSTUMO
875RUS POSMERTNYÏ
875SPA PÓSTUMO
875SWE EFTERLAMNED

876AAA POSTLUDE
876CZE DOHRA
876DAN POSTLUDIUM, EFTERSPIL
876DUT POSTLUDIUM, NASPEL
876FRE POSTLUDE
876GER NACHSPIEL
876HUN UTÓJÁTÉK
876ITA POS(T)LUDIO
876POL POSTLUDIUM
876POR POSLÚDIO
876RUS FINAL
876SPA POSTLUDIO
876SWE POSLUDIUM

877AAA PRACTICE, TO
877CZE CVIČITI SE
877DAN PRAKTISERE
877DUT PRACTISEREN
877FRE PRATIQUER, ÉTUDIER
877GER PRAKTIZIEREN
877HUN PRAKTIZÁLNI
877ITA ESERCITARSI
877POL PRAKTYKOWAĆ
877POR PRATICAR
877RUS PRAKTIKOVAT'
877SPA PRACTICAR, ESTUDIER
877SWE PRAKTISERA

878AAA PRAY, TO
878CZE PROSITI, MODLITI SE
878DAN BEDE
878DUT BIDDEN
878FRE PRIER
878GER BETEN, ERBITTEN
878HUN IMÁDKOZNI
878ITA PREGARE
878POL MODLIĆ SIĘ
878POR ROGAR, SUPLICAR
878RUS PROSIT'
878SPA REZAR
878SWE BEDJA

879AAA PRAYER
879CZE PROSBA, MODLITBA
879DAN BEDENDE
879DUT GEBED
879FRE PRIÈRE
879GER GEDET
879HUN IMA
879ITA PREGHIERA, PREGHERIA
879POL MODLITWA
879POR ROGO, SÚPLICA
879RUS PROS BA
879SPA REZO
879SWE BÖN

880AAA PREAMBLE
880CZE ÚVOD
880DAN FORTALE, INDLEDNING
880DUT INLEIDING
880FRE PRÉAMBULE
880GER EINLEITUNG
880HUN BEVEZETÉS
880ITA PREAMBOLO
880POL WSTĘP
880POR PREÂMBULO
880RUS PREAMBULA
880SPA PREÁMBULO
880SWE FÖRETAL, INLEDNING

881AAA PRECENTOR
881CZE VEDOUCÍ
881DAN FORSANGER, KANTOR
881DUT VOORSANGER, KOORLEIDER
881FRE CONDUCTEUR D'UN CHOEUR
881GER CHORALMEISTER, KANTOR
881HUN KÁNTOR
881ITA PRECENTORE, CABISCHOL
881POL PRZEWODNIK CHÓRU
881POR PRECENTOR, PRECHANTRE
881RUS REGENT KHORA
881SPA CAPISCOL
881SWE KANTOR

882AAA PRECISE
882CZE URČITY, PŘESNÝ
882DAN PRAECIS
882DUT NAUWKEURIG
882FRE PRÉCIS
882GER PRÄCIS
882HUN PONTOS
882ITA PRECISO
882POL DOKŁADNY
882POR PRECISO
882RUS TOCHNYĬ
882SPA PRECISO
882SWE PRECIS

883AAA PREFACE
883CZE PŘEDMLUVA
883DAN PRAEFATION, FORTALE
883DUT VOORREDE
883FRE PRÉFACE
883GER VORREDE
883HUN ELŐSZÓ
883ITA PREFAZIONE, PREFAZIO
883POL PREFACJA
883POR PREFÁCIO
883RUS PREDISLOVIE
883SPA PREFACIO, PRÓLOGO·
883SWE FÖRETAL

884AAA PRELUDE
884CZE PRELUDIUM
884DAN PRAELUDIUM, FORSPIL
884DUT VOORSPEL
884FRE PRÉLUDE
884GER VORSPIEL, PRÄLUDIUM
884HUN ELŐJÁTÉK
884ITA PRELUDIO
884POL PRELUDJUM
884POR PRELÚDIO
884RUS PRELIUDIIA
884SPA PRELUDIO
884SWE PRELUDIUM, FÖRSPEL

885AAA PREPARATION
885CZE PŘÍPRAVA
885DAN FORBERENDELSE
885DUT VOORBEREIDING
885FRE PRÉPARATION
885GER VORBEREITUNG
885HUN PREPARÁCIÓ
885ITA PREPARAZIONE
885POL PRZYGOTOWANIE
885POR PREPARAÇÃO
885RUS PRIGOTOVLENIE
885SPA PREPARACIÓN
885SWE FÖRBEREDELSE

886AAA PREPARE, TO
886CZE PŘEPRAVITI
886DAN FORBEREDE
886DUT INSTUDEREN
886FRE PRÉPARER
886GER VORBEREITEN
886HUN ELKÉSZÍTENI
886ITA PREPARARE
886POL PRZYGOTOWYWAĆ
886POR PREPARAR
886RUS PRIGOTOVLIAT'
886SPA PREPARAR
886SWE FÖRBEREDA

887AAA PRESSING ON
887CZE NALÉHAVÝ
887DAN PRESSERENDE
887DUT DRINGEND
887FRE PRESSANT
887GER DRINGEND, TREIBEND
887HUN GYORSULVA
887ITA PRESSANTE
887POL PRZYŚPIESZAJĄĆ
887POR URGENTE
887RUS SPESHNYĬ
887SPA URGENTE
887SWE PRESSNING

888AAA PRETTY
888CZE ROZTOMILÝ
888DAN NYDELIGT
888DUT AARDIG
888FRE BEAU, BELLE
888GER HÜBSCH, ANMUTIG
888HUN CSINOS
888ITA LEGGIADRO
888POL NIECO
888POR BONITO, LINDO
888RUS PRELESTNYĬ
888SPA BONITO, LINDO
888SWE TÄCK

889AAA PRIME	893AAA PROGRESSION
889CZE PRIMA	893CZE PROGRESE
889DAN PRIM	893DAN FREMSKIDEN
889DUT PRIME	893DUT PROGRESSIE
889FRE PREMIÈRE	893FRE PROGRESSION
889GER PRIM	893GER FORTSCHREITUNG
889HUN PRÍM	893HUN FOKOZATOSAN
889ITA PRIMO, PRIMA	893ITA PROGRESSIONE
889POL PIERWSZA	893POL PROGRESYJA
889POR PRIMA	893POR PROGRESSÃO
889RUS PRIM	893RUS PROGRESSIIA
889SPA PRIMO, PRIMERA	893SPA PROGRESION
889SWE PRIMA	893SWE FORTGÅNG
890AAA PRINCIPAL	894AAA PROLOGUE
890CZE HLAVNÍ	894CZE PROLOG, PŘEDZPĚV
890DAN PRINCIPAL	894DAN PROLOG
890DUT PRINCIPAAL	894DUT PROLOOG
890FRE PRINCIPAL	894FRE PROLOGUE
890GER PRINZIPAL	894GER PROLOG
890HUN PRINCIPÁL	894HUN ELŐBESZÉD
890ITA PRINCIPALE	894ITA PROLOGO
890POL PRYNCYPAL	894POL PROLOG
890POR PRINCIPAL	894POR PRÓLOGO
890RUS PRINTSIPAL	894RUS PROLOG
890SPA PRINCIPAL	894SPA PRÓLOGO
890SWE HUVUDSAKLIG	894SWE PROLOG
891AAA PRINCIPLE	895AAA PROLONGATION
891CZE PRINCIP, POČÁTEK	895CZE PRODLOUŽENÍ, PRŮTAH
891DAN PRINCIP	895DAN FORLAENGELSE
891DUT PRINCIPE	895DUT PROLONGATIE
891FRE PRINCIPE	895FRE PROLONGATION
891GER PRINZIP	895GER VERLÄNGERUNG
891HUN ELV, ALAP	895HUN MEGHOSSZABBÍTÁS
891ITA PRINCIPIO	895ITA PROLUNGAZIONE
891POL ZASADA	895POL PROLONGOWANIE
891POR PRINCÍPIO	895POR PROLONGAÇÃO
891RUS PRINTSIP	895RUS PROLONGATSIIA
891SPA PRINCIPIO	895SPA PROLONGACIÓN
891SWE PRINCIP	895SWE FÖRLÄNGNING
892AAA PROGRAM	896AAA PROLONG, TO
892CZE PROGRAM	896CZE PRODLOUŽITI
892DAN PROGRAM	896DAN FORLAENGE
892DUT PROGRAM(MA)	896DUT VERLENGEN
892FRE PROGRAMME	896FRE PROLONGER
892GER PROGRAMM	896GER VERLÄNGERN
892HUN PROGRAMM(ZENE)	896HUN MEGHOSSZABBÍTNI
892ITA PROGRAMMA	896ITA PROLUNGARE
892POL PROGRAMOWA	896POL PRZEDŁUŻAĆ
892POR PROGRAMA	896POR PROLONGAR
892RUS PROGRAMMA(IA)	896RUS PRODLEVAT'
892SPA PROGRAMA	896SPA PROLONGAR
892SWE PROGRAM	896SWE PROLONGERA, FÖRLÄNGA

897AAA PROMPTER
897CZE NÁPOVĚDA
897DAN SUFFLØR
897DUT SOUFFLEUR
897FRE SOUFFLEUR
897GER SOUFFLEUR
897HUN SUGÓ
897ITA SUGGERITORE
897POL SUFLER
897POR PONTO
897RUS SUFLĚR
897SPA APUNTADOR
897SWE SUFFLÖR

898AAA PRONOUNCE, TO
898CZE VYSLOVOVATI
898DAN UDTALE
898DUT UITSPREKEN
898FRE PRONONCER
898GER AUSSPRECHEN
898HUN KIEJTENI
898ITA PRONUNZIARE
898POL WYMAWIAĆ
898POR PRONUNCIAR
898RUS PROIZNOSIT'
898SPA PRONUNCIAR
898SWE UTTALA

899AAA PSALM
899CZE ŽALM
899DAN SALME
899DUT PSALM
899FRE PSAUME
899GER PSALM
899HUN ZSOLTÁR
899ITA SALMO
899POL PSALMO
899POR SALMO
899RUS PSALOM
899SPA SALMO
899SWE PSALM

900AAA PSALMODY
900CZE ZPÍVÁNÍ ŽALMŮ
900DAN SALMESANG
900DUT PSALMGEZANG
900FRE PSALMODIE
900GER PSALMGESANG
900HUN SZOLTÁRÉNEK
900ITA SALMODIA
900POL PSALMODIA
900POR PSALMODIA
900RUS PENIE PSALMOV
900SPA SALMODIA
900SWE PSALMODI, PSALMSÅNG

901AAA PSALTER
901CZE ŽALTÁŘ
901DAN SALMER
901DUT PSALMBOEK
901FRE PSAUTIER
901GER PSALTER
901HUN ZSOLTÁRKÖNYV
901ITA SALTER(I)O, SALTIERA
901POL PSAŁTERZ
901POR SALTERIO
901RUS PSALTYR'
901SPA SALTERIO
901SWE PSALTARE

902AAA PULSE
902CZE PULS
902DAN PULS
902DUT POLS
902FRE POULS
902GER PULS(SCHLAG)
902HUN PULZUS
902ITA POLSO
902POL PULS
902POR PULSO
902RUS PUL'S
902SPA PULSE
902SWE PULS

903AAA PULSATION
903CZE TEPOT
903DAN PULSERING
903DUT KLOPPING
903FRE PULSATION
903GER PULSATION
903HUN ÉRVERÉS
903ITA PULSAZIONE
903POL PULSACJA
903POR PULSAÇÃO
903RUS PUL'SATSIIA
903SPA PULSACION
903SWE PULSSLAG

904AAA PUPIL, STUDENT
904CZE ŽÁK
904DAN PUPIL
904DUT PUPIL
904FRE DISCIPLE, ÉLÈVE
904GER SCHULER
904HUN GYÁMGYERMEK
904ITA ALLIEVO
904POL PUPIL, UCZEŃ
904POR DISCIPULO, ALUNO
904RUS UCHENIK
904SPA DISCÍPULO, ALUMNO
904SWE PUPILL

905AAA PURE   909AAA QUARTET
905CZE ČISTÝ   909CZE KVARTETO
905DAN REN   909DAN KVARTET
905DUT REIN   909DUT QUARTETT
905FRE PUR(E), CLAIRE   909FRE QUATUOR
905GER REIN   909GER QUARTETT
905HUN TISZTA   909HUN KVARTETT
905ITA PURO   909ITA QUARTETTO
905POL CZYSTY   909POL KWARTET
905POR PURO   909POR QUARTETO
905RUS CHISTYĬ   909RUS KVARTET
905SPA PURO   909SPA CUARTETO
905SWE PUR, REN   909SWE KVARTETT

906AAA QUADRILLE   910AAA QUASI
906CZE ČTVERYLKA   910CZE SKORO
906DAN KVADRILLE   910DAN LIGESOM, KVASI-
906DUT QUADRILLE   910DUT BIJNA, QUASI
906FRE QUADRILLE, CONTREDANSE   910FRE QUASI, PRESQUE
906GER QUADRILLE   910GER BEINAHE, GLEICHSAM
906HUN QUADRILLE   910HUN CSAKNEM, MINTEGY
906ITA QUADRIGLIA   910ITA QUASI
906POL KADRYL   910POL PRAWIE
906P6R QUADRILHA   910POR QUASI
906RUS KADRIL'   910RUS POCHTI
906SPA CUADRILLA, CONTRADANZA   910SPA CUASI-
906SWE KADRILJ   910SWE KVASI-

907AAA QUALITY, TONE   911AAA QUICK
907CZE BARVA TÓNU   911CZE RYCHLE
907DAN KLÀNGFARVE   911DAN LEVENDE
907DUT KLANKKLEUR   911DUT LEVENDIG
907FRE TIMBRE, COULEUR DU SON   911FRE VITE, RAPIDE
907GER KLANGFARBE   911GER LEBENDIG, LEBHAFT
907HUN HANGSZÍN   911HUN SÜRGE, GYORSAN
907ITA COLORE DEL SUONO   911ITA CELERE, VELOCE, VIVO
907POL TEMBR   911POL SZYBKO
907POR TIMBRE   911POR VIVO, PRESTO
907RUS TEMBR   911RUS ZHIVOĬ
907SPA COLOR DEL SONIDO   911SPA PRESTO, RÁPIDO
907SWE KLANGFÄRG   911SWE LEVANDE

908AAA QUARTER NOTE, CROTCHET   912AAA QUIET
908CZE ČTVRTOVÁ NOTA   912CZE KLIDNÝ
908DAN FJERDEDELSNODE   912DAN ROLIGT
908DUT KWARTNOOT   912DUT RUSTIG
908FRE NOIRE   912FRE QUIET
908GER VIERTELNOTE   912GER STILL, RUHIG
908HUN NEGYEDHANGJEVY   912HUN NYÜGODTAN
908ITA NERA, SEMIMINIMA   912ITA QUIETO
908POL ĆWIERĆNUTA   912POL SPOKOJNIE
908POR NEGRA, SEMÍNIMA   912POR QUIETO
908RUS CHETVERT   912RUS SPOKOĬNYĬ, TIKHIĬ
908SPA NEGRA, SEMÍNIMA   912SPA QUIETO
908SWE FJERDEDELNOT   912SWE STILLE

913AAA QUINTET
913CZE KVINTET(O)
913DAN KVINTET
913DUT QUINTET
913FRE QUINTETTE, QUINTUOR
913GER QUINTETT
913HUN KVINTETT
913ITA QUINTETTO
913POL KWINTET
913POR QUINTETO
913RUS KVINTET
913S7A QUINTETO
913SWE KVINTETT

914AAA RAGE
914CZE ZUŘIVOST, HNĚV
914DAN RASERI
914DUT WOEDE
914FRE RAGE
914GER RASEREI, WUT(H)
914HUN DÜH
914ITA RABBIA, FURIA
914POL SZAŁ
914POR FÚRIA
914RUS HNEV
914SPA RABIA, FURIA
914SWE RASERI

915AAA RAISE, TO
915CZE SEJMOUTI, SUNDATI
915DAN HAEVE
915DUT OPBEUREN
915FRE LEVER, MONTER
915GER AUFHEBEN, ERHEBEN
915HUN EMELNI
915ITA LEVARE, ALZARE
915POL PODNIEŚĆ
915POR LEVANTAR
915RUS PODNIMAT'
915SPA LEVANTAR
915SWE HÄFVA

916AAA RAPID
916CZE RYCHLÝ, DRAVÝ
916DAN RASKT, LIVLIGT
916DUT SNEL
916FRE RAPIDE
916GER SCHNELL, RASCH
916HUN SEBESEN
916ITA RAPIDO
916POL PREDKO
916POR RÁPIDO
916RUS BYSTRYĬ
916SPA RÁPIDO
916SWE SNABB

917AAA RATHER
917CZE SPÍŠE
917DAN TEMMELING
917DUT NOG SNELLER, EER
917FRE PRESQUE, ASSEZ
917GER EIN WENIG, GLEICHSAM
917HUN SZAPORÁBBAN
917ITA PIUTTOSTO, ALQUANTO
917POL JAKBY, NIEMAL
917POR UM PUOCO
917RUS SKOREĬ
917SPA CASI
917SWE LIKSOM, NÄSTAN

918AAA REAL
918CZE SKUTEČNÝ
918DAN VIRKELIG
918DUT REAAL, WERKELIJK
918FRE RÉELLE
918GER WIRKLICH, ECHT(E)
918HUN IGAZI, VALÓDI
918ITA REALE
918POL REALNY
918POR REAL
918RUS REAL'NYĬ
918SPA REAL
918SWE VERKLIG

919AAA REALIZE, TO
919CZE REALIZOVATI
919DAN REALISERE
919DUT REALISEREN
919FRE RÉALISER
919GER REALISIEREN, AUSFÜHREN
919HUN VALÓSITNI
919ITA REALIZZARE
919POL REALIZOWAĆ
919POR REALIZAR
919RUS REALIZOVAT'
919SPA REALIZAR
919SWE REALISERA

920AAA RECAPITULATION
920CCZE REKAPITULACE
920CDAN REKAPULATION
920DUT RECAPITULATIE
920OFRE RÉCAPITULATION
920OGER REKAPITULATION
920OHUN HANYATLÁS
920OITA RICAPITOLAZIONE
920OPOL REKAPITULACJA
920OPOR RECAPITULAÇÃO
920ORUS REZIUMIROVANIE
920OSPA RECAPITULACIÓN
920OSWE REKAPITULERING

921AAA RECITAL
921CZE CONCERT SÓLOVÝ
921DAN KONSERT
921DUT VOORDRACHT
921FRE RÉCITAL
921GER VORTRAG
921HUN ELŐADÁS
921ITA RECITA,
921POL RECITAL
921POR RECITAL
921RUS KONTSÉRT
921SPA RECITAL
921SWE RECIT, KONSERT

922AAA RECITATIVE
922CZE RECITATIV
922DAN RECITATIV
922DUT RECITATIEF
922FRE RECITATIF
922GER REZITATIV, RECITATIV
922HUN ÉNEKBESZÉD
922ITA RECITATIVO
922POL RECYTATYW
922POR RECITATIVO
922RUS RECHITATIV
922SPA RECITADO
922SWE RECITATIV

923AAA RECORDER
923CZE FLAŽOLET
923DAN BLOKFLØJTE, RØRFLØJTE
923DUT BLOKFLUIT
923FRE FLAGEOLET
923GER REKORDER
923HUN CÖLÖPFLÓTA
923ITA FISTOLA, FLAGIOLETTO
923POL FLECIK
923POR FLAUTIM
923RUS FLAZHOLET
923SPA CARAMILLO
923SWE FLAGEOLETT

924AAA RECORD(ING), DISK
924CZE DESKA
924DAN DISKOS
924DUT GRAMMOFOONPLAAT
924FRE DISQUE
924GER SCHALLPLATTE
924HUN HANGLEMEZ
924ITA DISCO
924POL NAGRANIE
924POR DISCO
924RUS PLASTINKA
924SPA DISCO
924SWE GRAMMOFONSKIVA

925AAA REED
925CZE JAZÝČEK, TAKÉ
925DAN RØR
925DUT RIETJE
925FRE ANCHE, LANGUETTE
925GER RÖHRE, ZUNGE, BLATT
925HUN NYELV
925ITA ANCIA, LINGUETTA
925POL STROIK
925POR PALHETA, CANA
925RUS IAZYCHOK
925SPA LENGÜETA, CAÑA
925SWE TUNGA

926AAA REDUCE, TO
926CZE SMENŠITI
926DAN FORMINSKE
926DUT REDUCEREN
926FRE RÉDUIRE
926GER REDUZIEREN
926HUN LESZÁLLÍTANI
926ITA RIDURRE
926POL REDUKOWAĆ
926POR REDUZIR
926RUS UMEN'SHAT'
926SPA REDUCIR
926SWE REDUCERA

927AAA REDUCTION
927CZE ÚPRAVA
927DAN FORMINDSKELSE
927DUT REDUCTIE
927FRE RÉDUCTION
927GER REDUZIERUNG
927HUN LESZÁLLÍTAS
927ITA RIDUZIONE
927POL REDUKCJA
927POR REDUÇÃO
927RUS REDUKTSIIA
927SPA REDUCCIÓN
927SWE REDUKTION, REDUCERING

928AAA REFINED
928CZE RAFINOVANÝ
928DAN RAFFINERET
928DUT GEAFFINEERD
928FRE RAFFINÉ
928GER RAFFINIERT
928HUN FÍNOMÍTOTT
928ITA RAFFINATO
928POL RAFINOWANY
928POR REFINADO
928RUS RAFINIROVANNYĬ
928SPA REFINADO
928SWE FINOMITOTT

929AAA REFRACTION
929CZE REFRAKCIA
929DAN REFRAKTION
929DUT STRALLBREKING
929FRE RÉFRACTION
929GER STRAHLENBRECHUNG
929HUN SUGÁRTÖRÉS
929ITA RIFRAZIONE
929POL REFRAKCJA
929POR REFRAÇÃO
929RUS REFRAKTSIIA
929SPA REFRACCIÓN
929SWE STRÅLBRYTNING

930AAA REFRAIN
930CZE REFRÉN
930DAN REFRAEN, RITORNEL
930DUT REFREIN
930FRE REFRAIN, RITOURNELLE
930GER REFRAIN, KEHRREIM
930HUN REFRÉN
930ITA RITORNELLO, RITORNO
930POL REFREN
930POR REFRÃO, ESTRIBILHO
930RUS REFREN
930SPA RETORNELO, ESTRAMBOTE
930SWE REFRÄNG

931AAA REGAL
931CZE PŘENOSNÉ VARHÁNKY
931DAN KONGELIG
931DUT KONINKLIJK
931FRE RÉGALE
931GER REGAL, KÖNIGLICH
931HUN KIS
931ITA REGALE
931POL KRÓLEWSKI
931POR RÉGIO
931RUS REGALIIA
931SPA REGIO
931SWE KUNGLIG

932AAA REGISTER
932CZE REJSTŘIK
932DAN REGISTER
932DUT REGISTER
932FRE RÉGISTRE
932GER REGISTER
932HUN REGISZTER
932ITA REGISTRO
932POL REJESTR
932POR REGISTRO
932RUS REGISTR
932SPA REGISTRO
932SWE REGISTER

933AAA REGULAR
933CZE PRAVIDELNÝ
933DAN REGELMAESSIG
933DUT REGALMATIG
933FRE RÉGULIER
933GER REGELMÄSSIG
933HUN SZERZETES
933ITA REGOLARE, PRECISO
933POL REGULARNY
933POR REGULAR
933RUS REGULIARNYĬ
933SPA REGULAR
933SWE REGALBUNDEN

934AAA REHEARSAL
934CZE OPAKAVÁNÍ
934DAN PRØVE
934DUT REPETITIE
934FRE RÉPÉTITION
934GER PROBE, WIEDERHOLUNG
934HUN ZENEI PRÓBA
934ITA PROVA, RIPETIZIONE
934POL PRÓBA
934POR ENSAIO
934RUS REPETITSIIA
934SPA ENSAYO
934SWE UPPLÄSNING

935AAA REHEARSE, TO
935CZE OPAKOVATI
935DAN PRØVE
935DUT REPETEREN
935FRE RÉPÉTER
935GER PROBEN, PROBIEREN
935HUN PRÓBAKÉNT ELŐADNI
935ITA RIPETERE, PROVARE
935POL ODBYWAĆ PRÓBE
935POR ENSAIAR
935RUS REPETIROVAT'
935SPA ENSÁYAR
935SWE UPPLÄSA

936AAA REINFORCE, TO
936CZE ZESÍLITI
936DAN FORSTAERKE
936DUT VERSTERKEN
936FRE RENFORCER
936GER VERSTÄRKEN
936HUN MEGERŐSÍTNI
936ITA RINFORZARE
936POL WZMACNIAĆ
936POR REFORÇAR
936RUS USILIVAT'
936SPA REFORZAR
936SWE FÖRSTÄRKA

937AAA RELATIVE
937CZE POMĚRNÝ, PARALELNÍ
937DAN RELATIV
937DUT RELATIEF
937FRE RELATIF
937GER RELATIV
937HUN ROKON, RELATÍV
937ITA RELATIVA
937POL PARALELE
937POR RELATIVO
937RUS PARALLEL'
937SPA RELATIVA
937SWE RELATIV, PARALLEL

938AAA RELAX, TO
938CZE POVOLOVATI
938DAN SLAPPE, LØSNE
938DUT VERSLAPPEN, ONTSPANNEN
938FRE RELÂCHER
938GER NACHLASSEN
938HUN HAGYOMÁNYOZNI
938ITA RILASSARE, RILASCIARE
938POL ODPRĘŻAC, OSŁABIAĆ
938POR RELAXAR
938RUS OSLABLIAT'
938SPA RELAJAR
938SWE SLAPPA

939AAA RELIGIOUS
939CZE NÁBOŽNÝ
939DAN GUDSDYRKELSE
939DUT GODSDIENSTIG
939FRE RELIGIEUX
939GER ANDÄCHTIG, RELIGIÖS
939HUS ÁNÍTATTAL
939ITA RELIGIOSO
939POL NABOŻNIE
939POR RELIGIOSO
939RUS RELIGIOZNYÏ
939SPA RELIGIOSO
939SWE RELIGIÖS

940AAA REMAIN, TO
940CZE ZUSTATI
940DAN BLIVE
940DUT BLIJVEN
940FRE RESTER
940GER BLEIBEN
940HUN MARADNI
940ITA RESTARE, RIMANERE
940POL POZOSTAWAĆ
940POR RESTAR
940RUS OSTAVAT'SIA
940SPA QUEDAR
940SWE FÖRBLIFVA

941AAA REMOVE, TO
941CZE POSUNOUTI
941DAN BEVAEGE
941DUT WEGNEMEN
941FRE ENLEVER
941GER WEGNEHMEN
941HUN ELVENNI
941ITA SPOSTARE
941POL ZDEJMOWAĆ
941POR REMOVER
941RUS SNIMAT'
941SPA REMOVER
941SWE BORTTAGA

942AAA REPEAT
942CZE OPAKOVÁNÍ
942DAN REPRISE
942DUT REPRISE
942FRE REPRISE
942GER WIEDERHOLUNG
942HUN VISSZATÉRÉS
942ITA RIPRESA, REPLICA
942POL REPETYCJA, POWTÓRKA
942POR REPETIGÃO
942RUS POVTORENIE
942SPA REPETICIÓN
942SWE REPRIS, UPPREPNING

943AAA REPEAT, TO
943CZE OPAKOVATI
943DAN REPETERE
943DUT REPETEREN
943FRE RÉPÉTER
943GER WIEDERHOLEN
943HUN ISMÉTELNI
943ITA RIPETERE
943POL POWTARZAĆ
943POR REPETIR
943RUS REPETIROVAT'
943SPA REPETIR
943SWE UPPREPA

944AAA REPERCUSSION
944CZE OPAKOVANÝ UHOZ
944DAN TILBAGESTØDELSE
944DUT REPERCUSSIO
944FRE RÉPERCUSSION
944GER REPERKUSSION
944HUN REPERKUSSZIÓ
944ITA RIPERCUSSIONE
944POL REPERKUSJA
944POR REPERCUSSÃO
944RUS OTRAZHENIE
944SPA REPERCUSIÓN
944SWE ÅTERSTUDSNING

945AAA REPERTORY
945CZE REPERTOIR
945DAN REPERTOIRE
945DUT REPERTOIRE
945FRE RÉPERTOIRE
945GER SPIELPLAN
945HUN MÜSOR
945ITA REPERTORIO
945POL REPERTUAR
945POR REPERTÓRIO
945RUS REPERTUAR
945SPA REPERTORIO
945SWE REPERTOAR

946AAA REPOSE
946CZE ODPOČINEK
946DAN HVILE
946DUT RUST
946FRE REPOS
946GER RUHE
946HUN NYUGALOM
946ITA RIPOSO
946POL ODPOCZYNEK
946POR REPOUSO
946RUS OTDYKH
946SPA REPOSO
946SWE VILA

947AAA RESOLUTE
947CZE ROZHODNÝ
947DAN BESLUTSOM
947DUT VASTBESLOTEN
947FRE RÉSOLU
947GER RESOLUT, ENTSCHLOSSEN
947HUN HATÁROZOTT, ELTÖKÉLT
947ITA RISOLUTO
947POL STANOWCZO, REZOLUTNY
947POR RESOLUTO
947RUS RESHITEL'NYĬ
947SPA RESUELTO
947SWE BESLUTSAM, BESTÄMT

948AAA RESOLUTION
948CZE ROZHODNOST
948DAN RESOLUTION
948DUT RESOLUTIE
948FRE RÉSOLUTION
948GER RESOLUTION
948HUN HATÁROZAT
948ITA RISOLUZIONE
948POL REZOLUTNOŚĆ
948POR RESOLUÇÃO
948RUS REZOLIUTSIIA
948SPA RESOLUCIÓN
948SWE RESOLUTION

949AAA RESONANT
949CZE REZONANTNÍ
949DAN RESONANTS, GENLYDENDE
949DUT KLINKEND
949FRE RÉSON(N)ANT
949GER WIEDERKLÄNGLICH
949HUN VISZHANGZÓ
949ITA RISONANTE, SONABILE
949POL RESONANCYJNY
949POR RESOANTE
949RUS REZONIRUIUSHCHIĬ
949SPA RESONANTE
949SWE GENLJUDANDE

950AAA REST
950CZE PŘESTÁVKE, PAUZA
950DAN PAUSE
950DUT RUSTTEKEN
950FRE PAUSE
950GER PAUSE, SCHWEIGEZEICHEN
950HUN SZÜNET
950ITA FERMATA, PAUSA
950POL PAUZA, KORONA
950POR PAUSA
950RUS PAUZA
950SPA PAUSA
950SWE PAUS

951AAA RESTRAIN, TO
951CZE ZDRŽOVATI
951DAN TILBAGE
951DUT TERUGHOUDEN
951FRE RETENIR, CONTENIR
951GER ZURÜCKHALTEN
971HUN VISSZATARTANI
951ITA TRATTENERE
951POL POWŚCIĄGNĄĆ
951POR RESTRINGIR
951RUS SDERZHIVAT'
951SPA RESTRINGER, RESTRIÑIR
951SWE BEHÅLLA, ÅTERHÅLLA

952AAA RETARDATION
952CZE OPOŽDĚNÍ
952DAN FORSINKELSE
952DUT TERUGHOUDING
952FRE RETARDATION
952GER RETARDATION
952HUN RETARDÁCIÓ
952ITA RITARDAZIONE
952POL OPÓŹNIENIE
952POR RETARDACAO
952RUS OPOZDANIE
952SPA RETARDACIÓN
952SWE FÖRSENING

953AAA RETARD, TO
953CZE ZDRŽETI, ZPOMALENÍ
953DAN FORSINKE
953DUT VERTRAGEN
953FRE RETARDER
953GER EINSCHLAFEN, VERZÖGERN
953HUN KÉSLELTETNI
953ITA RITARDARE
953POL OPÓŹNIAĆ
953POR RETARDAR
953RUS ZADERZHIVAT'
953SPA RETARDER
953SWE FÖRSENA

954AAA RETROGRADE
954CZE ZPĚTNY
954DAN RETROGRAD
954DUT ACHTERWAARTS
954FRE RÉTROGRADE
954GER RÜCKGÄNGIG
954HUN HANYATLÓ
954ITA RETROGRADO
954POL IMITACJA RUCHEM RAKA
954POR RETRÓGRADO
954RUS RETROGRADNYÏ
954SPA RETRÓGRADO
954SWE TILLBAKASKRIDANDE

955AAA RETURN
955CAE NÁVRAT
955DAN RETURNERING
955DUT TERUGTEER
955FRE RETOUR
955GER RÜCKKEHR, WIEDERKEHR
955HUN VISSZATÉRÉS
955ITA RITORNO, REDITA
955POL POWRÓT
955POR VOLTA
955RUS VOZVRASHCHENIE
955SPA VUELTA
955SWE ÅTERKONST

956AAA RETURN, TO
956CZE VRÁTITI SE
956DAN RETURNERE
956DUT TERUGKOMEN
956FRE RETOURNER
956GER ZURÜCKKEHREN
956HUN VISSZATÉRNI
956ITA RITORNARE
956POL POWRACAĆ
956POR VOLTAR
956RUS VOZVRASHCHAT'SÎA
956SPA VOLVER
956SWE ÅTERVÄNDA

957AAA REVEIL(LE)
957CZE PROBUZENI, VOJENSKÝ
957DAN REVEILLE
957DUT MORGENSIGNAAL
957FRE RÉVEIL(LE), SONNERIE
957GER MORGENSIGNAL, WECKEN
957HUN ÉBRESZTŐ SZIGNÁL
957ITA SVEGLIA
957POL PRZEBUDZENIE SIĘ
957POR ALVORADA
957RUS PRODUZHDENIE
957SPA DIANA, TOQUE DE·DIANA
957SWE REVELJ

958AAA REVERBERATE, TO
958CZE ODRÁŽETI
958DAN GENLYDE
958DUT WEERKAASTEN
958FRE RÉVERBÉRER
958GER ZURÜCKWERFEN
958HUN VISSZAVETNI
958ITA RIVERBERARE
958POL PODDAWAĆ
958POR REVERBERAR
958RUS OTRAZHAT'
958SPA REVERBERAR
958SWE GENLJUDA

959AAA REVERIE
959CZE SNĚNÍ
959DAN DRØMMERI, FANTASTERI
959DUT DROMENIJ
959FRE RÉVERIE
959GER TRÄUMEREI
959HUN ÁLMODOZÁS
959ITA SOGNO, FANTASTICHERIA
959POL MARZENIE
959POR DEVANEIO, SONHO
959RUS MECHTY
959SPA SOÑO, FANTASÍA
959SWE DROMMERI

960AAA REVIEW
960CZE REVUE
960DAN REVY
960DUT REVUE
960FRE REVUE
960GER NACHPRÜFUNG
960HUN SZEMLE
960ITA RIVISTA
960POL REWIA
960POR REVISTA
960RUS REVÍU
960SPA REVISTA
960SWE REVY

961AAA REVISION
961CZE REVIZE
961DAN REVIDERET
961DUT REVISIE
961FRE REVISION
961GER REVISION
961HUN ÁTNÉS
961ITA REVISIONE
961POL REWIZJA
961POR REVISÃO
961RUS REVIZIIA
961SPA REVISIÓN, REPASO
961SWE REVISION

962AAA RHAPSODY
962CZE RAPSODIE
962DAN RHAPSODI
962DUT RAPSODIE
962FRE RAPSODIE
962GER RHAPSODIE
962HUN RAPSZÓDIA
962ITA RAPSODIA
962POL RAPSODJA
962POR RAPSÓDIA
962RUS RAPSODIIA
962SPA RAPSODIA
962SWE RAPSODI

963AAA RHYTHM
963CZE RYTMUS
963DAN RHYTME
963DUT RITMUS, RITME
963FRE R(H)YTHME
963GER RHYTHMUS
963HUN RITMUS, HANGEDOM
963ITA RITMO
963POL RYTM
963POR RITMO
963RUS RITM
963SPA RITMO
963SWE RYTM

964AAA RIGHT
964CZE PRAVÁ
964DAN RET
964DUT RECHT
964FRE DROITE
964GER RECHTE
964HUN JOBB KÉZ
964ITA DESTRA
964POL PRAWY
964POR DIREITO
964RUS PRAVAIA
964SPA DERECHA
964SWE RÄTT

965AAA RIGOROUS
965CZE PŘÍSNÝ
965DAN STRAENGT
965DUT STRENG
965FRE RIGOUREUX
965GER STRENG
965HUN SZIGORÚAN
965ITA RIGOROSO
965POL SUROWY
965POR RIGOROSO
965RUS SUROVYĬ
965SPA RIGOROSO
965SWE STRÄNG

966AAA RING, TO
966CZE SVONITI, SNÍTI
966DAN KLINGE, RINGE
966DUT KLINKEN, AANBELLEN
966FRE SONNER, RETENTIR
966GER SCHALLEN, BERINGEN
966HUN CSENGETNI
966ITA SONARE, SQUILLARE
966POL DZWENIĆ
966POR RETINIR
966RUS ZVONIT'
966SPA RETIÑIR, RIMBOMBAR
966SWE INRINGA

967AAA ROBBED
967CZE RUBÁTO
967DAN RUBATO
967DUT RUBATO
967FRE DEROBÉ
967GER GERAUBTES ZEITMASS
967HUN CSAPONGVA
967ITA RUBATO
967POL SWOBODNIE CO DO TEMPA
967POR RUBATO
967RUS RUBATO
967SPA DESCOMPASADO
967SWE RUBATO

968AAA ROBUST
968CZE ROBUSTNÍ, STATNÝ
968DAN ROBUST
968DUT STERK
968FRE ROBUSTE
968GER ROBUST, STARK
968HUN ERÖS
968ITA ROBUSTO
968POL KRZEPKI
968POR ROBUSTO
968RUS KREPKIĬ
968SPA ROBUSTO
968SWE STARK

969AAA ROLL, DRUMROLL
969CZE VÍŘENÍ
969DAN TROMMEHVIRVEL
969DUT ROLLO, TROMMROFFEL
969FRE ROULEMENT
969GER WIRBEL, TROMMELWIRBEL
969HUN DOBPERGÉS
969ITA ROLLO, RULLO
969POL WERBEL
969POR RUFO
969RUS BARABANNAĨA DROB'
969SPA REDOBLE
969SWE TRUMVIRFVEL

970AAA ROLL, TO
970CZE VÍŘIVĚ BUBNOVATI
970DAN SLÅ TROMMEHVIRVLER
970DUT ROLLEN, ROFFELEN
970FRE ROULER
970GER WIRBELN
970HUN DÖRÖGNI
970ITA RULLARE
970POL BIĆ WERBEL NA
970POR TOCAR RUFOS
970RUS OTBIVAT' DROB'
970SPA REDOBLAR
970SWE SLÅ HVIRFLA, VIRVLA

971AAA ROMANCE
971CZE ROMANCE, PÍSEŇ
971DAN ROMANCE
971DUT ROMANCE, ROMANZE
971FRE ROMANCE
971GER ROMANZE
971HUN ROMÁNC
971ITA ROMANZA
971POL ROMANS
971POR ROMANCA, RIMANCE
971RUS ROMANS
971SPA ROMANCE
971SWE ROMANS

972AAA RONDO
972CZE RONDÓ
972DAN RONDO
972DUT RONDO
972FRE RONDEAU
972GER RONDO
972HUN KÖRMÜ
972ITA RONDÒ
972POL RONDO
972POR RONDÓ
972RUS RONDO
972SPA RONDÓ
972SWE RONDO

973AAA ROOT
973CZE ZÁKLADNÍ
973DAN GRUNDTONE, BASSTEMME
973DUT GRONDTOON, FONDEMENT
973FRE FONDAMENTALE
973GER GRUNDSTIMME, GRUNDTON
973HUN ALAP
973ITA FONDAMENTALE
973POL A KORDU
973POR FUNDAMENTAL
973RUS OSNOVNAĨA NOTA AKKORDA
973SPA BASE, BAJO FUNDAMENTAL
973SWE GRUND

974AAA ROSIN
974CZE KALAFUNA
974DAN KOLOFONIUM
974DUT HARS
974FRE COLOPHANE
974GER KOLOPHONIUM, HARZ
974HUN GYANTA
974ITA COLOFONIA
974POL KALAFONIA
974POR COLOFÓNIA
974RUS KANIFOL'
974SPA COLOFONIA
974SWE HARTS

975AAA ROUGH
975CZE DRSNÝ, HRUBÝ
975DAN RU
975DUT RUW
975FRE RUDE
975GER RAUH
975HUN ZORD
975ITA RUVIDO, VILLANO
975POL SZORSTKI
975POR ÁSPERO
975RUS GRUBYĬ
975SPA RUDO, ÁSPERO
975SWE RÅ

976AAA ROULADE, RUN, SHAKE
976CZE RULÁDA, ZPĚVNI OZDOBA
976DAN ROULADE
976DUT GORGELTRILLER, ROLLER
976FRE ROULADE, VOLATE
976GER GURGELTRILLER, LAUF
976HUN FUTÁS
976ITA GORGHEGGIO, VOLATA
976POL RULADA
976POR GORJEIO
976RUS RULADA
976SPA GORJEO
976SWE RULAD

977AAA ROW   981AAA RUSTIC
977CZE RADA   981CZE VENKOVSKÝ, SELSKÝ
977DAN RAD   981DAN LANDLET
977DUT RIJ   981DUT LANDELIJK
977FRE RANG   981FRE CHAMPÊTRE, RUSTIQUE
977GER REIHE   981GER LÄNDLICH, BÄUERLICH
977HUN REND   981HUN FALUSIASAN
977ITA FILA   981ITA RUSTICO
977POL RZAD   981POL SIELANKOWO
977POR FILA   981POR RÚSTICO
977RUS RIÁD   981RUS DEREVENSKII
977SPA FILA   981SPA RÚSTICO
977SWE RAD   981SWE LANTLIGT

978AAA ROYAL   982AAA SACKBUT
978CZE SKUTEČNÝ   982CZE POLNICE, STARÝ POZOUNU
978DAN KONGELIG   982DAN TRAEKBASUN
978DUT KONINKLIJK   982DUT BAZUIN
978FRE ROYAL   982FRE SAQUEBOUTE
978GER KÖNIGLICH   982GER SACKBUT
978HUN KIRÁLYI   982HUN PÚZON
978ITA REGIO   982ITA SAQUEBUTE
978POL KRÓLEWSKI   982POL SAKBUT
978POR REGIO   982POR SACABUXA
978RUS KOROLEVSKII   982RUS TROMBON
978SPA REGIO   982SPA SACABUCHE
978SWE KUNGLIG   982SWE DRAGBASUN

979AAA ROYALTY, ROYALTIES   983AAA SACRED
979CZE AUTORSKA PRÁVA   983CZE POSVÁTNY
979DAN FORFATTERET   983DAN HELLIG
979DUT KROONPRIVILENIEN   983DUT HEILIG
979FRE DROIT D'AUTEUR   983FRE SACRÉ
979GER TANTIEMEN   983GER HEILIG
979HUN TANTIEMAN   983HUN EGYHÁZI
979ITA DIRITTI D'AUTORE   983ITA SACRO
979POL HONORIUM AUTORSKIE   983POL KOŚCIELNY
979POR DIREITO DE AUTOR   983POR SAGRADO
979RUS AVTORSKII HONORAR   983RUS DUKHOVNYI
979SPA DERECHO DE AUTOR   983SPA SAGRADO
979SWE AVGIFT   983SWE HELIG

980AAA RULE   984AAA SAD
980CZE PRAVIDLO   984CZE SMUTNÝ
980DAN REGEL   984DAN SØRGENDE
980DUT REGEL   984DUT TREURIG, DROEVIG
980FRE REGLE   984FRE TRISTE
980GER REGEL   984GER TRAURIG
980HUN SZABÁLY   984HUN SZOMORÚ
980ITA REGOLA   984ITA MESTO, DUOLO
980POL REGUŁA   984POL SMUTNIE
980POR REGRA   984POR TRISTE
980RUS PRAVILO   984RUS GRUSTNYI
980SPA REGLA   984SPA TRISTE
980SWE REGEL   984SWE SORGSEN

985AAA	SAME	989AAA	SAXOPHONE	
985CZE	TENTÝŽ, TATÁŽ	989CZE	SAXOFON	
985DAN	SAMME	989DAN	SAKSOFON	
985DUT	GELIJK	989DUT	SAXOFOON	
985FRE	MÊME	989FRE	SAXOPHONE	
985GER	DER(DAS)(DIE)SELBE	989GER	SAXOPHON	
985HUN	AZ, UGYANAZ	989HUN	SZAXOFÓN	
985ITA	STESSA, MEDESIMO	989ITA	SAXOFONO, SASSOFONO	
985POL	TEN SAM	989POL	SAKSOFON	
985POR	MESMA	989POR	SAXOFONE	
985RUS	TOT ZHE	989RUS	SAKSOFON	
985SPA	MISMA	989SPA	SAXOFÓN	
985SWE	SAMME	989SWE	SAXOFON	
986AAA	SARABAND	990AAA	SCALE	
986CZE	SARABANDA	990CZE	ŠKÁLA, STUPNICE	
986DA5	SARABANDE	990DAN	SCALA, SKALA	
986DUT	SARABANDE	990DUT	TOONLADDER	
986FRE	SARABANDE	990FRE	GAMME, ECHELLE	
986GER	SARABANDA	990GER	TONLEITER	
986HUN	SZARABANDA	990HUN	HANGSOR	
986ITA	SARABANDA	990ITA	SCALA	
986POL	SARABANDA	990POL	SKALA	
986POR	SARABANDA	990POR	ESCALA	
986RUS	SARABANDA	990RUS	GAMMA	
986SPA	ZARABANDA	990SPA	ESCALA	
986SWE	SARABANDE	990SWE	SKALA	
987AAA	SARRUSOPHONE	991AAA	SCAN, TO	
987CZE	SARUSOFON	991CZE	SKANDOVATI	
987DAN	SARRUSOFON	991DAN	SKANDERE	
987DUT	SARUSOPHONE	991DUT	SCANDEREN	
987FRE	SARRUSSOPHONE	991FRE	SCANDER	
987GER	SARRUSOPHON	991GER	DURCHSEHEN	
987HUN	SZARRUSZOFÓN	991HUN	ÁTNÉZNI	
987ITA	SARRUSSOFONO	991ITA	SCANDERE	
987POL	SARRUSOFON	991POL	SKANDOWAĆ	
987POR	SARRUSOFONE	991POR	ESCANDIR	
987RUS	SARRUSOFON	991RUS	SKANDIROVAT'	
987SPA	SARRUSÓFONO	991SPA	ESCANDIR	
987SWE	SARRUSOFON	991SWE	SKANDERA	
988AAA	SAXHORN	992AAA	SCENE	
988CZE	SAXŮV ROH	992CZE	SCÉNA, JEVIŠTÉ	
988DAN	SAXHORN	992DAN	SCENE	
988DUT	SAXHOORN	992DUT	TAFEREEL, SCÈNE	
988FRE	SAXHORN	992FRE	SCÈNE	
988GER	SAXHORN	992GER	SZENE, BÜHNE	
988HUN	SZAXKÜRTÖK	992HUN	SZÍNPAD	
988ITA	SAXCORNO	992ITA	SCENA	
988POL	SAKXHORN	992POL	SCENA	
988POR	SAXHORNE	992POR	CENA	
988RUS	SAKSHORN	992RUS	STSENA	
988SPA	BOMBARDINO	992SPA	ESCENA	
988SWE	SAXHORN	992SWE	SCEN	

993AAA SCHOOL   997AAA SCOTCH, SCOTTISH
993CZE ŠKOLA   997CZE SKOTSKA
993DAN SKOLE   997DAN SKOTSK
993DUT SCHOOL   997DUT SCHOTS
993FRE ÉCOLE   997FRE ÉCOSSAISE
993GER ECHULE   997GER SCHOTTISCH
993HUN ISKOLA   997HUN SCOZZESE, SKÓT
993ITA SCUOLA   997ITA SCOZZESE
993POL SZKOLA   997POL SZKOCKI
993POR ESCOLA   997POR ESCOCESA
993RUS SHKOLA   997RUS EKOSSEZ
993SPA ESCUELA   997SPA ESCOCESA
993SWE SKOLA   997SWE SKOTSKA

994AAA SCORE   998AAA SECOND
994CZE PARTITURA   998CZE SEKUNDA
994DAN PARTITUR   998DAN SEKUND
994DUT PARTITUUR   998DUT SECUNDA, TWEEDE STEM
994FRE PARTITION   998FRE SECONDE
994GER PARTITUR   998GER SEKUNDE
994HUN PARTITÚRA   998HUN SZEKUND
994ITA PARTITURA, PARTIZIONE   998ITA SECONDA
994POL PARTYTURA, PARTYCJA   998POL SEKUNDA
994POR PARTITURA   998POR SEGUNDA
994RUS PARTITURA   998RUS SEKUNDA
994SPA PARTITURA, PARTICIÓN   998SPA SEGUNDA
994SWE PARTITUR   998SWE SEKUNDA

995AAA SCORE, TO   999AAA SECTION
995CZE ORKESTROVATI   999CZE SEKCIA
995DAN INSTRUMENTERE   999DAN SEKTION
995DUT OP NOTEM ZETTEN   999DUT SECTIE
995FRE ECRIRE, ORCHESTRER   999FRE SECTION, COUPURE
995GER IN NOTEN SETZEN   999GER SEKTION, ABSCHNITT
995HUN HANGRZEREKNI   999HUN OSZTÁLY
995ITA ORCHESTRARE   999ITA SEZIONE, TAGLIO
995POL PARTOWAĆ   999POL SEKCJA
995POR ORQUESTRAR   999POR SECGÃO
995RUS ORKESTROVAT'   999RUS SECHENIE
995SPA ORQUESTAR   999SPA SECCIÓN
995SWE ORKESTRERA   999SWE AFDELNING

996AAA SCORN   1000AAA SEMI-
996CZE OPOVRŽENI   1000CZE POLO-
996DAN FORAGT   1000DAN SEMI-, HALV-
996DUT VERACHTING   1000DUT DEMI-, HALV-
996FRE MÉPRIS, DÉDAIN   1000FRE SEMI-, DEMI-
996GER VERACHTUNG, ZORN   1000GER HALB-
996HUN MEGVETÉS   1000HUN FÉL-
996ITA SDEGNO   1000ITA SEMI-
996POL POGARDA   1000POL POŁ-
996POR DESDÉM   1000POR SEMI-
996RUS PREZRENIE   1000RUS POLY-
996SPA DESDÉN   1000SPA SEMI-
996SWE FÖRAKT   1000SWE HALV-

1001AAA SEMIBREVE, WHOLE NOTE
1001CZE ČTYŘČTVRTOVÁ NOTA
1001DAN HELTAKTS NODE
1001DUT HELE NOOT
1001FRE RONDE
1001GER GANZE NOTE
1001HUN EGÉSZHANJEVY
1001ITA SEMIBREVE
1001POL CAŁA NUTA
1001POR SEMIBREVE
1001RUS TSELAIA NOTA
1001SPA SEMIBREVE
1001SWE HELNOT

1002AAA SEMI-TONE
1002CZE PŮLTÓN
1002DAN HALVTONE
1002DUT HALVE TOON
1002FRE DEMI-TON
1002GER HALB-TON
1002HUN FELHANG
1002ITA SEMITONO
1002POL PÓŁTON
1002POR SEMITOM
1002RUS POLUTON
1002SPA SEMITONO
1002SWE HALVTON

1003AAA SENSE
1003CZE SMYSL
1003DAN SANS
1003DUT GEVOEL
1003DUT SENS
1003GER SINN
1003HUN ÉRZÉK
1003ITA SENSO
1003POL ZMYSŁ, CZULE
1003POR SENTIDO
1003RUS SMYSL
1003SPA SENTIDO
1003SWE SINNE

1004AAA SENTIMENTAL
1004CZE SENTIMENTÁLNÍ
1004DAN FØLSOM
1004DUT SENTIMENTEEL
1004FRE SENTIMENTAL
1004GER EMPFINDLICH
1004HUN SZENTIMENTÁLIS
1004ITA SENTIMENTALE
1004POL UCZUSIOWY
1004POR SENTIMENTAL
1004RUS SENTIMENTAL'NYI
1004SPA SENTIMENTAL
1004SWE KANSLOFULL

1005AAA SEPARATE, TO
1005CZE ODDĚLITI
1005DAN SEPARERE, ADSKILLE
1005DUT AFSCHEIDEN
1005FRE SÉPARER
1005GER ABSETZEN, TRENNEN
1005HUN LETENNI
1005ITA SEPARARE
1005POL SEPAROWAĆ
1005POR SEPARAR
1005RUS OTDELIAT'
1005SPA SEPARAR
1005SWE SEPARERA, AVSKILJA

1006AAA SEPTET
1006CZE SEPTETO
1006DAN SEPTET
1006DUT SEPTET
1006FRE SEPTUOR
1006GER SEPTETT
1006HUN SZEPTÉT
1006ITA SEPTETO
1006POL SEPTET
1006POR SEPTOR
1006RUS SEPTET
1006SPA SEPTETO
1006SWE SEPTETT

1007AAA SEQUENCE
1007CZE SEKVENCE
1007DAN SEQUENTS
1007DUT SEQUENS
1007FRE SÉQUENCE, SUITE
1007GER SEQUENZ, REIHENFOLGE
1007HUN SORREND
1007ITA SEQUENZA
1007POL SEKWENS
1007POR SEQUÊNCIA
1007RUS SEKVENTSIIA
1007SPA SECUENCIA
1007SWE SEKVENS

1008AAA SERENADE
1008CZE SERENÁDA
1008DAN SERENADE, AFTENMUSIK
1008DUT SERENATA
1008FRE SÉRÉNADE
1008GER STÄNDCHEN, ABENDMUSIK
1008HUN SZERENÁD
1008ITA SERENATA
1008POL SERENADA
1008POR SERENATA, SERENADA
1008RUS SERENADA
1008SPA SERENADA, SERENATA
1008SWE SERENAD

1009AAA SERENE   1013AAA SEVEN
1009CZE JASNÝ   1013CZE SEDM
1009DAN KLAR   1013DAN SYV
1009DUT KLAAR, HELDER   1013DUT ZEVEN
1009FRE SEREIN   1013FRE SEPT
1009GER KLAR, HEITER   1013GER SIEBEN
1009HUN DERÜSEN   1013HUN HÉT
1009ITA SERÈNO   1013ITA SETTE
1009POL POGODNIE   1013POL SIEDEM
1009POR SERENO   1013POT SETE
1009RUS IASNYĬ   1013RUS SEM'
1009SPA SERENO   1013SPA SIETE
1009SWE KLAR   1013SWE SJU

1010AAA SERIES   1014AAA SEVERE
1010CZE SÉRIE   1014CZE PŘÍSNÝ
1010DAN SERIE   1014DAN STRENG
1010DUT SERIE   1014DUT STRENG
1010FRE SÉRIE   1014FRE SÉVÈRE
1010GER SERIE, REIHE   1014GER STRENG, KUNSTGERECHT
1010HUN SOR   1014HUN SZIGORÚ
1010ITA SERIE   1014ITA SEVERO
1010POL SERIA   1014POL SUROWY
1010POR SÉRIE   1014POR SEVERO
1010RUS SERIIA   1014RUS STROGIĬ
1010SPA SERIE   1014SPA SEVERO
1010SWE SERIE   1014SWE STRÄNG

1011AAA SERIOUS   1015AAA SEXTET
1011CZE VÁŽNÝ   1015CZE SEXTETO
1011DAN ALVORLIG   1015DAN SEKSTET
1011DUT ERNSTIG   1015DUT SEXTET
1011FRE SÉRIEUX   1015FRE SEXTUOR
1011GER ERNSTHAFT   1015GER SEXTETT
1011HUN KOMOLY   1015HUN SZEXTÉTT
1011ITA SERIO(SO)   1015ITA SEXTETTO
1011POL POWAŻNIE   1015POL SEKSTET
1011POR SÉRIO   1015POR SECTETO
1011RUS SER'ĖZNYĬ   1015RUS SEKSTET
1011SPA SERIO   1015SPA SEXTETO
1011SWE ALLVARLIG   1015SWE SEXTETT

1012AAA SERPENT   1016AAA SHARP
1012CZE SERPENT   1016CZE KŘÍŽEK
1012DAN SERPENT   1016DAN KRYDS
1012DUT SERPENT   1016DUT KRUIS
1012FRE SERPENT   1016FRE DIÈSE
1012GER SERPENT, SCHLANGENROHR   1016GER DIESIS
1012HUN SZERPENT   1016HUN KERESZT
1012ITA SERPENTE, SERPENTONE   1016ITA DIESIS
1012POL SERPENT   1016POL KRZYŻYK
1012POR SERPENTÃO   1016POT SUSTENIDO
1012RUS SERPENT   1016RUS DIEZ
1012SPA SERPENTÓN   1016SPA SOSTENIDO
1012SWE SERPENT   1016SWE KORS

1017AAA SHARP, TO
1017CZE OPATŘITI NOTA KŘÍŽKEM
1017DAN HØJNE
1017DUT VAN EEN KRUIS VOORZIEN
1017FRE DIÉSER
1017GER DURCH KREUZ ERHÖHEN
1017HUN FŐLEMELNI
1017ITA DIESARE
1017POL PODWYŻSZAĆ O PÓŁ TONU
1017POR SUSTENIZAR
1017RUS STAVIT' DIEZ
1017SPA SOSTENIZAR
1017SWE HÖJA EN HALV TON

1018AAA SHAWM
1018CZE ŠALMAJ
1018DAN SKALMEJE
1018DUT SCHALMEI
1018FRE CHALUMEAU
1018GER SCHALMEI
1018HUN SCHALMEI
1018ITA SCIALUMO, CHIARINO
1018POL SZAŁAMAJE
1018POR CHARAMELA, DULÇAINA
1018RUS SVIREL'
1018SPA CHIRIMÍA, DULZAINA
1018SWE SHALMEJA

1019AAA SHIFT, TO
1019CZE ZMĚNITI
1019DAN SKIFTE
1019DUT VERANDEREN
1019FRE CHANGER
1019GER VERÄNDERN
1019HUN VALTOZNI
1019ITA CAMBIARE
1019POL ZAMIENIAĆ
1019POR CAMBIAR
1019RUS MENIAT'
1019SPA CAMBIAR
1019SWE SKIFTA

1020AAA SHORT
1020CZE KRÁTKÝ
1020DAN KORT
1020DUT KORT
1020FRE COURT, RÉDUITE
1020GER KURZ
1020HUN RÖVID
1020ITA CORTO, RIDOTTA
1020POL KRÓTKI
1020POR CURTO
1020RUS KRATKIY, KOROTKIY
1020SPA CORTO
1020SWE KORT

1021AAA SHRILL
1021CZE OSTRÝ
1021DAN SKARP
1021DUT SCHERP
1021FRE AIGUÉ, POINTU
1021GER SCHRILL, SCHARF
1021HUN ÉLES, FÜLHASÍTÓ
1021ITA ACUTO
1021POL OSTRY
1021POR AGUDO
1021RUS OSTRYY
1021SPA AGUDO
1021SWE SKARP

1022AAA SIGH
1022CZE VZDECH
1022DAN SUK
1022DUT ZUCHT
1022FRE SOUPIR
1022GER SEUFZER
1022HUN SOHAJ
1022ITA SOSPIRO
1022POL WESTCHNIENIE
1022POR SUSPIRO
1022RUS VZDOKH
1022SPA SUSPIRO
1022SWE SUSA

1023AAA SIGH, TO
1023CZE VZDYCHATI
1023DAN SUKKE
1023DUT ZUCHTEN
1023FRE SOUPIRER
1023GER SEUFZEN
1023HUN SOHJTOZNI
1023ITA SOSPIRARE
1023POL WESTCHNAĆ
1023POR SUSPIRAR
1023RUS VZDYKHAT'
1023SPA SUSPIRAR
1023SWE SUCKA

1024AAA SIGN
1024CZE ZNAMENÍ, ZNAČKA
1024DAN TEGN, NODETEGN
1024DUT TEKEN
1024FRE SIGNE
1024GER STANGE, ZEICHEN
1024HUN SZÁMOZOTT BASZUS
1024ITA SEGNO
1024POL SNAK
1024POR SINAL
1024RUS ZNAK
1024SPA SIGNO
1024SWE TECKEN

1025AAA SIGNATURE(S)
1025CZE ZNAMENÍ, ZNAČKA
1025DAN SIGNATURER
1025DUT SIGNATUR
1025FRE SIGNATURE, SIGNE
1025GER VORZEICHNUNG
1025HUN ELÖJEL
1025ITA SEGNA, SEGNI
1025POL PODPIS
1025POR ASSINATURA
1025RUS ZNACHOK, PODPIS
1025SPA SIGNATURA
1025SWE KLAV

1026AAA SILENT
1026CZE MLČELIVÝ
1026DAN STILLE
1026DUT RUST
1026FRE SILENCIEUX
1026GER SCHWEIGEN
1026HUN HALLGATAG
1026ITA SILENZIO
1026POL MILCZĄCY
1026POR SILENCIO
1026RUS MOLCHALIVYY
1026SPA SILENCIO
1026SWE STILLA

1027AAA SIMILAR
1027CZE PODOBNÝ
1027DAN LIGNENDE
1027DUT OP DEZELFDE MANIER
1027FRE SIMILAIRE, SEMBLABLE
1027GER ÄHNLICH, GERADE
1027HUN HAZONLÓAN
1027ITA SIMILE, RETTO
1027POL PODOBNIEŻ
1027POR SIMILAR, DO MESMO MODO
1027RUS PODOBNYI
1027SPA SIMILAR, RECTO
1027SWE LIKNANDE

1028AAA SIMPLE
1028CZE PROSTÝ, JEDNODUCHY
1028DAN SIMPELT, ENFOLDIGT
1028DUT EENVOUDIG
1028FRE SIMPLE
1027GER EINFACH, SCHLICHT
1028HUN EGYSZERÜ
1028ITA SEMPLICE, SCHIETTO
1028POL PROSTO
1028POR SIMPLES
1028RUS PROSTOY
1028SPA SIMPLE
1028SWE ENKELT, OKONSTLAT

1029AAA SINCERE
1029CZE UPRIMNÝ
1029DAN OPRIGTIGT
1029DUT OPRECHT
1029FRE SINCÈRE
1029GER AUFRICHTIG
1029HUN ÖSZINTE
1029ITA SINCERO
1029POL SZCZERY
1029POR SINCERO
1029RUS ISKRENNIY
1029SPA SINCERO
1029SWE UPPRIKTIG

1030AAA SINGLE
1030CZE JEDNOTLIVÝ
1030DAN ENKELT
1030DUT ENKEL, ALLEEN
1030FRE SEUL
1030GER EINFACH, ALLEIN
1030HUN EGYEDÜL
1030ITA SINGOLO, SOLO
1030POL SAM, DOSŁOWNIE
1030POR ÚNICO
1030RUS ODINOCHNYY
1030SPA SINGLE, ÚNICO
1030SWE ENSAM, ENDA

1031AAA SING, TO
1031CZE ZPÍVATI
1031DAN SYNGE
1031DUT ZINGEN
1031FRE CHANTER
1031GER SINGEN
1031HUN ÉNEKELNI
1031ITA CANTARE
1031POL ŚPIEWAĆ
1031POR CANTAR
1031RUS PET'
1031SPA CANTAR
1031SWE SJUNGA

1032AAA SIREN
1032CZE SIRÉNA
1032DAN SIRENE
1032DUT SIRENE
1032FRE SIRÈNE
1032GER SIRENE
1032HUN SZIRENA
1032ITA SIRÈNA
1032POL SYRENA
1032POR SEREIA
1032RUS SIRENA
1032SPA SIRENA
1032SWE SIREN

1033AAA SIX
1033CZE ŠEST
1033DAN SEKS
1033DUT ZES
1033FRE SIX
1033GER SECHS
1033HUN HAT
1033ITA SEI
1033POL SZEŚĆ
1033POR SEIS
1033RUS SHEST'
1033SPA SEIS
1033SWE SEX

1034AAA SIXTEENTH NOTE
1034CZE ŠESTNÁCTINA
1034DAN SEKSTENDELSNODE
1034DUT ZESTIENDE NOOT
1034FRE DOUBLE CROCHE
1034GER SECHZEHNTEL NOTE
1034HUN TIZENHATODKÓTA
1034ITA SEMICROMA
1034POL SZESNASTKA
1034POR SEMICOLCHEIA
1034RUS DVUVIAZNAIA NOTA
1034SPA SEMICORCHEA
1034SWE SEXTONDELS NOT

1035AAA SKETCH
1035CZE SKIZZA, NÁČRT
1035DAN SKITSE
1035DUT SCHETS
1035FRE ESQUISSE, EBAUCHE
1035GER SKIZZE, ENTWURF
1035HUN VÁZLAT
1035ITA SCHIZZO
1035POL SZKIC
1035POR ESBÔCO
1035RUS ESKIZ
1035SPA BOSQUEJO
1035SWE SKISS

1036AAA SKILL
1036CZE ZRUČNOST
1036DAN DYGTIGHED
1036DUT VAARDIGHEID
1036FRE HABILETÉ
1036GER FERTIGHEIT
1036HUN ÜGYESSEG
1036ITA MAESTRIA, ABILITÀ
1036POL ZRECZNOSĆ
1036POR HABILIDADE
1036RUS LOVKOST'
1036SPA HABILIDAD, TALENTO
1036SWE SLICKLIGHET

1037AAA SKIN
1037CZE KŮŽE
1037DAN SKIND
1037DUT VEL
1037FRE PEAU
1037GER FELL
1037HUN BÖR
1037ITA PELLE
1037POL SKÓRA
1037POR PELE
1037RUS KOZHA
1037SPA PIEL
1037SWE SKINN

1038AAA SKIP
1038CZE SKOK
1038DAN SPRING, SJIPPE
1038DUT SPRING, SPRONGETJE
1038FRE SAUT
1038GER SPRUNG, HUPF
1038HUN UGRÁS
1038ITA SALTO
1038POL SKOK
1038POR SALTO
1038RUS SKIP, SKACHOK
1038SPA SALTO
1038SWE SKUTT

1039AAA SKIP, TO
1039CZE SKÁKATI
1039DAN SPRINGE, SJIPPE
1039DUT SPRINGEN
1039FRE SAUTER, SAUTILLER
1039GER SPRINGEN, HÜPFEN
1039HUN UGRANI
1039ITA SALTARE
1039POL SKAKAĆ
1039POR SALTAR
1039RUS SKAKAT'
1039SPA SALTAR
1039SWE SPRINGA, SKUTTA

1040AAA SLACKEN, TO
1040CZE ZPOMALOVATI
1040DAN SLAPPE
1040DUT VERSLAPPEN
1040FRE RALENTIR
1040GER NACHLASSEN, VERZÖGERN
1040HUN LASSITNI
1040ITA RALENTARE
1040POL ZWALNIAĆ
1040POR AFROIXAR, AFROUXAR
1040RUS OSLABLIAT'
1040SPA AFLOJAR, RETRASAR
1040SWE SLAPPNA

Small, little   133

1041AAA SLEIGHBELL(S)   1045AAA SLOW (DOWN), TO
1041CZE ROLNIČKA   1045CZE ZPOMALOVATI, ZPOMALITI
1041DAN BJAELDE   1045DAN FORHALE
1041DUT KLOKJES   1045DUT LANGZAMER WORDEND
1041FRE GRELOT, SONNETTE   1045FRE RETARDER, RALENTIR
1041GER SCHLITTENGLOCKE   1045GER LANGSAMMER WERDEN
1041HUN CSENGETYŰ   1045HUN LASSITNI
1041ITA SONAGLIO   1045ITA RAL(L)ENTARE
1041POL DZWONECZEK U SAŃ   1045POL ZWALNIAĆ
1041POR CASCABEL   1045POR RETARDAR
1041RUS BUBENCHIK   1045RUS ZADERZHIVAT'
1041SPA CASCABEL, SONAJERO   1045SPA RETRASAR, RETARDAR
1041SWE BJÄLLRA   1045SWE UPPEHALLA

1042AAA SLIDE   1046AAA SLUR
1042CZE KLOUZAVÉ   1046CZE VÁZÁNÍ, LIGATURA
1042DAN GLIDEN   1046DAN LEGATOSPIL
1042DUT GLIJDEN, PORTAMENTO   1046DUT KOPPELBOOG
1042FRE GLISSEMENT   1046FRE LIGATURE
1042GER PORTAMENTO   1046GER BINDEZEICHEN
1042HUN CSÚSZÁS   1046HUN KÖTJEL
1042ITA GLISSANDO, PORTAMENTO   1046ITA LEGATURA
1042POL SUWAK   1046POL ŚPIEW
1042POR PORTAMENTO   1046POR LIGADURA
1042RUS SKOL'ZHENIE, PORTAMENTO   1046RUS LIGATURA
1042SPA DESLIZ, PORTAMENTO   1046SPA LIGADO
1042SWE GLID   1046SWE LEGATO

1043AAA SLIDE(INSTRUMENT)   1047AAA SLUR, TO.
1043CZE ZAVÍRACÍ VENTIL   1047CZE VÁZATI
1043DAN GLIDER   1047DAN SPILLE LEGATO
1043DUT SCHUIF   1047DUT SLEPPEN, BINDEN
1043FRE COULISSE   1047FRE LIER
1043GER VENTIL   1047GER TÖNE BINDEN, VERBINDEN
1043HUN CSÚSZÓ ALKATRÉSZ   1047HUN KÖTNI
1043ITA TIRO   1047ITA LEGARE
1043POL OZDOBNIK   1047POL ŚPIEWAĆ, GRAĆ
1043POR VARA   1047POR MODULAR
1043RUS KLAPAN   1047RUS IGRAT' LEGATO
1043SPA VARA   1047SPA LIGAR LAS NOTAS
1043SWE SLIDVENTIL   1047SWE SPELA LEGATO

1044AAA SLOW   1048AAA SMALL, LITTLE
1044CZE POMALÝ   1048CZE MALÝ
1044DAN LANGSOMT   1048DAN LILLE
1044DUT LANGZAAM   1048DUT KLEIN
1044FRE LENT   1048FRE PETITE
1044GER LANGSAM   1048GER KLEINE
1044HUN LASSÚ   1048HUN APRÓ
1044ITA LENTO, ADAGIO   1048ITA PICCOLA
1044POL DOSŁOWNIE   1048POL MAŁY
1044POR LENTO   1048POR PEQUENA
1044RUS MEDLENNYY   1048RUS MALEN'KIY
1044SPA LENTO   1048SPA PEQUEÑA
1044SWE LÅNGSAMT   1048SWE LITEN

1049AAA SMOOTH		1053AAA SOFT	
1049CZE HLADKÝ		1053CZE MĚKKÝ	
1049DAN GLAT		1053DAN SVAGT	
1049DUT EENVOUDIG		1053DUT ZACHT	
1049FRE LISSE, EN FLATTANT		1053FRE ÉTEINT, PIANO	
1049GER GLATT, SCHMEICHELND		1053GER SANFT, PIANO, LEISE	
1049HUN SIMÁN		1053HUN LÁGY	
1049ITA LISCIO		1053ITA PIANO, MOLLE	
1049POL GŁADKI		1053POL MIĘKKI	
1049POR LISO		1053POR PIANO	
1049RUS GLADKIĬ		1053RUS MAGKIĬ	
1049SPA LISONJEANDO		1053SPA PIANO, EXTINTO	
1049SWE GLATT		1053SWE SVAGT	
1050AAA SMOTHER, TO		1054AAA SOLEMN	
1050CZE DUSITI		1054CZE SLAVNOSTNÍ	
1050DAN DAEMPE		1054DAN HØJTIDELIG	
1050DUT DAMP		1054DUT PLECHTIG	
1050FRE ÉTOUFFER		1054FRE SOLONNEL	
1050GER DÄMPFEN		1054GER FEIERLICH	
1050HUN ELFOJTANI		1054HUN ÜNNEPÉLYES	
1050ITA SOFFOCARE		1054ITA SOLENNE	
1050POL ZADUSIĆ		1054POL UROCZYŚCIE	
1050POR SUFOCAR		1054POR SOLENE	
1050RUS DUSHIT'		1054RUS TORZHESTVENNYĬ	
1050SPA SOFOCAR		1054SPA SOLEMNE	
1050SWE DÄMPA		1054SWE HÖGTIDLIG	
1051AAA SO		1055AAA SOL-FA, TO	
1051CZE TAK		1055CZE SOLFEDŽOVATI	
1051DAN SÅ		1055DAN SYNGE TRAEFFEØVELSER	
1051DUT ZEER, ZO		1055DUT ZINGEN SOLFEGGIO	
1051FRE AINSI		1055FRE SOLFIER	
1051GER SO		1055GER SOLFEGGIEREN	
1051HUN ÍGY		1055HUN SZOLMIZÁLNI	
1051ITA TANTO, COSÌ		1055ITA SOLFEGGIARE	
1051POL TYLE, TAK		1055POL SOLFEMIZOWAĆ	
1051POR ASSIM		1055POR SOLFEJAR	
1051RUS TAK		1055RUS PET' SOL'FEDZHIO	
1051SPA ASÍ		1055SPA SOLFEAR	
1051SWE SÅ		1055SWE SJUNGA	
1052AAA SOB, TO		1056AAA SOLFEGE	
1052CZE VZLYKATI		1056CZE SOLFEDŽE	
1052DAN HULKE		1056DAN TRAEFFEØVELSER	
1052DUT ZUCHTEN		1056DUT SOLFEGGIO	
1052FRE SANGLOTER		1056FRE SOLFÈGE	
1052GER SCHLUCHZEN		1056GER GESANGÜBUNG	
1052HUN ZOKOGNI		1056HUN SZOLFÉZS	
1052ITA SINGHIOZZARE		1056ITA SOLFEGGIO	
1052POL SZLOCHAĆ, ŁKAĆ		1056POL SOLFEŻ	
1052POR SOLUÇAR		1056POR SOLFEO	
1052RUS RYDAT'		1056RUS SOL'FEDZHIO	
1052SPA SOLLOZAR		1056SPA SOLFEO	
1052SWE SNYFTA		1056SWE TONTRÄFFNINGSÖVNING	

1057AAA SOLMISATION
1057CZE SOLMISACE
1057DAN TRAEFFEØVELSE
1057DUT SOLMISATIE
1057FRE SOLMISATION
1057GER SOLMISATION
1057HUN SZOLMIZÁS
1057ITA SOLMISAZIONE
1057POL SOLMIZACJA
1057POR SOLMIZAÇÃO
1057RUS SOLMIZATSIIA
1057SPA SOLFA
1057SWE HÖGTIDLIGHÅLANDE

1058AAA SOMBER
1058CZE TEMNÝ
1058DAN DYSTER, MØRK
1058DUT SOMBER
1058FRE SOMBRE, ÉPAIS
1058GER DÜSTER
1058HUN KOMOR
1058ITA FOSCO, OSCURO
1058POL CIEMNY
1058POR SOMBRIO
1058RUS TĚMNYĬ
1058SPA SOMBRIO
1058SWE DYSTER, MÖRK

1059AAA SOME
1059CZE NĚKTERÝ, NĚJAKÝ
1059DAN NOGEN
1059DUT ENIGE
1059FRE QUELQUE
1059GER ETWAS
1059HUN NÉMELY
1059ITA QUALCHE
1059POL JAKIŚ
1059POR ALGUM
1059RUS NEKIĬ
1059SPA ALGO, ALGUNO
1059SWE NÅGON

1060AAA SOMEWHAT
1060CZE DOSTI
1060DAN NOGET
1060DUT IETWAT
1060FRE UN PEU, QUELQUE PEU
1060GER ETWAS
1060HUN NÉMILEG
1060ITA UN POCO, ALQUANTO
1060POL TROCKĘ, NIECO
1060POR UM TANTO, UM POUCO
1060RUS NEMNOGO
1060SPA UN POCO, ALGO
1060SWE NÅGOT

1061AAA SONATA
1061CZE SONÁTA
1061DAN SONATE
1061DUT SONATE
1061FRE SONATE
1061GER SONATE
1061HUN SZONÁTA
1061ITA SONATA
1061POL SONATA
1061POR SONATA
1061RUS SONATA
1061SPA SONATA
1061SWE SONAT

1062AAA SONG
1062CZE SPĚV, PÍSEŇ
1062DAN SANG
1062DUT GESANG, ZANG, LIED
1062FRE CHANSON
1062GER GESANG, LIED
1062HUN ÉNEK, DAL
1062ITA CANZONE, CANTO
1062POL PIEŚŃ, ŚPEIW
1062POR CANÇÃO
1062RUS PESNIA
1062SPA CANCIÓN
1062SWE SÅNG

1063AAA SONOROUS
1063CZE ZVUČNÝ
1063DAN KLANGFULD
1063DUT KLANKVOL
1063FRE SONORE
1063GER KLANGVOLL
1063HUN HANGOS
1063ITA SONORO
1063POL DŹWIĘCZNIE
1063POR SONORO
1063RUS ZVUCHNYĬ
1063SPA SONORO
1063SWE KLANGFULL

1064AAA SOON
1064CZE RYCHLE
1064DAN SNART
1064DUT SNEL
1064FRE TÔT
1064GER BALD
1064HUN NEMSOKÁRA
1064ITA TOSTO, PRESTO
1064POL PRĘDKO
1064POR LOGO
1064RUS SKORO
1064SPA PRONTO
1064SWE SNART

1065AAA SORROW
1065CZE SMUTEK, ŻAL
1065DAN SORGMODIGHED
1065DUT DROEFHEID
1065FRE TRISTESSE
1065GER SORGE
1065HUN GOND
1065ITA DOLORE
1065POL SMUTEK, BOLEŚNIE
1065POR TRISTEZA
1065RUS PECHAL', GORE
1065SPA TRISTEZA, DOLOR
1065SWE SORG

1066AAA SOUL
1066CZE DUŠE, DUCH
1066DAN SJAEL
1066DUT ZIEL
1066ERE ÂME
1066GER SEELE
1066HUN LELEK
1066ITA ANIMA, SPIRITO
1066POL DUSZA
1066POR ALMA
1066RUS DUSHA
1066SPA ALMA
1066SWE SJÄL

1067AAA SOUND
1067CZE SVUK
1067DAN LYD, KLANG
1067DUT GELUID, TOON
1067FRE SON
1067GER TON, KLANG
1067HUN HANG
1067ITA S(U)ONO
1067POL DŹWIĘK
1067POR SONIDO, SAO
1067RUS ZVUK
1067SPA SON
1067SWE LJUD, KLANG, SON(D)

1068AAA SOUND BOARD
1068CZE ŘEHTAČKA VELIKONOČNÍ
1068DAN RESONANSBUND
1068DUT KLANKBODEN, ZANGBODEM
1068FRE TABLE, ABAT-VOIX
1068GER RESONANZBODEN
1068HUN HANGFENÉK
1068ITA TAVOLA, TAVOLETTA
1068POL PŁYTA RESONANSOWA
1068POR TAMPA, TAMPO
1068RUS REZONANSAÍA DOSKA
1068SPA CAJA DE RESONANCIA
1068SWE RESONNSBORD, LJUDSKÄRM

1069AAA SOUND HOLE(S)
1069CZE SLUCH
1069DAN LYDHUL
1069DUT KLANKGAT, GALMGAT
1069FRE ORIELLE, OUÏE
1069GER SCHALLOCK
1069HUN F-LYUKAK, HANGRÉS
1069ITS ORECCHIO, ROSA
1069POL OTWÓR
1069POR OUVIDO, ESPELHO
1069RUS IMET SLUX
1069SPA OIDO, ROSA
1069SWE LJUDHÅL

1070AAA SOUND POST
1070CZE DESKA
1070DAN STEMMEPIND
1070DUT STAPEL
1070FRE TABLE, L·AME
1070GER STIMMPFOSTEN
1070HUN LELEK
1070ITA TAVOLA
1070POL PODPÓRKA REZONANSOWA
1070POR ALMA
1070RUS DÉKA
1070SPA ALMA
1070SWE STÄMME

1071AAA SOUND, TO
1071CZE ZVUČETI
1071DAN SONDERE, LYDE
1071DUT SONDEREN
1071FRE SONNER
1071GER TÖNEN, ERTÖNEN
1071HUN HANGOZTATNI
1071ITA SONDARE, SUONARE
1071POL DŹWIĘCZEĆ
1071POR SONDAR
1071RUS ZVUCHAT' ZVONIT'
1071SPA SONAR, TOCAR
1071SWE SONDERA, LÅTA LJUDA

1072AAA SPACE
1072CZE MEZERA
1072DAN MELLEMRUM
1072DUT TUSSENRUIMTE
1072FRE ESPACE
1072GER ZWISCHENRAUM, RAUM
1072HUN VONALKÖZ
1072ITA SPAZIO
1072POL SPACJA
1072POR ESPAÇO
1072RUS RASSTOÍANIE
1072SPA ESPACIO
1072SWE MELLENRUM

1073AAA SPAN
1073CZE VZDÁLENOST
1073DAN SPAND
1073DUT SPAN
1073FRE ÉCART
1073GER SPANNE, GESPANN
1073HUN ARASZ
1073ITA SPANNA
1073POL PRZĘSŁO, PRZECIĄG
1073POR PALMO
1073RUS PIAD'
1073SPA PALMO
1073SWE SPANN

1074AAA SPARKLING
1074CZE JISKŘIVÝ
1074DAN GNISTRENDE
1074DUT SCHITTEREND
1074FRE ÉTINCELLEMENT
1074GER GLÄNZEND
1074HUN FÉNYES
1074ITA SCINTILLANTE
1074POL ISKRZĄCY
1074POR CINTILANTE
1074RUS SVERKANIE
1074SPA CENTELLEANTE
1074SWE GLÄNSANDE

1075AAA SPEECH
1075CZE MLUVA, ŘEV
1075DAN TALE(EVNE)
1075DUT SPRAAK
1075FRE PAROLE
1075GER SPRACHE
1075HUN SESZÉD
1075ITA PAROLA
1075POL MOWA
1075POR PALAVRA
1075RUS RECH', SLOVO
1075SPA PALABRA
1075SWE TAL

1076AAA SPECIES
1076CZE DRUH
1076DAN ART
1076DUT SPECIE
1076FRE ESPÈCE
1076GER ART
1076HUN FAJ, NEM
1076ITA SPECIE
1076POL RODZAJ
1076POR ESPÉCIE
1076RUS VID, SORT
1076SPA ESPÉCIE
1076SWE ART

1077AAA SPEED
1077CZE RYCHLOST
1077DAN HURTIGHED, HASTIGHED
1077DUT SNELHEID, SPOED
1077FRE CÉLÉRITÉ, VÉLOCITÉ
1077GER SCHNELLIGHEIT, EILE
1077HUN SIETSÉG, GYORSASÁG
1077ITA FRETTA, CELERITÀ
1077POL SZYBKOŚĆ
1077POR PRESA
1077RUS SKOROST'
1077SPA CELERIDAD, PRISA
1077SWE HASTIGHED

1078AAA SPINET
1078CZE SPINET
1078DAN SPINET
1078DUT SPINET
1078FRE ÉPINETTE
1078GER SPINETT
1078HUN ZONGORA NEME
1078ITA SPINETTA
1078POL SZPINET
1078POR ESPINETA
1078RUS SPINET
1078SPA ESPINETA
1078SWE SPINETT

1079AAA SPIRIT
1079CZE DUCH
1079DAN AAND
1079DUT ZIEL
1079FRE ESPRIT, ANIMÉ
1079GER GEIST
1079HUN SZELLEM
1079ITA SPIRITO, ANIMA
1079POL DOWCIPNIE
1079POR ESPÍRITO
1079RUS DUKH
1079SPA ESPÍRITU
1079SWE ANDE

1080AAA SPRIGHTLY
1080CZE PROBUDILÝ, ŽIVÝ
1080DAN LIVLIG, VAAGEN
1080DUT VURIG, LEVENDIG
1080FRE ÉVEILLÉ
1080GER LEBHAFT, MUNTER
1080HUN ÉLÉNK
1080ITA DESTO, SVEGLIANDO
1080POL ŻYWY
1080POR ESPERTO
1080RUS ZHIVOY
1080SPA DESPIERTO
1080SWE LIVLIG

1081AAA STAFF
1081CZE OSNOVA LINKOVÁ
1081DAN NODESYSTEM, PENTAGRAM
1081DUT NOTENBALK
1081FRE PORTÉE
1081GER LINIENSYSTEM
1081HUN VONALRENDSZER
1081ITA RIGO, PENTAGRAMMA
1081POL PENTAGRAM
1081POR PENTAGRAMA
1081RUS NOTAIA LINEÏKA
1081SPA PENTAGRAMA, PAUTADA
1081SWE STAV

1082AAA STAGE
1082CZE SNIŽEC, JEVIŠTÉ
1082DAN SCENE(GULV)
1082DUT TAFEREEL
1082FRE SCÈNE
1082GER BÜHNE
1082HUN SZÍNPAD
1082ITA SCENA, PALCO(SCENICO)
1082POL SCENA, STAGIONE
1082POR CENA
1082RUS STZENA
1082SPA ESCENA, PALCO, TABLADO
1082SWE SCEN

1083AAA STANZA
1083CZE STROFA
1083DAN STANZA
1083DUT STANZA
1083FRE STANCE
1083GER STANZE
1083HUN STANZA
1083ITA STANZA
1083POL STROFA
1083POR ESTÂNCIA
1083RUS STANS, STROFA
1083SPA ESTANCIA
1083SWE STANS

1084AAA STATELY
1084CZE OKÁZALY
1084DAN PRAGTFULDT
1084DUT STATIG
1084FRE ECLATANT
1084GER STATIÖS, PRACHTVOLL
1084HUN DISZES
1084ITA FASTOSO
1084POL WSPANIAŁY
1084POR SOPERBO, ALTIVO
1084RUS GROMKIÏ
1084SPA FASTUOSO
1084SWE STÅTLIG, PRAKFULL

1085AAA STEADY
1085CZE STÁLÝ
1085DAN STADIG
1085DUT BESTENDIG
1085FRE STABLE
1085GER FEST, STETIG
1085HUN SZILARD
1085ITA STABILE, FERMO
1085POL STAŁY
1085POR FIRME
1085RUS STABIL'NYÏ
1085SPA ESTABLE, FIRME
1085SWE STADIG

1086AAA STEEL
1086CZE OCEL
1086DAN STÅL
1086DUT STAAL
1086FRE ACIER
1086GER STAHL
1086HUN ACZÉL
1086ITA ACCIAIO
1086POL STAL
1086POR AÇO
1086RUS STAL'
1086SPA ACERO
1086SWE STÅL

1087AAA STEP
1087CZE KROK
1087DAN GRAD
1087DUT GRAAD, TOONTRAP
1087FRE PAS, DEGRÉ
1087GER SCHRITT, GRAD, STUFE
1087HUN HANGFOK
1087ITA GRADO, PASSO
1087POL KROK
1087POR DEGRAU, PASSO
1087RUS GRADUS, SHAG
1087SPA GRADO, PASO
1087SWE STEG

1088AAA STERN
1088CZE PŘÍSNÝ
1088DAN STRENG
1088DUT STRENG
1088FRE SÉVÈRE
1088GER STRENG
1088HUN KOMOLY
1088ITA SEVERO
1088POL SUROWIE
1088POR SEVERO
1088RUS STROGIÏ
1088SPA SEVERO
1088SWE STRÄNG

1089AAA STIFF
1089CZE TUHÝ, ZTUHLÝ
1089DAN STIV
1089DUT STIJF
1089FRE RAIDE, PINCÉ
1089GER STEIF, HÄRT
1089HUN MEREV
1089ITA RIGIDO, STECCHITO
1089POL SZTYWNY
1089POR RÍGIDO, TÊSO
1089RUS ZHËSTKIY
1089SPA RÍGIDO, TIESO
1089SWE STYV

1090AAA STIFLE, TO
1090CZE DUSITI
1090DAN KVAELE
1090DUT VERSTIKKEN
1090FRE ÉTOUFFER
1090GER DÄMPFEN, ERSTICKEN
1090HUN ELFOJTANI
1090ITA SOFFOCARE
1090POL DUSIĆ
1090POR SUFOCAR, ABAFAR
1090RUS DUSHIT)
1090SPA SOFOCAR
1090SWE KVÄVA

1091AAA STOP
1091CZE FERMÁTA, KORUNA
1091DAN PAUSE
1091DUT SLUITTEKEN
1091FRE COURONNE, PAUSE
1091GER FERMATE, HALT
1091HUN MEGÁLLÁS
1091ITA FERMATA
1091POL KLAPKA
1091POR SUSTIMENTO
1091RUS KORONA
1091SPA FERMATA
1091SWE FERMAT

1092AAA STORMY
1092CZE BOUŘNÝ
1092DAN STORMENDE
1092DUT ONSTUIMIG
1092FRE TEMPÉTUEUX
1092GER STÜRMISCH
1092HUN VIHAROS
1092ITA TEMPESTOSO
1092POL BURZOWY
1092POR TEMPESTUOSO
1092RUS BURNYY
1092SPA TEMPESTUOSO
1092SWE STORMANDE

1093AAA STRAIN
1093CZE ÚSILI
1093DAN ANSTRENGELSE
1093DUT SPANNING
1093FRE EFFORT
1093GER ANSTRENGUNG
1093HUN DALLAM
1093ITA SFORZO
1093POL NAPIĘCIE
1093POR ESFÔRÇO
1093RUS USILIE
1093SPA ESFUERZO
1093SWE SPÄNNING, STRÄKNING

1094AAA STRICT
1094CZE TĚSNÝ, PŘESNÝ
1094DAN STRENG
1094DUT STRENG
1094FRE ÉTRIOT, STRICT
1094GER STRENG
1094HUN SZIGORÚ
1094ITA STRETTO, ESATTO
1094POL ŚCISŁY
1094POR ESTRITO
1094RUS TESNYY
1094SPA ESTRICTO
1094SWE STRÄNG

1095AAA STRING
1095CZE STRUNA
1095DAN STRENG
1095DUT SNAAR
1095FRE CORDE
1095GER SAITE
1095HUN HÚR
1095ITA CORDA
1095POL STRUNA
1095POR CORDA
1095RUS STRUNA
1095SPA CUERDA
1095SWE STRÄNG

1096AAA STRING, TO
1095CZE STRUNAMI
1096DAN PAASAETTE STRENGE
1096DUT BESNAREN
1096FRE ACCORDER
1096GER BESAITEN
1096HUN HÚRÓZNI
1096ITA FORNIRE DI CORDE A
1096POL STROIĆ
1096POR ENCORDOAR
1096RUS NATIAGIVAT' STRUNY NA
1096SPA ENCORDAR
1096SWE STRÄNGA

1097AAA STROKE	1101AAA STUDY
1097CZE ÚHOZ, RÁZ	1101CZE ETÝDA, STUDIUM
1097DAN SLAG	1101DAN STUDERING, STUDIUM
1097DUT SLAG	1101DUT ETUDE, STUDIE(STUK)
1097FRE COUP	1101FRE ÉTUDE
1097GER SCHLAG, STOSS	1101GER STUDIE, ETÜDE
1097HUN SCAPÁS	1101HUN GYAKORLAT
1097ITA COLPO	1101ITA STUDIO
1097POL UDERZENIE	1101POL ETIUDA, STUDIUM
1097POR GOLPE, BATIDO	1101POR ESTUDO
1097RUS UDAR	1101RUS ETIÚD, IZUCHENIE
1097SPA GOLPE, BATIDO	1101SPA ESTUDIO
1097SWE SLAG	1101SWE STUDIUM
1098AAA STRONG	1102AAA STUDY, TO
1098CZE SILNÉ	1102CZE STUDOVATI
1098DAN STAERK, KRAFTIG	1102DAN STUDERE
1098DUT STERK	1102DUT STUDEREN
1098FRE FORTE(MENT)	1102FRE ÉTUDIER
1098GER STARK, KRÄFTIG	1102GER STUDIEREN
1098HUN ERŐS	1102HUN TANULNI
1098ITA FORTE	1102ITA STUDIARE
1098POL SILNIE	1102POL STUDIOWAĆ
1098POR FORTE	1102POR ESTUDAR
1098RUS SIL'NYǏ	1102RUS IZUCHAT'
1098SPA FUERTE	1102SPA ESTUDIAR
1098SWE STARK, KRAFTIG	1102SWE STUDERA
1099AAA STROPHE	1103AAA STYLE
1099CZE STROFA, SLOKA	1103CZE SLOH
1099DAN STROFE	1103DAN STIL
1099DUT STROFE	1103DUT STIJL
1099FRE STROPHE	1103FRE STYLE
1099GER STROPHE	1103GER STIL
1099HUN VERSSZAK	1103HUN STÍLUS
1099ITA STROFA	1103ITA STILE
1099POL STROFA	1103POL STYL
1099POR ESTROFE	1103POR ESTILO
1099RUS STROFA	1103RUS STIL'
1099SPA ESTROFA	1103SPA ESTILO
1099SWE STROF	1103SWE STIL
1100AAA STRUCTURE	1104AAA SUB-
1100CZE STRUKTURA	1104CZE SUB-, POD-
1100DAN BYGNINGSMADE	1104DAN SUB-, UNDER-
1100DUT STRUCTUUR	1104DUT ONDER-, SUB-
1100FRE STRUCTURE	1104FRE SUB-
1100GER BAU	1104GER UNTER-
1100HUN ÉPÍTÉS	1104HUN ALÁ-
1100ITA STRUTTURA	1104ITA SOTTO-, SUB-
1100POL STRUKTURA	1104POL SUB-, POD-
1100POR ESTRUTURA	1104POR SUB-
1100RUS STRUKTURA	1104RUS SUB-, POD-
1100SPA ESTRUCTURA	1104SPA SUB-
1100SWE BYG(G)NAD	1104SWE UNDER-

1105AAA SUBJECT
1105CZE NÁMĚT, SUBJEKT
1105DAN TEMA, SUBJEKT
1105DUT THEMA(INZET)
1105FRE SUJET
1105GER THEIL, THEMA, SUBJEKT
1105HUN TÉMA
1105ITA SOGGETTO, PROPOSTA
1105POL TEMAT
1105POR SÚDITO, TEMA
1105RUS TEMA, SIUZHET
1105SPA SUJETO, TEMA
1105SWE TEMA

1106AAA SUBLIME
1106CZE VZNEŠENÝ
1106DAN SUBLIM
1106DUT VERHEVEN
1106FRE SUBLIME
1106GER ERHABEN
1106HUN MAGASZTOS
1106ITA SUBLIME
1106POL WZNOISŁY
1106POR SUBLIME
1106RUS VOZVYSHENNYĬ
1106SPA SUBLIME
1106SWE SUBLIM

1107AAA SUBSEQUENT
1107CZE NÁSLEDUJÍCÍ
1107DAN FØLGENDE, PAAFØLGENDE
1107DUT VOLGEND
1107FRE SUBSÉQUENT
1107GER FOLGEND
1107HUN KÖVETKEZŐ
1107ITA SUSSEGUENTE
1107POL NASTĘPNY
1107POR SUBSEQÜENTE
1107RUS POSLEDUIUSHCHIĬ
1107SPA SUBSECUENTE
1107SWE FÖLJANDE

1108AAA SUDDEN
1108CZE NÁHLÝ, IHNED
1108DAN PLUDSELIG
1108DUT PLOTSELING
1108FRE SUBIT, DE SUITE
1108GER PLÖTZLICH, SOGLEICH
1108HUN HIRTELEN
1108ITA SUBITO
1108POL NAGLE
1108POR SÚBITO
1108RUS NAGLO
1108SPA SÚBITO
1108SWE PLÖTSLIG

1109AAA SUITE
1109CZE SUITA, PARTIE
1109DAN SUITE
1109DUT SUITE
1109FRE SUITE
1109GER SUITE, PARTITA
1109HUN SZVIT
1109ITA PARTITA, CASSATIO
1109POL SUITA
1109POR SUITE
1109RUS SIUITA
1109SPA SUITE, SÉGUITO
1109SWE SVIT

1110AAA SUPER-
1110CZE NAD-, PŘE-
1110DAN SUPER-, OVER-
1110DUT SUPER-, OVER-
1110FRE SUR-, SUS-
1110GER SUPER-, OBER-
1110HUN LEG-, FEL-
1110ITA SOVRA-
1110POL NAD-
1110POR SUPER-
1110RUS SUPER-, PERE-
1110SPA SUPER-
1110SWE ÖVER-

1111AAA SUPERIOR
1111CZE HOŘEJŠÍ, VYŠŠÍ
1111DAN HØJERE
1111DUT SUPERIEUR
1111FRE SUPÉRIEUR
1111GER HÖHER
1111HUN FELSŐ
1111ITA SUPERIORE
1111POL WYŻSZY
1111POR SUPERIOR
1111RUS VYSSHIĬ
1111SPA SUPERIOR
1111SWE HÖRARE

1112AAA SUPPLEMENT
1112CZE DOPLNEK, DODATEK
1112DAN SUPPLEMENT
1112DUT SUPPLEMENT, AANVULLING
1112FRE SUPPLÉMENT
1112GER ERGÄNZUNG
1112HUN KIEGÉSZÍTÉS
1112ITA SUPPLEMENTO
1112POL DODATEK
1112POR SUPLEMENTO
1112RUS DOPOLNENIE
1112SPA SUPLEMENTO
1112SWE SUPPLEMENT

1113AAA	SUPPLICATE, TO	1117AAA	SWEET
1113CZE	PROSITI	1117CZE	SLADKÝ
1113DAN	BEDE	1117DAN	SØD
1113DUT	SMEKEN	1117DUT	LIEFLIJK, ZOET
1113FRE	SUPPLIER	1117FRE	DOUX, MANSUET, SUAVE
1113GER	BITTEN	1117GER	SÜSS, SANFT, LIEBLICH
1113HUN	KÖNYÖRÖGNI	1117HUN	ÉDES
1113ITA	SUPPLICARE	1117ITA	DOLCE, MANSUETO
1113POL	PROSIĆ	1117POL	SŁODKO
1113POR	SUPLICAR	1117POR	DOCE
1113RUS	PROSIT'	1117RUS	SLADKIĬ
1113SPA	SUPLICAR	1117SPA	DULCE, SUAVE
1113SWE	BEDJA	1117SWE	SÖT

1114AAA	SURPRISE	1118AAA	SYLLABLE
1114CZE	PŘEKRAPENÍ	1118CZE	SLABIKA
1114DAN	OVERRASKELSE	1118DAN	STAVELSE
1114DUT	VERRASSING	1118DUT	LETTERGREEP
1114FRE	SURPRISE	1118FRE	SYLLABE
1114GER	ÜBERRASCHUNG	1118GER	SILBE
1114HUN	MEGLEPÉS	1118HUN	SZÓTAG
1114ITA	SORPRESA	1118ITA	SILLABA
1114POL	ZASKOCZENIE	1118POL	SYLABA
1114POR	SURPRÊSA	1118POR	SÍLABA
1114RUS	SIŪRPRIZ	1118RUS	SLOG
1114SPA	SORPRESA	1118SPA	SÍLABA
1114SWE	ÖVERRASKNING	1118SWE	STAVELSE

1115AAA	SUSPENSION	1119AAA	SYMMETRICAL
1115CZE	ZARAŽENÍ	1119CAE	SOUMĚRNÝ
1115DAN	OPHAENGNING	1119DAN	SYMMETRISK
1115DUT	OPHANGING	1119DUT	SYMMETRISCH
1115FRE	SUSPENSION	1119FRE	SYMÉTRIQUE
1115GER	FORHALT	1119GER	EBENMÄSSIG, SYMMETRISCH
1115HUN	FELFÜGGESZTÉS	1119HUN	SZIMMETRÍKUS
1115ITA	SOSPENSIONE	1119ITA	SIMMETRICO
1115POL	ZAWIESZENIE	1119POL	SYMETRYCZNY
1115POR	SUSPENSÃO	1119POR	SIMÉTRICO
1115RUS	SUSPENZIIĀ	1119RUS	SIMMETRICHNYĬ
1115SPA	SUSPENSIÓN	1119SPA	SIMÉTRICO
1115SWE	UPPHÄNGNING	1119SWE	SYMMETRISK

1116AAA	SUSTAIN, TO	1120AAA	SYMPATHETIC
1116CZE	PODPÍRATI, ZDRŽOVATI	1120CZE	SYMPATICKÝ
1116DAN	HOLDE	1120DAN	SYMPATETISK
1116DUT	UDHOLDEN	1120DUT	SYMPATHIEK
1116FRE	SOUTENIR, FILAR	1120FRE	SYMPATHIQUE
1116GER	AUSSPINNEN, AUSHALTEN	1120GER	SYMPATHISCH
1116HUN	FELTARTÓZTATNI	1120HUN	REZONÁLÓ
1116ITA	SOSTENERE, FILARE	1120ITA	SIMPATICO
1116POL	WYTRZMYWAĆ	1120POL	SYMPATYCZNY
1116POR	SUSTENAR	1120POR	SIMPÁTICA
1116RUS	PODDERZHIVAT'	1120RUS	SIMPATICHNYĬ
1116SPA	SOSTENER, HILAR	1120SPA	SIMPÁTICA
1116SWE	UTHÅLLA	1120SWE	SYMPATETISK

1121AAA	SYMPHONY		1125AAA	TABLATURE
1121CZE	SYMFONIE		1125CZE	TABULATURA
1121DAN	SYMFONI		1125DAN	TABULATUR
1121DUT	SYMFONIE		1125DUT	TABULATUUR
1121FRE	SYMPHONIE		1125FRE	TABULATURE
1121GER	SYMPHONIE		1125GER	TABULATUR
1121HUN	SZIMFÓNIA		1125HUN	TABULATÚRA
1121ITA	SINFONIA		1125ITA	TABULATURA, TAVOLA
1121POL	SYMFONJA		1125POL	TABULATURA
1121POR	SINFONIA		1125POR	TABLATURA
1121RUS	SIMFONIIA		1125RUS	TABLATURA
1121SPA	SINFONÍA		1125SPA	ENTABLATURA
1121SWE	SYMFONI		1125SWE	TABULATUR
1122AAA	SYNCOPATE, TO		1126AAA	TAIL
1122CZE	SYNKOPOVATI		1126CZE	KÓDA, ZÁVĚR
1122DAN	DANNE SYNKOPER		1126DAN	SLUTTORE, CODA
1122DUT	SYNCOP(ER)EN		1126DUT	AANHANGSEL, NASPEL
1122FRE	SYNCOPER		1126FRE	CODA, QUEUE
1122GER	SYNKOPIEREN		1126GER	ANHANG, ZUSATZ, SCHWEIF
1122HUN	SINCOPÁLNI		1126HUN	FÜGGELEK
1122ITA	SINCOPARE		1126ITA	CODA
1122POL	SYNKOPOWAĆ		1126POL	KODA
1122POR	SINCOPAR		1126POR	CAUDA
1122RUS	ISPOLNIAT' SINKOPAMI		1126RUS	KODA
1122SPA	SINCOPAR		1126SPA	COLA, REMATE
1122SWE	SYNKOPERA		1126SWE	SLUTDEL
1123AAA	SYNCOPE		1127AAA	TAIL-PIECE
1123CZE	SYNKOPA		1127CZE	STRUNÍK
1123DAN	SYNKOPE		1127DAN	STRENGEHOLDER
1123DUT	SYNKOPE		1127DUT	STAARTSTUK
1123FRE	SYNCOPE		1127FRE	CORDIER, TIRE CORDE
1123GER	SYNKOPE		1127GER	SAITENHALTER, -FESSEL
1123HUN	HANGUGRATÁS		1127HUN	HÚRTARTÓ
1123ITA	SINCOPA		1127ITA	CORDIERA, CORDAIO
1123POL	SYNKOPA		1127POL	STRUNNIK
1123POR	SÍNCOPA		1127POR	ESTANDARTE
1123RUS	SINKOPA		1127RUS	PODGRIFOK
1123SPA	SÍNCOPA		1127SPA	CORDAL
1123SWE	SYNKOP		1127SWE	VINJETT
1124AAA	SYSTEM		1128AAA	TAMBOURINE
1124CZE	SYSTÉM, SOUSTAVA		1128CZE	TAMBURÍNA
1124DAN	SYSTEM		1128DAN	TAMBURIN
1124DUT	SYSTEEM		1128DUT	TAMBOERIJN, HANDTROMMEL
1124FRE	SYSTÈME		1128FRE	TAMBOURIN
1124GER	SYSTEM		1128GER	TAMBURIN
1124HUN	SYSTEMA		1128HUN	CSÖRGŐDOB
1124ITA	SISTEMA		1128ITA	TAMBURELLO, TAMBURINO
1124POR	SISTEMA		1128POL	TAMBURINO
1124POR	SISTEMA		1128POR	TAMBORIL, PANDEIRO
1124RUS	SISTEMA		1128RUS	TAMBURIN
1124SPA	SISTEMA		1128SPA	TAMBORIL, PANDERO
1124SWE	SYSTEM		1128SWE	TAMBURIN

1129AAA TARANTELLA
1129CZE TARANTELA
1129DAN TARANTEL
1129DUT TARANTELLA
1129FRE TARANTELLE
1129GER TARANTELLE
1129HUN TARANTELLA
1129ITA TARANTELLA
1129POL TARANTELLA
1129POR TARANTELA
1129RUS TARANTELLA
1129SPA TARANTELA
1129SWE TARANTELLA

1130AAA TASTE
1130CZE VKUS
1130DAN SMAG(SSANS)
1130DUT SMAAK
1130FRE GOÛT
1130GER GESCHMACK
1130HUN ÍZLÉS
1130ITA GUSTO
1130POL GUST
1130POR GÔSTO
1130RUS VKUS
1130SPA GUSTO
1130SWE SMAK(SINNE)

1131AAA TEARFUL
1131CZE PLAČTIVÉ
1131DAN BEGRAEDELIGT, TÅREFULD
1131DUT KLAGEND
1131FRE EN PLEURANT, PLAINTIF
1131GER WEINEND, TRÄNENREICH
1131HUN SIRÁNKOZVA
1131ITA PIANGENDO, LAGRIMOSO
1131POL PLACZLIWIE
1131POR CHOROSO
1131RUS PLACHUSHIY
1131SPA LLOROSO
1131SWE TÅRFYLLD

1132AAA TECHNIC
1132CZE TECHNIKA
1132DAN TEKNIK
1132DUT TECHNIEK
1132FRE TECHNIQUE
1132GER TECHNIK
1132HUN TECHNIKA
1132ITA TECNICA
1132POL TECHNIKA
1132POR TÉCHNICA
1132RUS TEKHNIKA
1132SPA TÉCHNICA
1132SWE TEKNIK

1133AAA TEMPERAMENT
1133CZE TEMPEROVÁNÍ
1133DAN TEMPERAMENT
1133DUT TEMPERAMENT
1133FRE TEMPÉRAMENT
1133GER TEMPERAMENT
1133HUN TEMPERAMENTUM
1133ITA TEMPERAMENTO
1133POL TEMPEROWANY
1133POR TEMPERAMENTO
1133RUS TEMPERAMENT
1133SPA TEMPERAMENTO
1133SWE TEMPERAMENT

1134AAA TEMPER, TO
1134CZE TEMPEROVATI
1134DAN TEMPERE
1134DUT TEMPEREN
1134FRE TEMPÉRER
1134GER TEMPERIEREN
1134HUN HANGOLNI
1134ITA TEMPERARE, MODULARE
1134POL TEMPEROWAĆ
1134POR TEMPERAR
1134RUS TEMPERIROVAT'
1134SPA TEMPERAR
1134SWE TEMPERA

1135AAA TEMPESTUOUS
1135CZE BOUŘNÝ
1135DAN STORMENDE
1135DUT ONSTUIMIG
1135FRE TEMPÉTUEUX, TONNERRE
1135GER STÜRMISCH
1135HUN VIHAROS
1135ITA TEMPESTOSO, PROCELLA
1135POL BURZLIWY
1135POR TEMPESTUOSO
1135RUS BURNYY
1135SPA TEMPESTUOSO
1135SWE STORMIG

1136AAA TEMPO
1136CZE TEMPO, ČAS, DOBA
1136DAN TEMPO, TAKT
1136DUT TIJDMAAT
1136FRE TEMPS
1136GER ZEITMASS
1136HUN IDŐ(MÉRTÉK)
1136ITA TEMPO
1136POL TEMPO, DOSŁOWNIE
1136POR TEMPO
1136RUS TEMP
1136SPA TIEMPO
1136SWE TID, TEMPO

1137AAA TEN
1137CZE DESET
1137DAN TI
1137DUT TIEN
1137FRE DIX
1137GER ZEHN
1137HUN TÍZ
1137ITA DIECI
1137POL DZIESIĘĆ
1137POR DEZ
1137RUS DESIAT'
1137SPA DIEZ
1137SWE TIO

1138AAA TENDER
1138CZE NĚŽNÝ, NAPNOUTI
1138DAN TENDER, ZART, FINT
1138DUT TE(D)ER
1138FRE TENDRE
1138GER ZÄRTLICH
1138HUN GYENGÉDEN
1138ITA TENERO
1138POL CZUŁY
1138POR TENRO
1138RUS NEZHNYÏ
1138SPA TIERNO
1138SWE ÖMTÅLIG

1139AAA TENOR
1139CZE TENOR
1139DAN TENOR
1139DUT TENOR
1139FRE TÉNOR
1139GER TENOR
1139HUN TENOR
1139ITA TENORE
1139POL TENOR
1139POR TENOR
1139RUS TENOR
1139SPA TENOR
1139SWE TENOR

1140AAA TENSION
1140CZE NAPĚTÍ
1140DAN SPAENDING
1140DUT SPANNING
1140FRE TENSION
1140GER SPANNUNG
1140HUN FESZÜLTÉG
1140ITA TENSIONE
1140POL NAPIĘCIE
1140POR TENÇÃO
1140RUS NAPRIAZHENIE
1140SPA TENSIÓN
1140SWE SPÄNNING

1141AAA TERNARY
1141CZE POTROJNÝ
1141DAN TRESTOFFET, TREDELT
1141DUT DREITALLIG
1141FRE TERNAIRE
1141GER TERNÄR
1141HUN HÁRMAS
1141ITA TERNARIO
1141POL POTRÓJNY
1141POR TERNÁRIO
1141RUS TROÏNOÏ
1141SPA TERNARIO
1141SWE TREFALDIG

1142AAA TERRIFY, TO
1142CZE PODĚSITI
1142DAN FORFAERDE
1142DUT VERSCHRIKKEN
1142FRE TERRIFIER
1142GER ERSCHRECKEN
1142HUN MEGRETTENTENI
1142ITA ATTERRIRE, SPAVENTARE
1142POL PRZERAŹAĆ
1142POR ATERRAR, TERRIFICAR
1142RUS UZHASAT'
1142SPA ATERRAR
1142SWE FÖRSKRÄCKA

1143AAA TERTIAN
1143CZE TERCIE
1143DAN ANDENDAGSFEBER
1143DUT TERTIAAN
1143FRE TIERCE
1143GER TERTIÄR
1143HUN HARMADNAPI
1143ITA TERZANA
1143POL TERCJANA
1143POR TERÇÃO
1143RUS TERTSIÏA
1143SPA TERCIANO
1143SWE ANNANDAGS

1144AAA TETRA-
1144CZE TETRA-, ČTYR-
1144DAN TETRA-
1144DUT VIER-
1144FRE TÉTRA-
1144GER VIER-, TETRA-
1144HUN NEGY-
1144ITA TETRA-
1144POL CZTERO-
1144POR TETRA-
1144RUS TETRA-, CHETYRËKH
1144SPA TETRA-
1144SWE FYRTA-

1145AAA	TEXT	1149AAA	THEME
1145CZE	TEXT	1149CZE	THEMA
1145DAN	TEKST	1149DAN	TEMA
1145DUT	TEKST	1149DUT	THEMA
1145FRE	TEXTE	1149FRE	THÈME
1145GER	TEXT	1149GER	THEMA
1145HUN	SZÖVEG	1149HUN	TÓSZÓ
1145ITA	TESTO	1149ITA	TEMA
1145POL	TEKST	1149POL	TEMAT
1145POR	TEXTO	1149POR	TEMA
1145RUS	TEKST	1149RUS	TEMA
1145SPA	TEXTO	1149SPA	TEMA
1145SWE	TEXT	1149SWE	TEMA
1146AAA	TEXTURE	1150AAA	THEN
1146CZE	TEXTURA	1150CZE	TEHDY, TU
1146DAN	TEKSTUR, VAEVNING	1150DAN	DA
1146DUT	TESTITUUR	1150DUT	DAN
1146FRE	TESSITURE	1150FRE	ALORS, DONC, PUIS
1146GER	TEXTUR, REIHENFOLGE	1150GER	DANN, DAMALS, SODANN
1146HUN	SZÖVET	1150HUN	AZTÁN
1146ITA	TESSITURA	1150ITA	ALLORA, DOPO, POI
1146POL	TEKSTURA	1150POL	WŁEDY
1146POR	TEXTURA	1150POR	ENTÃO
1146RUS	TESSITURA	1150RUS	TOGDA
1146SPA	TEXTURA	1150SPA	ENTONCES, EN SEGUIDA
1146SWE	VÄFNING	1150SWE	DÅ
1147AAA	THAN	1151AAA	THEORY
1147CZE	NEŽ, ZE	1151CZE	THEORIE
1147DAN	END	1151DAN	THEORI
1147DUT	DAN	1151DUT	THEORIE
1147FRE	QUE	1151FRE	THEORIE
1147GER	WELCHER, WIE, ALS	1151GER	THEORIE
1147HUN	MINT	1151HUN	TEÓRIA
1147ITA	CHE	1151ITA	TEORIA
1147POL	NIŻ	1151POL	TEORJA
1147POR	QUE	1151POR	TEORIA
1147RUS	CHEM, ESHCHÉ	1151RUS	TEORIIA
1147SPA	QUE	1151SPA	TEORÍA
1147SWE	ÄN	1151SWE	TEORI
1148AAA	THEATER	1152AAA	THIN
1148CZE	DIVADLO	1152CZE	TENKÝ
1148DAN	TEATER	1152DAN	TYND
1148DUT	SCHOUWBURG	1152DUT	SWAK
1148FRE	THÉÂTRE	1152FRE	GRÊLE, MINCE
1148GER	THEATER	1152GER	DÜNN, SCHWACH
1148HUN	JÁTÉKSZÍN	1152HUN	GYENGE
1148ITA	TEATRO	1152ITA	GRACILE, TENUE
1148POL	TEATR	1152POL	CIENKI
1148POR	TEATRO	1152POR	DELGADO, TENUE
1148RUS	TEATR	1152RUS	TONKII
1148SPA	TEATRO	1152SPA	DELGADO, GRACIL
1148SWE	TEATER	1152SWE	TUNN

1153AAA THIRD
1153CZE TERCIE
1153DAN TERZ
1153DUT TERTS
1153FRE TIERCE
1153GER TERZ
1153HUN TERC
1153ITA TERZA
1153POL TERCJA
1153POR TERCEIRA, TERCA
1153RUS TERTSIIA
1153SPA TERCERA, TERCIA
1153SWE TERS

1154AAA THIS
1154CZE TEN
1154DAN DENNE
1154DUT DEZE
1154FRE CE(T)(TE)
1154GER DIESE(R)
1154HUN EZ
1154ITA QUESTO
1154POL TEN
1154POR ESTE
1154RUS ETOT
1154SPA ESTE, ESE
1154SWE DENNE

1155AAA THOROUGHBASS
1155CZE GENERÁLNÍ BAS
1155DAN GENERALBAS
1155DUT GENERALE BAS
1155FRE BASSE CONTINUE
1155GER UNUNTERBROCHENER BASS
1155HUN SZÁMZOTT ALHANG
1155ITA BASSO CONTINUO
1155POL BAS CYFROWANY
1155POR BAIXO CONTÍNUO
1155RUS BASSO KONTINUO
1155SPA BAJO CONTINUO
1155SWE KONTINISERLIG BAS

1156AAA THOUGHTFUL
1156CZE ZADUMANÝ, PŘEMÝŠLIVÝ
1156DAN TANKEFULD
1156DUT DENKEND
1156FRE PENSIF, RÉFLÉCHI
1156GER GEDANKENVOLL, DENKLICH
1156HUN ELMÉLYEDVE
1156ITA PENSIEROSO
1156POL ZAMYŚLONY
1156POR PENSATIVO
1156RUS ZADUMCHIVYĬ
1156SPA PENSATIVO
1156SWE TANKFULL

1157AAA THREATEN, TO
1157CZE HROZITI
1157DAN TRUE
1157DUT DREIGEN
1157FRE MENACER
1157GER DROHEN
1157HUN FENYEGETNI
1157ITA MINACCIARE
1157POL GROZIĆ
1157POR AMEAÇAR
1157RUS GROZIT'
1157SPA AMENAZAR
1157SWE HOTA

1158AAA THREE
1158CZE TŘI
1158DAN TRE
1158DUT DRIE
1158FRE TROIS
1158GER DREI
1158HUN HÁROM
1158ITA TRE
1158POL TRZY
1158POR TRÊS
1159RUS TRI
1158SPA TRES
1158SWE TRE

1159AAA THROAT
1159CZE HRDLO
1159DAN HALS
1159DUT HALS
1159FRE GORGE
1159GER HALS, KEHLE
1159HUN TÖRÖK
11592TA GOLA
1159POL GARDŁO
1159POR GARGANTA
1159RUS GORLO
1159SPA GARGANTA
1159SWE HALS

1160AAA THROUGH
1160CZE PRO, V(E)
1160DAN IGENNEM
1160DUT VOOR, DOOR
1160FRE DANS, À TRAVERS
1160GER DURCH
1160HUN ÁT
1160ITA PER, ATTRAVERSO
1160POL PRZEZ, POPRZEZ
1160POR ATRAVÉS DE, DIRETO
1160RUS CHEREZ, SKVOZ'
1160SPA A TRAVÉS DE
1160SWE GENOM, FÖR

1161AAA	THROUGHOUT		1165AAA	THUS
1161CZE	VESKRZE		1165CZE	TAK
1161DAN	HELT IGNENNEM		1165DAN	SÅLEDES
1161DUT	GEHEEL		1165DUT	DUS
1161FRE	JUSQU'AU BOUT		1165FRE	AINSI
1161GER	DURCHAUS		1165GER	SO, GLEICHFALLS
1161HUN	EGÉSZEN ÁT		1165HUN	ÍGY
1161ITA	PER TUTTA LA DURATA		1165ITA	COSÌ
1161POL	PRZEZ		1165POL	TAK
1161POR	POR TODO		1165POR	ASSIM
1161RUS	POVSIUDU		1165RUS	TAK
1161SPA	POR TODO		1165SPA	ASÍ
1161SWE	ALLTIGENOM		1165SWE	SÅ
1162AAA	THROW, TO		1166AAA	TIE
1162CZE	HÁZETI		1166CZE	VÁZÁNÍ
1162DAN	KASTE		1166DAN	LIGATUR
1162DUT	WERPEN		1166DUT	BOOG
1162FRE	JETER		1166FRE	LIAISON
1162GER	WERFEN		1166GER	BINDUNG, LIGATUR
1162HUN	DOBNI		1166HUN	KÖTŐÍV
1162ITA	GETTARE		11662TA	LEGATURA
1162POL	RZUCIĆ		1166POL	ŁĄCZNIK
1162POR	ATIRAR		1166POR	LIGADURA
1162RUS	BROSAT'		1166RUS	LIGATURA, LIGA
1162SPA	TIRAR		1166SPA	LIGADURA
1162SWE	KASTA		1166SWE	BINDNING
1163AAA	THUMB		1167AAA	TIE, TO
1163CZE	PALEC		1167CZE	VÁZATI (SE)
1163DAN	TOMMELFINGER		1167DAN	BINDE
1163DUT	DUIM		1167DUT	BINDEN
1163FRE	POUCE		1167FRE	LIER, ENCHAÎNER
1163GER	DAUMEN		1167GER	VERBINDEN, BINDEN
1163HUN	HÜVELYKUJJ		1167HUN	BEKÖTNI, KÖTNI
1163ITA	POLLICE		1167ITA	LEGARE
1163POL	DUŻY PALEC		1167POL	ŁĄCZYĆ
1163POR	DEDO POLEGAR		1167POR	LIGAR
1163RUS	BOL'SHOI PALETS		1167RUS	VIAZAT'
1163SPA	PULGAR		1167SPA	LIGAR, ENCADENAR
1163SWE	TUMME		1167SWE	FÖRBINDA, BINDA
1164AAA	THUNDER		1168AAA	TIME
1164CZE	HŘÍMÁNÍ		1168CZE	TEMPO, ČAS, DOBA
1164DAN	TORDENSKRALD		1168DAN	TEMPO, TAKT
1164DUT	DONDER		1168DUT	MAAT
1164FRE	TONNERRE		1168FRE	TEMPS
1164GER	DONNER		1168GER	ZEITMASS, TEMPO, TAKT
1164HUN	MENNYDÖRGÉS		1168HUN	TEMPÓ, ÜTEM
1164ITA	TUONO		1168ITA	TEMPO
1164POL	GRZMOT, GROM		1168POL	TAKT
1164POR	TROVÃO		1168POR	TEMPO
1164RUS	GROM		1168RUS	TEMP, TAKT
1164SPA	TRUENO		1168SPA	TIEMPO
1164SWE	ÅSKA		1168SWE	TAKT, TEMPO

1169AAA TIMID
1169CZE BOJÁCNÝ, BÁSLIVÝ
1169DAN SKY, FRYGTSOM
1169DUT SCHUW, BESCHROOMD
1169FRE TIMIDE, PEUREUX
1169GER FURCHTSAM, ERSCHROCKEN
1169HUN FÉLENK
1169ITA TIMIDO
1169POL BOJAŹLIWY
1169POR TÍMIDO
1169RUS POBKIÏ
1169SPA TÍMIDO
1169SWE SKYGG, RÄDD

1170AAA TINKLE, TO
1170CZE CINKATI, KLINKATI
1170DAN KLIRRE
1170DUT KLINKEN
1170FRE TINTER
1170GER KLINGELN, LÄUTEN
1170HUN CSILINGELNI
1170ITA TINTINNARE
1170POL DZWONIĆ
1170POR TINIR
1170RUS ZVONIT', ZVIÁKAT'
1170SPA TINTIN(E)AR, RETIÑIR
1170SWE KLINGA

1171AAA TIP
1171CZE KONEC, ŠPIČKA, HROT
1171DAN SPIDS, TOP
1171DUT STIP
1171FRE POINTE
1171GER SPITZE, PUNKT
1171HUN CSÚCS
1171ITA PUNTO
1171POL KONIEC
1171POR PONTA
1171RUS KONETS
1171SPA PUNTA
1171SWE SPETS

1172AAA TIRADE
1172CZE TIRÁDA
1172DAN TIRADE
1172DUT TIRADE, SNELLE LOOP
1172FRE TIRADE
1172GER TIRADE
1172HUN TIRÁDA
1172ITA TIRATA, TIRATO
1172POL TYRADA
1172POR TIRADA
1172RUS TIRADA
1172SPA TIRADO
1172SWE HARANG

1173AAA TIRE (OUT), TO
1173CZE UNAVITI
1173DAN TRAETTE
1173DUT VERMOEIEN
1173FRE LASSER, FATIGUER
1173GER ERMATTEN
1173HUN FÁRASZTANI
1173ITA FATICARE, STANCARE
1173POL ZNUZYĆ, WYCZERPYWAĆ
1173POR CANSAR
1173RUS UTOMLIÁT'
1173SPA CANSAR, FATIGAR
1173SWE TRÖTTA

1174AAA TO
1174CZE K(E), KU
1174DAN TIL
1174DUT TE
1174FRE À, AU
1174GER AN, AUF, ZU
1174HUN -HOZ, HEZ, -HOZ
1174ITA A
1174POL KU
1174POR A, PARA
1174RUS K, B, DO
1174SPA A(L)
1174SWE TILL

1175AAA TOCCATA
1175CZE TOKÁTA
1175DAN TOCCATA
1175DUT TOCCATA
1175FRE TOCCATE
1175GER TOCCATE, TOKKATE
1175HUN TOKKÁTA
1175ITA TOCCATA
1175POL TOKATA
1175POR TOCATA
1175RUS TOKKATA
1175SPA TOCATA
1175SWE TOCCATA

1176AAA TOGETHER
1176CZE DOHROMADY, SPOLEČNĚ
1176DAN SAMMEN
1176DUT SAMEN(SPEL)
1176FRE ENSEMBLE
1176GER ZUSAMMEN
1176HUN EGYÜTT
1176ITA INSIEME, ASSIEME
1176POL ENSAMBL, RAZEM
1176POR CONJUNTO, JUNTAMENTE
1176RUS ANSAMBL'
1176SPA UNIDAMENTE
1176SWE TILLSAMMAMS

1177AAA TONALITY	1181AAA TOO
1177CZE TONALITA	1181CZE PŘILIŠ, TÉŽ
1177DAN TONALITET	1181DAN ALTFOR
1177DUT TONALITEIT	1181DUT TE VEEL
1177FRE TONALITÉ	1181FRE TROP, AUSSI
1177GER TONCHARACTER	1181GER VIEL, ZU SEHR
1177HUN HANGNEM	1181HUN NAGYON
1177ITA TONALITÀ	1181ITA TROPPO
1177POL TONACJA	1181POL ZA WIELE, TEŻ
1177POR TONALIDADE	1181POR MUITO, DEMASIADO
1177RUS TONAL'NOST'	1181RUS TOZHE
1177SPA TONALIDAD	1181SPA DEMASIADO
1177SWS TONALITET	1181SWE ALLTFÖR
1178AAA TONE	1182AAA TOUCH
1178CZE TÓN(INA)	1182CZE DOTKNUTÍ, KLÁVESA
1178DAN TONE	1182DAN ANSLAG
1178DUT TOON	1182DUT AANSLAG
1178FRE TON	1182FRE TOUCHE
1178GER TON	1182GER ANSCHLAG
1178HUN HANG	1182HUN ÉRINTÉS
1178ITA TONO	1182ITA TOCCO, TOCCATA
1178POL TON	1182POL UDERZENIE, KLAWISZ
1178POR TOM	1182POR TOQUE
1178RUS TON	1182RUS TUSHE, PRIKOSNOVENIE
1178SPA TONO	1182SPA TOQUE
1178SWE TON	1182SWE ANSLAG
1179AAA TONGUE	1183AAA TOUCH, TO
1179CZE JAZYK	1183CZE HRÁTI
1179DAN TUNGE	1183DAN SPILLE PAA
1179DUT TONG	1183DUT AANSLAAN
1179FRE LANGUE	1183FRE TOUCHER
1179GER ZUNGE	1183GER ANSCHLAGEN, ANGREIFEN
1179HUN NYELV	1183HUN ÉRINTENI
1179ITA LINGUA	1183ITA TOCCARE
1179POL JĘZYK, STROIK	1183POL UDERZAĆ W
1179POR LÍNGUA	1183POT TOCAR
1179RUS IAZYK	1183RUS PRIKASAT'SIA
1179SPA LENGUA	1183SPA TOCAR
1179SWE TUNGA	1183SWE SLÅ AN, TUSCHERA
1180AAA TONIC	1184AAA TOWARD
1180CZE TÓNIKA	1184CZE NA(D)
1180DAN GRUNDTONE, TONICA	1184DAN MOD
1180DUT TONICA, TOON	1184DUT OP
1180FRE TONIQUE	1184FRE SUR
1180GER GRUNDTON, TONIKA	1184GER GEGEN, NACH, AUF
1180HUN TONIKA, HANGZÓ	1184HUN FELÉ
1180ITA TONICA	1184ITA SUL
1180POL TONICZNY	1184POL NA, PRZY
1180POR TÓNICA	1184POR PARA, POR
1180RUS TONIKA	1184RUS NA
1180SPA TÓNICA	1184SPA HACIA, PARA, POR
1180SWE TONIKA	1184SWE MOT, PÅ

1185AAA	TRAGIC	1189AAA	TRANSCRIPTION
1185CZE	TRAGICKÝ	1189CZE	TRANSKRIPCE
1185DAN	TRAGISK	1189DAN	TRANSCRIPTION
1185DUT	TRAGISCH	1189DUT	TRANSCRIPTIE
1185FRE	TRAGIQUE	1189FRE	TRANSCRIPTION
1185GER	TRAGISCH	1189GER	TRANSKRIPTION
1185HUN	TRAGIKAI	1189HUN	ÁTÍRÁS
1185ITA	TRAGICO	1189ITA	TRASCRIZIONE
1185POL	TRAGICZNY	1189POL	TRANSKRYPCJA
1185POR	TRÁGICO	1189POR	TRANSCRIÇÃO
1185RUS	TRAGICHESKIĬ	1189RUS	TRANSKRIPTSIIA
1185SPA	TRÁGICO	1189SPA	TRANSCRIPCIÓN
1185SWE	TRAGISK	1189SWE	TRANSKRIPTION
1186AAA	TRANQUIL	1190AAA	TRANSFIGURE, TO
1186CZE	KLIDNÝ, POKOJNÝ	1190CZE	PROMENITI
1186DAN	ROLIGT	1190DAN	FORKLARE
1186DUT	RUSTIG	1190DUT	HERSCHEPPEN
1186FRE	TRANQUILLE	1190FRE	TRANSFIGURER
1186GER	BESCHAULICH, RUHIG	1190GER	VERKLÄREN
1136HUN	NYUGODTAN	1190HUN	ÁTVÁLTOZTATNI
1186ITA	TRANQUILLO	1190ITA	TRASFIGURARE
1186POL	SPOKOJNIE	1190POL	PRZEMIENIAĆ
1186POR	TRANQUILO	1190POR	TRANSFIGURAR
1186RUS	SPOKOĬNYĬ	1190RUS	VIDOIZMENIAT'
1186SPA	TRANQUILO	1190SPA	TRANSFIGURAR
1186SWE	LUNGT	1190SWE	OMGESTALTA
1187AAA	TRANS-	1191AAA	TRANSFORM, TO
1187CZE	PŘE-, TRANS-	1191CZE	PŘEMĚNITI
1187DAN	OVER-	1191DAN	FORVANDLE
1187DUT	OVER-	1191DUT	TRANSFORMEREN
1187FRE	TRANS-	1191FRE	TRANSFORMER
1187GER	ÜBER-	1191GER	VERWANDELN
1187HUN	TRANZ-	1191HUN	ATALAKÍTNI
1187ITA	TRANS-, TRAS-	1191ITA	TRASFORMARE
1187POL	TRANS-	1191POL	PRZEKSZTAŁCAĆ
1187POR	TRANS-, TRAS-	1191POR	TRANSFORMAR
1187RUS	TRANS-	1191RUS	PREVRASHCHAT'
1187SPA	TRANS-	1191SPA	TRANSFORMAR
1187SWE	ÖVER-	1191SWE	FÖRVANDLA
1188AAA	TRANSCRIBE, TO	1192AAA	TRANSIENT
1188CZE	TRANSKRIBOVATI	1192CZE	PŘECHODNÝ
1188DAN	TRANSCRIBERE	1192DAN	FÖRBIGÅENDE
1188DUT	OVERSCHRIJVEN	1192DUT	VOORBIJGAAND
1188FRE	TRANSCRIRE	1192FRE	TRANSITOIRE
1188GER	ABSCHREIBEN	1192GER	VORÜBERGEHEND
1188HUN	ÁTIRNI	1192HUN	MULÉKONY
1188ITA	TRASCRIVERE	1192ITA	TRANSITORIO
1188POL	TRANSKRYBOWAĆ	1192POL	PRZEJŚCIOWY
1188POR	TRANSCREVER	1192POR	TRANSITÓRIO
1188RUS	TRANSKRIBIROVAT'	1192RUS	PEREKHODNYĬ
1188SPA	TRANSCRIBIR	1192SPA	TRANSITORIO
1188SWE	AFSKRIFTA	1192SWE	ÖVERGÅENDE

1193AAA	TRANSITION	1197AAA	TREBLE	
1193CZE	PŘECHOD	1197CZE	SOPRÁN, DISKANT	
1193DAN	OVERGANG	1197DAN	SOPRAN	
1193DUT	OVERGANG	1197DUT	SOPRAAN	
1193FRE	TRANSITION	1197FRE	DESSUS, DE DESSUS	
1193GER	ÜBERGANG	1197GER	DISCANTSTIMME, SOPRAN	
1193HUN	ATMENET	1197HUN	SZOPRÁN	
1193ITA	TRANSIZIONE	1197ITA	SOPRANO	
1193POL	PREJŚCIE	1197POL	SOPRAN	
1193POR	TRANSIÇÃO	1197POR	TIPLE	
1193RUS	PEREKHOD	1197RUS	DISKANT	
1139SPA	TRANSICIÓN	1197SPA	TIPLE	
1193SWE	ÖVERGÅNG	1197SWE	DISKANT, SOPRAN	
1194AAA	TRANSMIT, TO	1198AAA	TREMBLE, TO	
1194CZE	PŘENÉSTI	1198CZE	TŘÁSTI SE	
1194DAN	TRANSMITTERE	1198DAN	SKAELVE	
1194DUT	OVERBRENGEN	1198DUT	TRILLEN	
1194FRE	TRANSMETTRE	1198FRE	TREMBLER	
1194GER	ÜBERSENDEN	1198GER	ZITTERN, BEBEN	
1194HUN	MEGKÜLDENI	1198HUN	RESZKETNI	
1194ITA	TRASMETTERE	1198ITA	TREMARE	
1194POL	TRANSMITOWAĆ	1198POL	TRZĄŚĆ	
1194P6R	TRANSMITIR	1198POR	TREMER	
1194RUS	TRANSLIROVAT'	1198RUS	TRIASTIS'	
1194SPA	TRANSMITIR	1198SPA	TREMBLAR	
1194SWE	ÖVERSÄNDA	1198SWE	SKÄLVA	
1195AAA	TRANSPOSE, TO	1199AAA	TREMENDOUS	
1195CZE	TRANSPONOVATI	1199CZE	HROZIVĚ	
1195DAN	TRANSPONERE	1199DAN	FRYGTELLIG	
1195DUT	TRANSPONEREN	1199DUT	GEDUCHT	
1195FRE	TRANSPOSER	1199FRE	TERRIBLEMENT	
1195GER	TRANSPONIEREN	1199GER	SCHRECKLICH	
1195HUN	ÁTTENNI	1199HUN	IJESZTŐ	
1195ITA	TRASPORTARE	1199ITA	TREMENDO	
1195POL	TRANSPONOWAĆ	1199POL	OGROMNY	
1195POR	TRANSPORTAR	1199POR	TREMENDO	
1195RUS	TRANSPONIROVAT'	1199RUS	GROZNO	
1195SPA	TRANSPORTAR	1199SPA	TREMENDO	
1195SWE	TRANSPONERA	1199SWE	FÖRSKRÄCKLIG	
1196AAA	TRANSPOSITION	1200AAA	TREMOLO	
1196CZE	TRANSPOSICE	1200CZE	TREMOLO	
1196DAN	TRANSPOSITION	1200DAN	SKAELVEN, BAEVENDE	
1196DUT	TRANSPOSITIE	1200DUT	TREMOLO	
1196FRE	TRANSPOSITION	1200FRE	TRÉMOLO	
1196GER	TRANSPONIEREN	1200GER	SCHWEBUNG, TREMOLO	
1196HUN	TRANSZONÁLÓ	1200HUN	RESZKÉTES	
1196ITA	TRASPOSIZIONE	1200ITA	TREMOLO	
1196POL	TRANSPOZYCJA	1200POL	DRŻĄC	
1196POR	TRANSPORTE	1200POR	TRÉMULO	
1196RUS	TRANSPOZITSIIA	1200RUS	TREMOLO	
1196SPA	TRANSPOSICIÓN	1200SPA	TREMOLO	
1196SWE	TRANSPONERING	1200SWE	TREMOLO	

1201AAA TRIAD   1205AAA TRILL, TO
1201CZE TROJZVUK   1205CZE TRYLKOVATI
1201DAN TREKLANG   1205DAN TRILLE
1201DUT DRIEKLANK   1205DUT TRILLEN
1201FRE TRIADE   1205FRE TRILLER
1201GER DREIKLANG   1205GER TRILLERN
1201HUN HARMASHANGZAT   1205HUN TRILLÁZNI
1201ITA TRIADA   1205ITA TRILLARE
1201POL TRYJADA   1205POL TRELOWAĆ
1201POR TRÍADE   1205POR TRINAR
1201RUS TRIADA   1205RUS PUSKAT' TRELI
1201SPA TRIADA   1205SPA TRINAR
1201SWE TREKLANG   1205SWE DRILLA

1202AAA TRIANGLE   1206AAA TRIO
1202CZE TRIANGL   1206CZE TRIO
1202DAN TREKANT   1206DAN TRIO
1202DUT TRIANGEL   1206DUT TRIO
1202FRE TRIANGLE   1206FRE TRIO
1202GER TRIANGEL, DREIECK   1206GER TERZETT, TRIO
1202HUN HÁROMSZÖG   1206HUN TRIO
1202ITA TRIANGOLO   1206ITA TRIO
1202POL TRJANGUL   1206POL TRIO
1202POR TRIÂNGULO   1206POR TRIO
1202RUS TREUGOL'NIK   1206RUS TRIO
1202SPA TRIÁNGULO   1206SPA TRÍO
1202SWE TRIANGEL   1206SWE TRIO

1203AAA TRIFLE   1207AAA TRIPLE
1203CZE BAGATELA   1207CZE TROJNY
1203DAN BAGATEL   1207DAN TREDOBBELT
1203DUT BAGATEL(LA)   1207DUT TRIPPELMAAT
1203FRE BAGATELLE   1207FRE TRIPLE, TERNAIRE
1203GER KLEINIGKEIT, BAGATELLE   1207GER DREIFACH, DREIZEITIGE
1203HUN POTOMSÁG   1207HUN HÁRMAS, HÁRMOSZOROS
1203ITA BAGATELLA   1207ITA TRIPLO
1203POL FRASZKA, ZABAWKA   1207POL POTRÓJNY
1203POR BAGATELA   1207POR TRIPLO, TRÍPLICE
1203RUS BEZDELITSA, PUSTIAK   1207RUS TROYNOY
1203SPA BAGATELA   1207SPA TRIPLE
1203SWE BAGATELL   1207SWE TREDUBBEL, TREFALDIG

1204AAA TRILL   1208AAA TRIPLET
1204CZE TRYLEK   1208CZE TRIOLA
1204DAN TRILLE   1208DAN TRIOL
1204DUT TRILLER   1208DUT TRIOOL
1204FRE TRILLE   1208FRE TRIOLET
1204GER TRILLE(R)   1208GER TRIOLE, DRILLINGE
1204HUN TRILLA   1208HUN HÁROMSZOROS VERSSZAK
1204ITA TRILLO   1208ITA TRIOLA, TRIPLETTA
1204POL TRYL   1208POL TROJKA
1204POR TRINADO   1208POR TERCÉTO
1204RUS TREL'   1208RUS TRIOL'
1204SPA TRINO, TRINADO   1208SPA TRESILLO
1204SWE DRILL   1208SWE TRIOL

1209AAA	TRIUMPH		1213AAA	TROUPE
1209CZE	VÍTĚZOSLÁVA		1213CZE	TRUPA
1209DAN	TRIUMF		1213DAN	TRUP
1209DUT	TRIOMF		1213DUT	TROEP
1209FRE	TRIOMPHE		1213FRE	TROUPE
1209GER	TRIUMPH		1213GER	TRUPPE
1209HUN	DIADAL		1213HUN	SZÍNTÁRSULAT
1209ITA	TRIONFO		1213ITA	COMPAGNIA
1209POL	TRIUMF		1213POL	TRUPA
1209POR	TRIUNFO		1213POR	TRUPE
1209RUS	TRIUMF		1213RUS	TRUPPE
1209SPA	TRIUNFO		1213SPA	CAMPAÑÍA
1209SWE	TRIUMF		1213SWE	TRUPP
1210AAA	TROCHEE		1214AAA	TRUMPET
1210CZE	TROCHEJ		1214CZE	TRUBKA
1210DAN	TROKAE		1214DAN	TROMPET
1210DUT	TROCHEE		1214D4T	TROMPET
1210FRE	TROCHÉE		1214FRE	TROMPETTE
1210GER	TROCHÄUS		1214GER	TROMPETE
1210HUN	TROCHEUS		1214HUN	TROMBITA
1210ITA	TROCHEO		1214ITA	TROMBA
1210POL	TROCHEJ		1214POL	TRĄBKA
1210POR	TROQUEU		1214POR	TROMPETE, TROMBETA
1210RUS	TROKHEĬ		1214RUS	TRUBA
1210SPA	TROQUEO		1214SPA	TROMPETA
1210SWE	TROUK(I)		1214SWE	TRUMPET
1211AAA	TROMBONE		1215AAA	TUBA
1211CZE	POZOUN		1215CZE	TÚBA
1211DAN	BASUN, TRAEKBASUN		1215DAN	TUBA
1211DUT	BAZUIN		1215DUT	TUBA
1211FRE	TROMBONE		1215FRE	TUBA
1211GER	POSAUNE		1215GER	TUBA
1211HUN	HARSONA		1215HUN	TUBA
1211ITA	TROMBONE		1215ITA	TUBA
1211POL	PUZON		1215POL	TUBA
1211POR	TROMBONE		1215POR	TUBA
1211RUS	TROMBON		1215RUS	TUBA
1211SPA	TROMBÓN		1215SPA	TUBA
1211SWE	BASUN, DRAGBASUN		1215SWE	BASTUBA
1212AAA	TROPE		1216AAA	TUBE
1212CZE	CÍRKEVNÍ TÓNINA		1216CZE	PIŠŤALA
1212DAN	TROPE		1216DAN	RØR, TUBE
1212DUT	TROOP, TROPUS		1216DUT	TUBE, PIJP
1212FRE	TROPE		1216FRE	TUBE
1212GER	TROPE		1216GER	ROHR, TUBE
1212HUN	TROPUS		1216HUN	TUBUS, CSŐ
1212ITA	TROPO		1216ITA	TUBO
1212POL	TROPY		1216POL	TUB(K)A
1212POR	TROPO		1216POR	TUBO
1212RUS	TROP		1216RUS	TRUBA
1212SPA	TROPO		1216SPA	TUBO
1212SWE	FIGURLIGT TALESÄTT		1216SWE	TUB

1217AAA TUMULT
1217CZE HLUK
1217DAN TUMULT
1217DUT TUMULT
1217FRE TUMULTE
1217GER TUMULT
1217HUN LÁRMA
1217ITA TUMULTO
1217POL GWARNO, TUMULT
1217POR TUMULTO
1217RUS SHUM, DRAKA, BUĬSTVO
1217SPA TUMULTO
1217SWE TUMULT

1218AAA TUNE, TO
1218CZE NALADITI
1218DAN STEMME
1218DUT STEMMEN
1218FRE ACCORDER
1218GER STIMMEN, ACCORDIEREN
1218HUN HANGOLNI
1218ITA ACCORDARE
1218POL NASTROIĆ
1218POR AFINAR
1218RUS NASTRAIVAT)
1218SPA AFINAR
1218SWE STÄMMA

1219AAA TUNING FORK
1219CZE LADIDLO
1219DAN STEMMEGAFFEL
1219DUT STEMVORK
1219FRE DIAPASON
1219GER STIMMGABEL
1219HUN HANGVILLA
1219ITA DIAPASON
1219POL WIDEŁKI STROIKOWE
1219POR DIAPASĂO
1219RUS DIAPAZON
1219SPA DIAPASÓN
1219SWE STÄMGAFFEL

1220AAA TURKISH
1220CZE TURECKÝ
1220DAN TYRKISK, TURCA
1220DUT TURKS
1220FRE TURC, À LA TURQUE
1220GER TÜRKISCH
1220HUN TÖRÖK
1220ITA TURCA, ALLA TURCA
1220POL TURECKI
1220POR TURCA
1220RUS TURETSKIĬ
1220SPA TURCA
1220SWE TURKISK

1221AAA TURN
1221CZE OBRAT)TE, SKUPINKA
1221DAN DOBBELTSLAG
1221DUT DOPPELSLAG
1221FRE TOUNEZ, GRUPPETTO
1221GER DOPPELSCHLAG, BIEGUNG
1221HUN HAJLÍTÁS
1221ITA GRUPPETTO
1221POL OBIEGNIK
1221POR GRUPETO
1221RUS FIORITURA
1221SPA GRUPETO, GLOPETE
1221SWE FIORITUR

1222AAA TWELVE
1222CZE DVANÁCT
1222DAN TOLV
1222DUT TWAALF
1222FRE DOUZE
1222GER ZWÖLF
1222HUN TIZENKÉT
1222ITA DODICI
1222POL DWANAŚCIE
1222POR DOZE
1222RUS DVENADTSAT)
1222SPA DOCE
1222SWE TOLV

1223AAA TWO
1223CZE DVE, DVA
1223DAN TO
1223DUT TWEE
1223FRE DEUX
1223GER ZWEI
1223HUN KETLŐ
1223ITA DUE
1223POL DWA
1223POR DOIS
1223RUS DVA, DVE
1223SPA DOS
1223SWE TVÅ

1224AAA TYMPAN(UM)
1224CZE KOTEL, BUBÍNEK UŠNÍ
1224DAN PAUKE, TROMMELHULE
1224DUT PAUKE, TROMMELVLIES
1224FRE TIMBALE
1224GER PAUKE
1224HUN DOB, FÜLDOB
1224ITA TIMPANO
1224POL KOTŁY
1224POR TÍMPANO, TIMBALE
1224RUS TIMPAN
1224SPA TÍMPANO
1224SWE PUKA, TRUMMA

1225AAA UNDER
1225CZE POD
1225DAN UNDER, NEDE
1225DUT ONDER
1225FRE SOUS
1225GER UNTER, UNTEN, DARUNTER
1225HUN ALATT
1225ITA SOTTO, AL DISOTTO
1225POL POD
1225POR DEBAIXO
1225RUS POD
1225SPA DEBAJO
1225SWE UNDER

1226AAA UNION
1226CZE SPOJENÍ, SLOUČENÍ
1226DAN FORBINDELSE
1226DUT UNIE
1226FRE UNION
1226GER UNION, VERBINDUNG
1226HUN EGYESÜLÉS
1226ITA UNIONE
1226POL UNIA
1226POR UNIÃO
1226RUS UNITA
1226SPA UNIÓN
1226SWE FÖRBINDNING

1227AAA UNISON
1227CZE UNISONO, INTERVAL PRIMY
1227DAN I ENKLANG
1227DUT EENKLANK, UNISONO
1227FRE UNISSON(S)
1227GER EINKLANG
1227HUN EGY HANGON
1227ITA UNIS(S)ONO
1227POL JEDNODZWIĘK
1227POR UNISSONO
1227RUS UNISON
1227SPA UNISONO
1227SWE ENKLANG

1228AAA UNIT
1228CZE JEDNOTA
1228DAN ENHED
1228DUT EENHEID
1228FRE UNITÉ
1228GER EINHEIT
1228HUN EGYSÉG
1228ITA UNITÀ
1228POL JEDNOSTKA
1228POR UNIDADE
1228RUS EDINITSA, EDINSTVO
1228SPA UNIDAD
1228SWE ENHET

1229AAA UNTIL
1229CZE AŽ, DO
1229DAN TIL
1229DUT TOT
1229FRE JUSQUE, JUSQU'À
1229GER BIS
1229HUN IG
1229ITA FINO
1229POL DO
1229POR ATÉ (A)
1229RUS DO
1229SPA HASTA
1229SWE TILL

1230AAA UPBEAT
1230CZE PŘEDTAKÍ
1230DAN OPTAKT
1230DUT OP MAAT
1230FRE ANACROUSE
1230GER ANAKRUSIS
1230HUN ÜTEMELŐZŐ
1230ITA ANACRUSI
1230POL PODNIESIENIE
1230POR ANACRUSE
1230RUS ANAKRUZA
1230SPA ANACRUSIS
1230SWE UPPTAKT

1231AAA UPRIGHT PIANO
1231CZE PIANINO
1231DAN OPRETSTAAENDE KLAVER
1231DUT PIANINO
1231FRE PIANO VERTICAL
1231GER WAND PIANO
1231HUN ZONGORA
1231ITA PIANOFORTE VERTICALE
1231POL PIANINO
1231POR PIANO DE ARMÁRIO
1231RUS PIANINO
1231SPA PIANINO
1231SWE PIANINO

1232AAA URGENT
1232CZE NALÉHAVÝ
1232DAN TRAENGE PAA
1232DUT URGENT
1232FRE URGENT
1232GER DRINGEND
1232HUN SÜRGŐS
1232ITA URGENTE
1232POL PILNIE
1232POR URGENTE
1232RUS SROCHNYĬ
1232SPA URGENTE
1232SWE TRÄNGANDE

1233AAA USE, TO
1233CZE POUŽÍVATI
1233DAN ANVENDE
1233DUT GEBRUIKEN
1233FRE USER DE
1233GER GEBRAUCHEN
1233HUN HASZNÁLNI
1233ITA USARE
1233POL UŻYWAĆ
1233POR USAR
1233RUS UPOTREBLIAT'
1233SPA USAR
1233SWE ANVÄNDA

1234AAA USUAL
1234CZE OBRYKLÝ
1234DAN SAEDVANLIG
1234DUT GEWOON
1234FRE USUEL, ACCOUTUMÉ
1234GER GEWÖHNLICH(ERWEISE)
1234HUN SZOKASOS
1234ITA USUALE, SOLITO
1234POL ZWYKŁY
1234POR USUAL
1234RUS OBYCHNYÍ
1234SPA USUAL
1234SWE VANLIG

1235AAA UTMOST
1235CZE KRAJNÍ
1235DAN YDERST
1235DUT UITERSTE
1235FRE EXTRÊME
1235GER ÄUSSERST
1235HUN LEGVÉGSŐ
1235ITA ESTREMA
1235POL SKRAJNY
1235POR ÚLTIMO
1235RUS KRAÍNIÍ
1235SPA EXTREMADO, ÚLTIMO
1235SWE YTTERST

1236AAA VAGUE
1236CZE NEURČITÝ
1236DAN UBESTEMT, VAG
1236DUT VAAG
1236FRE VAGUE
1236GER UNBESTIMMT
1236HUN HATÁROZATLAN
1236ITA VAGO
1236POL NIEJASNY
1236POR VAGO
1236RUS NEIASNYÍ
1236SPA VAGO
1236SWE OBESTÄMD

1237AAA VALVE
1237CZE ZAVÍRACÍ VENTIL
1237DAN VENTIL
1237DUT VENTIEL
1237FRE VALVE, SOUPAGE
1237GER VENTIL
1237HUN VENTIL
1237ITA VALVOLA
1237POL WENTYL
1237POR VÁLVULA
1237RUS VENTIL'
1237SPA VÁLVULA
1237SWE VENTIL

1238AAA VARIATION
1238CZE VARIACE
1238DAN VARIATION
1238DUT VARIATIE
1238FRE VARIATION
1238GER VARIATION, VERÄNDERUNG
1238HUN VARIÁCIÓ
1238ITA VARIAZIONE
1238POL WARIACJA
1238POR VARIAÇÃO
1238RUS VARIATSIIA
1238SPA VARIACIÓN
1238SWE FÖRÄNDRING

1239AAA VARIOUS
1239CZE RŮZNY, ROZMANITÝ
1239DAN ULIG, FORSKELLING
1239DUT VERSCHEIDEN
1239FRE DIVERS
1239GER VERSCHIEDEN(E)
1239HUN KÜLÖNBÖZŐ
1239ITA VARIO
1239POL ROŻNY
1239POR VÁRIO
1239RUS RAZNYÍ
1239SPA VARIO
1239SWE OLIK

1240AAA VAUDEVILLE
1240CZE VESELOHRA SE ZPĚVY
1240DAN VAUDEVILLE
1240DUT VAUDEVILLE
1240FRE VAUDEVILLE
1240GER VAUDEVILLE
1240HUN KABARÉ(FAJTA)
1240ITA CANZONETTA
1240POL WODEWIL
1240POR VAUDEVILLE
1240RUS VODEVIL'
1240SPA VAUDEVILLE
1240SWE VARIETÉ

1241AAA VEHEMENT
1241CZE PRUDKÝ
1241DAN HEFTIG
1241DUT VEHEMENTE, ONSTUIMIG
1241FRE VÉHÉMENT
1241GER HEFTIG
1241HUN HEVESEN
1241ITA VEEMENTE
1241POL GWAŁTOWNY
1241POR VEEMENTE
1241RUS SILNYĬ
1241SWE HÄFTIG

1242AAA VEILED, MUFFLED
1242CZE ZASTŘENÝ
1242DAN SKJULT, TILSLØRET
1242DUT GEVOILEERD
1242FRE VOILÉ
1242GER BEDECKT
1242HUN ELFOJTOTT
1242ITA VELATO
1242POL TŁUMIONE
1242POR VELADO
1242RUS ZAKRYTYĬ
1242SPA VELADO
1242SWE BETÄCKT

1243AAA VELOCITY
1243CZE RYCHLOST
1243DAN HASTIGHED
1243DUT SNELHEID
1243FRE VÉLOCITÉ
1243GER SCHNELLIGKEIT
1243HUN GYORSASÁG
1243ITA VELOCITÀ
1243POL SZYBKOŚĆ
1243POR VELOCIDADE
1243RUS SKOROST'
1243SPA VELOCIDAD
1243SWE HASTIGHET

1244AAA VELVETY
1244CZE SAMETOVĚ MĚKKÝ
1244DAN FLØJLSBLØD
1244DUT FLUWEELACHTIG
1244FRE VELOUTÉ
1244GER SAMMETARTIG
1244HUN BARSONYOS
1244ITA VELLUTATO
1244POL AKSAMITNY
1244POR AVELUDADO
1244RUS BARKHATNYĬ
1244SPA ATERCIOPELADO
1244SWE SAMMETSLIK

1245AAA VENT
1245CZE OTVOR
1245DAN LUFTHUL
1245DUT VENTIEL, LUCHGAT
1245FRE VENT
1245GER VENTIL
1245HUN FÚVÓK
1245ITA APERTURA
1245POL DZIURKA
1245POR ABERTURA
1245RUS KLAPAN
1245SPA ABERTURA
1245SWE LUFTHÅL

1246AAA VERSE
1246CZE VERŠ, SMEREM
1246DAN VERS
1246DUT VERS
1246FRE VERS
1246GER VERS
1246HUN VERS
1246ITA VERSO
1246POL WIERSZ(E)
1246POR VERSO
1246RUS STIKH
1246SPA VERSO
1246SWE VERS

1247AAA VERVE
1247CZE VERVA, ZIVOST
1247DAN VERVE
1247DUT VUUR, VERVE
1247FRE VERVE
1247GER SCHWUNG
1247HUN ÉLÉNK
1247ITA BRIO
1247POL WERWA
1247POR ESTRO
1247RUS ZHIVOST'
1247SPA BRÍO
1247SWE SCHVUNG

1248AAA VERY
1248CZE DOSTI
1248DAN MEGET
1248DUT ZEER
1248FRE TRÈS, ASSEZ, BEAUCOUP
1248GER SEHR, VIEL, GENUG
1248HUN IGEN
1248ITA ASSAI, STESSO, MOLTO
1248POL BARDZO
1248POR MUITO
1248RUS OCHEN'
1248SPA MUY, MUCHO
1248SWE MYCKET

1249AAA	VESPERS		1253AAA	VIOLA
1249CZE	VEČERNÍ		1253CZE	VIOLA
1249DAN	VESPER(TID), AFTENSANG		1253DAN	BRATSCH
1249DUT	DE VESPER		1253DUT	ALTVIOOL, VIOLA
1249FRE	VÊPRES		1253FRE	VIOLE, ALTO
1249GER	ABENDMUSIK		1253GER	BRATSCHE, VIOLE
1249HUN	VECSERNYE		1253HUN	MÉLYHEGEDŰ
1249ITA	VESPRI		1253ITA	VIOLA
1249POL	NIESZPORY		1253POL	ALTÓWKA, WIOLA
1249POR	VÉSPERAS		1253POR	VIOLA
1249RUS	VECHERNIA		1253RUS	VIOLA
1249SPA	VÍSPERAS		1253SPA	VIOLA
1249SWE	AFTONMUSIK		1253SWE	ALTFIOL, VIOLA
1250AAA	VIBRATE, TO		1254AAA	VIOLIN
1250CZE	CHVĚTI SE, KMITATI		1254CZE	HOUSLE
1250DAN	VIBRERE		1254DAN	VIOLIN
1250DUT	VIBREREN		1254DUT	VIOOL
1250FRE	VIBRER		1254FRE	VIOLON
1250GER	VIBRIEREN		1254GER	VIOLINE, GEIGE
1250HUN	REZGENI		1254HUN	HEGEDŰ
1250ITA	VIBRARE		1254ITA	VIOLINO
1250POL	WIBRAJĄĆ		1254POL	SKRZYPCE
1250POR	VIBRAR		1254POR	VIOLINO
1250RUS	VIBRIROVAT'		1254RUS	SKRIPKA
1250SPA	VIBRAR		1254SPA	VIOLÍN
1250SWE	VIBRERA		1254SWE	FIOL, VIOLIN
1251AAA	VIBRATION		1255AAA	VIOLONCELLO
1251CZE	VIBRACE		1255CZE	VIOLONČELO
1251DAN	VIBRATION		1255DAN	VIOLONCEL
1251DUT	VIBRATIE		1255DUT	VIOLONCEL(LO)
1251FRE	VIBRATION		1255FRE	VIOLONCELLE
1251GER	SCHWINGUNG		1255GER	VIOLONCELL
1251HUN	REZGŰ		1255HUN	GORDONKA
1251ITA	VIBRAZIONE		1255ITA	VIOLONCELLO
1251POL	WIBRACJA		1255POL	WIOLONCZELA
1251POR	VIBRAÇÃO		1255POR	VIOLONCELO
1251RUS	VIBRATSIIA		1255RUS	VIOLONCHEL'
1251SPA	VIBRACIÓN		1255SPA	VIOLONC(H)ELO
1251SWE	SVÄNGNING		1255SWE	VIOLONCELL
1252AAA	VIGOR		1256AAA	VIOLENT
1252CZE	RÁZNOST		1256CZE	PRUDKÝ
1252DAN	KRAFT		1256DAN	VOLDSOM
1252DUT	KRACHT		1256DUT	GEWELDIG
1252FRE	VIGUEUR		1256FRE	VIOLENT
1252GER	KRAFT		1256GER	GEWALTSAM
1252HUN	ERŐTELJESEN		1256HUN	HEVES
1252ITA	VIGORE		1256ITA	VIOLENTO
1252POL	WIGOR		1256POL	GWAŁTOWNY
1252POR	VIGOR		1256POR	VIOLENTO
1252RUS	SILA		1256RUS	SILNYI, NEISTOVYI
1252SPA	VIGOR		1256SPA	VIOLENTO
1252SWE	KRAFT		1256SWE	VÅLDSAM

1257AAA VIRGINAL
1257CZE VIRGINÁL
1257DAN JOMFRUSLAGS SPINET
1257DUT SPINET
1257FRE VIRGINAL
1257GER DOCKENKLAVIER
1257HUN TÖVISES ZONGORA
1257ITA CLAVICEMBALO
1257POL KLAWICYMBAŁ
1257POR ESPINETA
1257RUS SPINET
1257SPA ESPINETA
1257SWE SPINETT

1258AAA VIRTUOSO
1258CZE VIRTUOS
1258DAN VIRTUOS
1258DUT VIRTUOOS
1258FRE VIRTUOSE
1258GER VIRTUOS, KUNSTMEISTER
1258HUN VIRTUÓZ, MŰÉRTŐ
1258ITA VIRTUOSO
1258POL WIRTUOZ
1258POR VIRTUOSO
1258RUS VIRTUOZ
1258SPA VIRTUOSO
1258SWE VIRTUOS

1259AAA VIVACIOUS
1259CZE ŽIVÝ
1259DAN LIVLIGT, HURTIGT
1259DUT OPGEWEKT, LEVENDIG
1259FRE VIVACE, VIF
1259GER LEBHAFT, LEBENDIG
1259HUN ÉLÉNKEN
1259ITA VIVACE
1259POL ŻYWO
1259POR VIVAZ
1259RUS ZHIVOY
1259SPA VIVAZ
1259SWE LIVLIG

1260AAA VOCAL
1260CZE VOKÁLNÍ, HLASOVÝ
1260DAN VOCAL
1260DUT VOCAAL
1260FRE VOCAL
1260GER VOCAL, STIMMLICH
1260HUN SZÓBELI, SZÓLAM
1260ITA VOCALE
1260POL WOKALNY, GLOSOWY
1260POR VOCAL
1260RUS VOKAL'NYY
1260SPA VOCAL
1260SWE VOKAL

1261AAA VOCALISE
1261CZE VOKALISA
1261DAN VOCALISE
1261DUT VOCALISE
1261FRE VOCALISE
1261GER VOKALISA
1261HUN SZOLMIZÁLÁS
1261ITA VOCALIZZO
1261POL WOKALIZ
1261POR VOCALIZO
1261RUS VOKALIZ
1261SPA VOCALIZO
1261SWE VOKALIS

1262AAA VOCALIZE, TO
1262CZE VOKALIZOVATI
1262DAN VOKALISERE
1262DUT VOCALISEREN
1262FRE VOCALISER
1262GER VOKALISIEREN
1262HUN SKALÁRNI
1262ITA VOCALIZZARE
1262POL WOKALIZOWAĆ
1262POR VOCALIZAR
1262RUS VOKALIZIROVAT'
1262SPA VOCALIZAR
1262SWE VOKALISERA

1263AAA VOLUPTUOUS
1263CZE ROZLOŠNICKÝ
1263DAN VELLYSTIG
1263DUT WELLUSTIG
1263FRE VOLUPTUEUX
1263GER WOLLÜSTIG
1263HUN KÉJES
1263ITA VOLUTTUOSO
1263POL ZMYSŁOWY
1263POR VOLUPTUOSO
1263RUS SLADOSTRASTNYY
1263SPA VOLUPTUOSO
1263SWE VÄLLUSTIG

1264AAA VOWEL
1264CZE VOCÁLNÍ
1264DAN VOKAL
1264DUT KLINKER
1264FRE VOCAL
1264GER VOKAL
1264HUN ÖNHANGZÓ
1264ITA VOCALE
1264POL SAMOGŁOSKA
1264POR VOGAL
1264RUS VOKAL'NAYA
1264SPA VOCAL
1264SWE VOKAL

1265AAA WALTZ	1269AAA WARLIKE
1265CZE VALČIK	1269CZE BOJOVNÝ
1265DAN VALS	1269DAN KRIGERSK
1265DUT WALS	1269DUT KRIJGSHAFTIG
1265FRE VALSE(R)	1269FRE GUERRIER
1265GER WALZE(R)	1269GER KRIEGERISCH
1265HUN KERINGŐ	1269HUN HARCIAS
12652TA VALZER	1269ITA GUERRIERO, -EGGEVOLE
1265POL WALC	1269POL WOJENNY
1265POR VALSA	1269POR GUERREIRO
1265RUS VAL'S	1269RUS VOINSTVENNYĬ
1265SPA VALS	1269SPA GUERRERO
1265SWE VALS	1269SWE KRIGISK
1266AAA WALKING	1270AAA WARM
1266CZE KROKEM, ZVOLNA	1270CZE TEPLÝ, VŘELÝ
1266DAN GAAENDE, ANDANTE	1270DAN VARME
1266DUT GAANDE	1270DUT WARM
1266FRE AMBULANT	1270FRE CHAUD
1266GER GEHEND, SCHRITTMÄSSIG	1270GER WARM
1266HUN GYALOGLÓ	1270HUN MELEG
1266ITA ANDANTE, CAMMINANDO	1270ITA CALDA, CALOROSO
1266POL IDĄCY	1270POL CIEPŁY
1266POR ANDANTE	1270POR CALOROSO
1266RUS ANDANTE	1270RUS TEPLYĬ
1266SPA ANDANTE	1270SPA CALOROSO
1266SWE GÅENDE	1270SWE VARM
1267AAA WANTON	1271AAA WAVE
1267CZE ZLOMYSLNÝ	1271CZE VLNA
1267DAN LETSINDIG	1271DAN BØLGE
1267DUT DARTEEL	1271DUT GOLF
1267FRE ESPIÈGLE, MALIN	1271FRE ONDE
1267GER SCHALKHAFT	1271GER WOGE
1267HUN PAJKOS, CSINTALAN	1271HUN HAB
1267ITA MALIGNO	1271ITA ONDA
1267POL ZŁOŚLIWY	1271POL FALA
1267POR LICENCIOSO	1271POR ONDA
1267RUS ZLOBNYĬ, ZLOĬ	1271RUS VOLNA
1267SPA PICARESCO	1271SPA ONDA
1267SWE LÄTTSINNIG	1271SWE BÖLJA
1268AAA WARBLE, TO	1272AAA WAVER, TO
1268CZE CVRLIKATI, TRYLKOVATI	1272CZE KOLÍSATI
1268DAN SLÅ TRILLER	1272DAN VAKLE
1268DUT KWELEN	1272DUT WANKELEN
1268FRE GAZOUILLER	1272FRE ASSOUPLIR, VACILLER
1268GER ZWITSCHERN	1272GER SCHWANKEN
I268HUN ENEKELNI	1272HUN INGADOZNI
1268ITA GARRIRE	1272ITA VACILLARE
1268POL NUCIĆ	1272POL KOŁYSAĆ SIĘ
1268POR GORJEAR	1272POR ONDEAR
1268RUS IZDAVAT' TRELI	1272RUS KOLEBAT'SĬA
1268SPA GORJEAR	1272SPA VACILAR, ONDEAR
1268SWE DRILLA	1272SWE VACKLA

1273AAA WEAK
1273CZE SLABÝ
1273DAN SVAG
1273DUT ZWAK
1273FRE FAIBLE
1273GER SCHWACH, LEICHTER
1273HUN GYENGEN
1273ITA DEBOLE, FIACCO
1273POL SŁABY
1273POR FRACO
1273RUS SLABYǏ
1273SPA FLACO, DÉBIL, FLOJO
1273SWE SVAG

1274AAA WEARY
1274CZE UMDLENÝ
1274DAN TRAET
1274DUT VERMOEID
1274FRE FATIGUÉ, LAS
1274GER MÜDE, ERMATTET
1274HUN FÁRADT
1274ITA STANCO, AFFATICATO
1274POL ZNUŻONY
1274POR CANSADO, FATIGADO
1274RUS UTOMLÉNNYǏ
1274SPA CANSADO, FATIGADO
1274SWE TRÖTT

1275AAA WEEP, TO
1275CZE PLAKATI
1275DAN GRAEDE
1275DUT WENEN
1275FRE PLEURER
1275GER WEINEN
1275HUN SÍRATNI
1275ITA PIANGERE, LAGRIMARE
1275POL PŁAKAĆ
1275POR CHORAR
1275RUS PLAKAT'
1275SPA LLORAR
1275SWE GRÅTA

1276AAA WEIGHTY
1276CZE TĚŽKÝ
1276DAM VAEGTIG
1276DUT GEWICHTIG
1276FRE PESANT
1276GER GEWICHTIG, WUCHTIG
1276HUN SÚLOSAN
1276ITA PESANTE
1276POL CIĘŻKO
1276POR PESADO
1276RUS TĬAZHEL'YǏ
1276SPA PESADO
1276SWE VIKTIG

1277AAA WELL
1277CZE DOBŘE
1277DAN VEL, GODT
1277DUT WEL, GOED
1277FRE BIEN
1277GER GUT, WOHL
1277HUN JÓL
12772TA BEN(E), BUONO
1277POL DOBRZE
1277POR BEM
1277RUS KHOROSHO
1277SPA BIEN, BUEN(O)
1277SWE VÄL

1278AAA WHIMSY
1278CZE ROZMAR
1278DAN LUNE, GRILLE
1278DUT GRIL
1278FRE CAPRICE
1278GER GRILLE, LAUNE
1278HUN SZESZÉLY
1278ITA CAPRICCIO
1278POL KAPRYS
1278POR CAPRICHO
1278RUS KAPRIZ
1278SPA CAPRICHO
1278SWE KAPRIS

1279AAA WHISPER, TO
1279CZE ŠEP(O)TATI
1279DAN HVISKE
1279DUT FLUISTEREN
1279FRE CHUCHOTER
1279GER FLÜSTERN
1279HUN SUTTOGNI
1279ITA BISBIGLIARE
1279POL SZEPTAĆ
1279POR SUSSURRAR
1279RUS SHÉPTAT'
1279SPA SUSURRAR
1279SWE VISKA

1280AAA WHISTLE, TO
1280CZE HVÍZDATI, PÍSKATI
1280DAN FLØJTE
1280DUT FLUITEN
1280FRE SIFFLER
1280GER PFEIFEN
1280HUN FÜTYÖLNI
1280ITA FISCHIARE
1280POL GWIZDAĆ
1280POR SILVAR, SIBILAR
1280RUS SVISTAT'
1280SPA SILBAR
1280SWE VISSLA

1281AAA WHITE
1281CZE BÍLÝ
1281DAN HVID
1281DUT WIT
1281FRE BLANC
1281GER WEISS, REIN
1281HUN FEJÉR
1281ITA BIANCO
1281POL BIAŁY
1281POR BRANCO
1281RUS BELYY
1281SPA BLANCO
1281SWE VIT

1282AAA WHOLE
1282CZE CELÝ, VŠE(CHEN)
1282DAN HEL
1282DUT HEEL
1282FRE ENTIÈRE, TOUT
1282GER GANZ, HEIL
1282HUN EGÉSZ
1282ITA INTERO, TUTTO
1282POL CAŁA
1282POR INTEIRO, TODO
1282RUS TSELYY
1282SPA ENTERO, TODO
1282SWE HEL

1283AAA WIDE
1283CZE ŠIROKÝ
1283DAN BREDT
1283DUT BREED
1283FRE LARGE, AMPLE
1283GER BREIT, GEDEHNT
1283HUN SZÉLESEN
1283ITA LARGO
1283POL SZEROKO
1283POR LARGO
1283RUS SHIROKIY
1283SPA LARGO
1283SWE BRETT

1284AAA WILD
1284CZE DIVOKÝ
1284DAN VILD
1284DUT WILD
1284FRE SAUVAGE
1284GER WILD
1284HUN VAD
1284ITA SELVAGGIO
1284POL DZIKI
1284POR SELVAGEM
1284RUS DIKIY
1284SPA SALVAJE
1284SWE VILD

1285AAA WIND
1285CZE VZDUCH
1285DAN VIND
1285DUT WIND
1285FRE VENT
1285GER WIND
1285HUN SZÉL, FÚVÓ-
1285ITA VENTO
1235POL WIATR, DĘTE
1285POR VENTO
1285RUS DYKHANIE, VETER
1285SPA VIENTO
1285SWE VIND

1286AAA WITCH
1286CZE ČARODĚJNICE
1286DAN HEKS
1286DUT HEKS
1286FRE SORCIÈRE
1286GER HEXE
1286HUN BOSZORKÁNY
1286ITA STREGA
1286POL CSAROWNICA
1286POR BRUXA
1286RUS CHARODEYKA
1286SPA BRUJA
1286SWE HÄXA

1287AAA WITH
1287CZE S(E)
1287DAN MED
1287DUT MET
1287FRE AVEC
1287GER MIT
1287HUN -VAL, -VEL
1287ITA CON, COL
1287POL Z
1287POR COM
1287RUS S(O)
1287SPA CON
1287SWE MED

1288AAA WITHOUT
1288CZE BEZ
1288DAN UDEN
1288DUT ZONDER
1288FRE SANS
1288GER OHNE
1288HUN NÉLKÜL
1288ITA SENZA
1288POL BEZ
1288POR FORA
1288RUS BEZ
1288SPA SIN
1288SWE UTAN

1289AAA WOMAN   1293AAA WORK
1289CZE ŽENA   1293CZE OPUS, DÍLO
1289DAN KVINDE   1293DAN VAERK
1289DUT VROUW   1293DUT WERK
1289FRE FEMME   1293FRE OEUVRE
1289GER WEIB, FRAU   1293GER WERK
1289HUN NŐ, ASZSZONY   1293HUN MŰ
1289ITA DONNA   1293ITA OPERA
1289POL ZONA   1293POL PRACA
1289POR MULHER   1293POR OBRA
1289RUS ZHENSHCHINA   1293RUS OPUS
1289SPA MUJER   1293SPA OBRA
1289SWE KVINNA   1293SWE VERK

1290AAA WONDERFUL   1294AAA WRATH
1290CZE OBDIVUHODNÝ   1294CZE HNĚV
1290DAN FORUNDERLIG   1294DAN VREDE
1290DUT WONDERBAAR   1294DUT TOORN
1290FRE MERVEILLEUX   1294FRE COURROUX, COLÈRE
1290GER WUNDERBAR   1294GER WUT(H), ZORN
1290HUN CSUDALATOS   1294HUN HARAG
1290ITA MERAVIGLIOSO   1294ITA IRA, COLLERA
1290POL CUDOWNY   1294POL GNIEW
1290POR MARAVILHOSO   1294POR IRA, CÓLERA
1290RUS UDIVITEL'NYY   1294RUS GNEV
1290SPA MARAVILLOSA   1294SPA IRA, CÓLERA
1290SWE UNDERBAR   1294SWE VREDE

1291AAA WOOD   1295AAA XYLOPHONE
1291CZE DŘEVO   1295CZE XYLOFON
1291DAN SKOV   1295DAN XYLOFON
1291DAN HOUT   1295DUT XYLOFOON
1291FRE BOIS   1295FRE CLAQUEBOIS, PATOUILLE
1291GER HOLZ   1295GER ZILOFONE, STROHFIEDEL
1291HUN FA   1295HUN XILOFON
1291ITA LEGNO   1295ITA SILOFONO, STICCATO
1291POL DRZEWO   1295POL KSYLOFÓN
1291POR MADEIRA   1295POR XILOFONE
1291RUS DEREVO   1295RUS KSILOFON
1291SPA MADERA   1295SPA XILOFÓN(O), ESQUILETAS
1291SWE SKOG   1295SWE XYLOFON

1292AAA WORD   1296AAA YEARNING
1292CZE SLOVO   1296CZE TOUHA
1292DAN ORD   1296DAN LAENGSEL
1292DUT WOORD   1296DUT VERLANGEN
1292FRE PAROLE   1296FRE DÉSIR
1292GER WORT   1296GER SEHNSÜCHTIG
1292HUN SZÓ   1296HUN BUS
1292ITA PAROLA   1296ITA DESIDERIO
1292POL SŁOWO   1296POL TĘSKNOTA
1292POR PALAVRA   1296POR DESEJO
1292RUS SLOVO   1296RUS ZHELANIE
1292SPA PALABRA   1296SPA DESEO
1292SWE ORD   1296SWE LÄNGTAN

1297AAA YET
1297CZE JEŠTĚ
1297DAN ENDNU
1297DUT NOG EENS
1297FRE ENCORE
1297GER NOCH
1297HUN MÉG
1297ITA ANCORA
1297POL JESZCZE
1297POR TODAVIA, AINDA
1297RUS ESHCHĚ
1297SPA TODAVÍA, AÚN
1297SWE ÄNNU

1298AAA YODEL, TO
1298CZE JODLOVATI
1298DAN JODLE
1298DUT JODEL(E)N
1298FRE JODLER, IODLER, IOULER
1298GER JODELN
1298HUN GAJDOLNI
1298ITA FARE GRIDA DI GIOIA
1298POL JODLOWAĆ
1298POR GRITAR DI GIOIA
1298RUS PET' PO-TIROLSKI
1298SPA JODELN
1298SWE JODDLA

1299AAA ZEAL
1299CZE HORLIVOST
1299DAN IVER
1299DUT IJVER
1299FRE ZÈLE
1299GER EIFER
1299HUN BUZGALOM
1299ITA ZELO
1299POL GORLIWOŚĆ
1299POR ZÈLE
1299RUS RVENIE
1299SPA CELO, ARDOR
1299SWE IVER

1300AAA ZITHER
1300CZE KYTARA, CITERA
1300DAN CITER
1300DUT ZITHER, CITER
1300FRE CYTHARE, CISTRE
1300GER ZITHER
1300HUN CITERA
1300ITA CITARA, CETRA
1300POL CYT(A)RA
1300POR CÍTARA
1300RUS KIFARA, TSISTRA
1300SPA CÍTARA, CISTRO
1300SWE CITTRA

INDEX

214   Index

517POR HARPᴀ	283DAN HEERLIJK
517SWE HARPA	283DUT HEERLIJK
72DUT HARPACHTEN	1241DAN HEFTIG
73DUT HARPACTIG	139DUT HEFTIG
517DAN HARPE	1241GER HEFTIG
517DUT HARPE	569GER HEFTIG, INTENSIV
517FRE HARPE	1254HUN HEGEDÜ
73DAN HARPEGGIO,	152HUN HEGEDÜLÁB
73SWE HARPMÄSSIGT	146HUN HEGEDÜVONÓ, VONÓ
519ENG HARPSICHORD	983DUT HEILIG
505GER HARRE	983GER HEILIG
974DUT HARS	1286DAN HEKS
518ENG HARSH	1286DUT HEKS
134HUN HARSOGATNI	1282DAN HEL
1211HUN HARSONA	1282SWE HEL
511GER HART	527ENG HELD
24DUT HARTELIJK, WARM	319DUT HELDER
778GER HARTNÄCKIG	153DUT HELDER
974SWE HARTS	530DUT HELDHAFTIG
821DUT HARTSTOCHT	1001DUT HELE NOOT
822DUT HARTSTOCHTELIJK	528ENG HELICON
641HUN HASONLOAN	528DUT HELICON
520DAN HAST	528FRE HÉLICON
520GER HAST	528POR HÉLICON
520SWE HAST	983SWE HELIG
1229SPA HASTA	528CZE HELIKON
520ENG HASTE	528DAN HELIKON
1243DAN HASTIGHED	528GER HELIKON
1077SWE HASTIGHED	528HUN HELIKON
1243SWE HASTIGHET	528POL HELIKON
445DAN HASTIGT	528RUS HELIKON
1233HUN HASZNÁLNI	528SWE HELIKON
1033HUN HAT	983DAN HELLIG
948HUN HATÁROZAT	153GER HELL, KLAR
1236HUN HATÁROZATLAN	1001SWE HELNOT
275HUN HATÁROZOTTAN	1161DAN HELT IGNENNEM
947HUN HATÁROZOTT, ELTÖKELT	1001DAN HELTAKTS NODE
356HUN HATÁS	565HUN HELYETT
520FRE HÂTE	451HUN HELYETT
542FRE HÂTER, PRESSER	1DAN HENGIVENHED
96HUN HÁTTÉR	529DAN HER
521ENG HAUGHTY	13GER HERBHEIT
532FRE HAUT	354DUT HERDERSDICHT
776FRE HAUTBOIS	529ENG HERE
1286SWE HÄXA	530ENG HEROIC
826HUN HAZAFIÚI	530RUS HEROICHESKIÏ
1162CZE HÁZETI	530POR HERÓICO
1027HUN HAZONLOAN	530SPA HEROICO
522ENG HEAD	530FRE HÉROÏQUE
524ENG HEARTFELT	530GER HEROISH, HELDENMÄSSIG
523ENG HEAR, TO	530DAN HEROISK
525ENG HEAT	530SWE HEROISKT
526ENG HEAVY	1190DUT HERSCHEPPEN
70DAN HEDE	748DUT HERSTELLINGSTEKEN
1282DUT HEEL	441GER HERUNTERSTIMMEN

238

Index

983POL KOŚCIELNY
200POL KOŚCIÓŁ
775RUS KOSOĬ
142CZE KOST
142RUS KOST'
200CZE KOSTEL
607CZE KOTEL
1224CZE KOTEL, BUBÍNEK UŠNÍ
254RUS KOTIL'ON
254DAN KOTILLON
254GER KOTILLON
1046HUN KÖTJEL
607POL KOTŁOW
1224POL KOTŁY
233HUN KÖTNI
1047HUN KÖTNI
1166HUN KÖTŐÍV
254POL KOTYLION
215DUT KOUD
63CZE KOVADLINA
235HUN KÖVETKEZETES
1107HUN KÖVETKEZŐ
228HUN KÖVETKEZTETÉS
449HUN KÖVETNI
63POL KOWADLO
571HUN KOZBEJOVES
750HUN KÖZEL
754HUN KÖZELÉG
701HUN KÖZÉN
684HUN KÖZÉP
1037RUS KOZHA
574HUN KÖZJÁTÉK
179HUN KÖZPONTI
548HUN KÖZVETLEN
286POL KPIĄCY, IRONICZNY
452DUT KRACHT
1252DUT KRACHT
452DAN KRAFT
1252DAN KRAFT
452GER KRAFT
1252GER KRAFT
452SWE KRAFT
1252SWE KRAFT
201POL KRĄG
403RUS KRAĬNIĬ
1235RUS KRAĬNIĬ
1235CZE KRAJNÍ
727GER KRANKHAFT
122CZE KRÁSA
655RUS KRASIVYĬ
655CZE KRÁSNÝ
122RUS KRASOTA
1020RUS KRATKIĬ, KOROTKIĬ
151CZE KRÁTKÝ
1020CZE KRÁTKÝ

968RUS KREPKIĬ
435RUS KREPKIĬ
490CZE KŘÍDLOVÉ KLAVÍR
446CZE KŘÍDLOVKA
1269GER KRIEGERISCH
1269DAN KRIGERSK
1269SWE KRIGISK
1269DUT KRIJGSHAFTIG
261CZE KRITIK
261RUS KRITIK
261HUN KRITIKA
261DAN KRITIKER
261SWE KRITIKER
261GER KRITIKER, KUNSTRICHTER
1016CZE KŘÍŽEK
262CZE KŘIŽITI
752CZE KRK
260DUT KROES
811CZE KROK
1087CZE KROK
1087POL KROK
811POL KROK
1266CZE KROKEM, ZVOLNA
978POL KRÓLEWSKI
931POL KRÓLEWSKI
199HUN KROMATIKUS
199DAN KROMATISK
199SWE KROMATISK
979DUT KROONPRIVILENIËN
138SWE KROPP
1020POL KRÓTKI
619POL KRTAŃ
201RUS KRUG
201CZE KRUH
1016DUT KRUIS
262DUT KRUISEN
260DAN KRUSET
260SWE KRUSIG
1016DAN KRYDS
258CZE KRYTÝ
261POL KRYTYK
968POL KRZEPKI
262POL KRZYŻOWAĆ
1016POL KRZYŻYK
1295RUS KSILOFON
1295POL KSYLOFON
1174POL KU
87GER KÜHN, HERZHAFT
792HUN KUKUCS-ÜVEG
211HUN KULCS
609HUN KULCS
832HUN KULCS
642POL KULEĆ
642CZE KULHATI
305HUN KÜLÖNBÖZŐ

640DUT LICHT
255POL LICZENIE
256POL LICZYĆ
773POL LICZYĆ
638ENG LID
661HUN LÍD
821SWE LIDELSE
822SWE LIDELSEFULL
 24SWE LIDELSEFULLT
821DAN LIDENSKAB
822DAN LIDENSKABELIG
661RUS LIDIISKII
661ITA LIDIO
661POR LIDIO
661SPA LIDIO
661SWE LIDISK
648DAN LIDT, LILLE
661POL LIDYJSKI
654GER LIEBE
655GER LIEBLICH
624DUT LIED
624GER LIED, GESANG
654DUT LIEFDA
 45DUT LIEFELIJK
171DUT LIEFKOZEN
1117DUT LIEFLIJK, ZOET
662DUT LIER
233FRE LIER
1047FRE LIER
1167FRE LIER, ENCHAÎNER
1046SPA LIGADO
639POR LIGADURA
1166POR LIGADURA
1046POR LIGADURA
639SPA LIGADURA
1166SPA LIGADURA
1167POR LIGAR
1047SPA LIGAR LAS NOTAS
1167SPA LIGAR, ENCADENAR
639DAN LIGATUR
1166DAN LIGATUR
639CZE LIGATURA
639POL LIGATURA
1046RUS LIGATURA
639RUS LIGATURA
639HUN LIGATURA, KÖTÉS
1166RUS LIGATURA, LIGA
639ENG LIGATURE
1046FRE LIGATURE
639FRE LIGATURE, LIAISON
639GER LIGATUR, BINDBOGEN
639SWE LIGATUR, LEGATOBÅGE
639DUT LIGATUUR, LIGATURA
379DAN LIGE
640POR LIGEIRO

640SPA LIGERO
78DAN LIGESOM
37DAN LIGESOM
641DAN LIGESOM
910DAN LIGESOM, KVASI-
640ENG LIGHT
643FRE LIGNE
631FRE LIGNE AJOUTÉE
1027DAN LIGNENDE
643DUT LIJN, NOTENLIJN
379SWE LIKA
641ENG LIKE
1027SWE LIKNANDE
78SWE LIKSOM
641SWE LIKSOM
917SWE LIKSOM, NÄSTAN
603RUS LIKUIUSHCHII
1048DAN LILLE
642ENG LIMP, TO
643SWE LINA
643ENG LINE
643SPA LÍNEA
631SPA LÍNEA ADICIONAL
644DAN LINEAER
644DUT LINEAIR
644FRE LINÉAIRE
644SPA LINEAL
644ENG LINEAR
644GER LINEAR
644POR LINEAR
644SWE LINEAR
644ITA LINEARE
644CZE LINEÁRNÍ
644POL LINEARNY
644RUS LINEINYI
616ITA LINGUA
1179ITA LINGUA
616POR LINGUA
1179POR LINGUA
643POR LINHA
631POR LINHAS SUPLEMENTARES
643POL LINIA
631POL LINIA DODANA
643DAN LINIE
1081GER LINIENSYSTEM
643GER LINIE, NOTENLINIE
643RUS LINIIA
643CZE LINKA
629DUT LINKS
629GER LINK(E)
645ENG LIP
645DUT LIP
645GER LIPPE
662ITA LIRA
662POR LIRA

677FRE MAÎTRE
678FRE MAÎTRE CHANTEUR
667DAN MAJESTAETISK
667GER MAJESTÄTISCH
667SWE MAJESTÄTISK
667CZE MAJESTÁTNÍ
667POL MAJESTATYCZNIE
667ENG MAJESTIC
667POR MAJESTOSO
667DUT MAJESTUEUS
667GRE MAJESTUEUX
667SPA MAJESTUOSO
668FRE MAJEUR
668ENG MAJOR
669DUT MAKEN
669ENG MAKE, TO
248SWE MAKLIGT
220SWE MAKLIGT, BEKVÄMT
670ENG MALE
682DAN MÅLE
670FRE MÅLE
95CZE MALE KŘÍDLO
1048RUS MALEN'KIÏ
648RUS MALEN'KIÏ
1267ITA MALIGNO
693DAN MALING
1048CZE MALÝ
1048POL MAŁY
95POL MAŁY FORTEPIAN
648CZE MALÝ, MALO
648POL MAŁY, TROCHE
752FRE MANCHE
671ENG MANDOLIN
671DAN MANDOLIN
671HUN MANDOLIN
671SWE MANDOLIN
671CZE MANDOLÍNA
671POL MANDOLINA
671RUS MANDOLINA
671DUT MANDOLINE
671FRE MANDOLINE
671GER MANDOLINE
671ITA MANDOLINO, MANDOLA
670DAN MAND(L)IG
672SWE MANER
672RUS MANERA
672SPA MANERA, DE MODO
737SWE MÅNG
737DAN MANGE-
752ITA MANICO
672DUT MANIER
672ITA MANIERA
672POL MANIERA
672POR MANIERA
672FRE MANIÈRE, FAÇON

672GER MANIER, SPIELMANIEREN
670SWE MANLIG
670DUT MANNELIJK
672ENG MANNER
670GER MÄNNLICH
510ITA MANO
510SPA MANO
686POR MANSO
686SPA MANSO, SUAVE
686FRE MANSUET
686ITA MANSUETO
673DUT MANUAAL
673ENG MANUAL
673CZE MANUAL
673DAN MANUAL
673GER MANUAL
673HUN MANUÁL
673RUS MANUAL
673SWE MANUAL
673ITA MANUALE
752SPA MANUBRIO, MASTIL
673FRE MANUEL
510POR MÃO
664POR MÁQUINA
664SPA MÁQUINA
38HUN MÁR
940HUN MARADNI
1290POR MARAVILHOSO
1290SPA MARAVILLOSA
675POR MARCAR
675SPA MARCAR
675ITA MARCARE
274ITA MARCATO, DECISO
674ENG MARCH
674POR MARCHA
674SPA MARCHA
674FRE MARCHE
674ITA MARCIA
593SPA MARFIL
593POR MARFIM
675SWE MÄRKE
675GER MARKIEREN, HERVORHEBEN
675ENG MARK, TO
675FRE MARQUER
674DUT MARS
674DAN MARSCH
674GER MARSCH
674SWE MARSCH
674RUS MARSH
674POL MARSZ, CHOD
509POR MARTELAR
509FRE MARTELER
509ITA MARTELLARE
509SPA MARTILLAR
959POL MARZENIE

714ENG MODALITY
714POL MODALNOŚĆ
713POL MODALNY
715ENG MODE
715FRE MODE
608FRE MODE
716ENG MODEL
716DAN MODEL
716DUT MODEL
716POL MODEL
716RUS MODEL'
716FRE MODÈLE
716GER MODELL
716SWE MODELL
716ITA MODELLO
716POR MODELO
716SPA MODELO
717POR MODERADO
717SPA MODERADO
717ENG MODERATE
717ITA MODERATO
717FRE MODÉRÉ
718ENG MODERN
718DUT MODERN
718GER MODERN
728DAN MODERNE
718FRE MODERNE
718CZE MODERNÍ
718ITA MODERNO
718POR MODERNO
718SPA MODERNO
718SWE MODERN, NYMODIG
726FRE MODE, HUMEUR
719POR MODIFICAR
719SPA MODIFICAR
719ITA MODIFICARE
719DAN MODIFICERE
718FRE MODIFIER
719SWE MODIFIERA
719RUS MODIFITSIROVAT'
719GER MODIFIZIEREN
719ENG MODIFY, TO
878POL MODLIĆ SIĘ
879POL MODLITWA
715ITA MODO
608ITA MODO
608POR MODO
715POR MODO
608SPA MODO
715SPA MODO
672HUN MODOR
719HUN MÓDOSÍTANI
 43HUN MÓDOSÍTNI
714HUN MODOZAT
721POR MODULAÇÃO

721CZE MODULACE
721HUN MODULÁCIÓ
721SPA MODULACION
721POL MODULACJA
720POR MODULAR
1047POR MODULAR
720SPA MODULAR
720ITA MODULARE
720ENG MODULATE, TO
721DUT MODULATIE
721ENG MODULATION
721DAN MODULATION
721FRE MODULATION
721SWE MODULATION
721ITA MODULAZIONE
720FRE MODULER
720SWE MODULERA
720DAN MODULERE
720DUT MODULEREN
721RUS MODULIÁTSIIA
560RUS MODULIÁTSIIA
720GER MODULIEREN, DURCHFÜHREN
720RUS MODULIROVAT
720CZE MODULOVATI
720POL MODULOWAĆ
719POL MODYFIKOWAĆ
874DUT MOGELIJK
874GER MÖGLICH
634FRE MOINS
506FRE MOITIÉ, DEMI-
874SWE MÖJLIG
1026RUS MOLCHALIVYY
707GER MOLL
707SWE MOLL
707CZE MOLL, MENŠÍ
738ITA MOLTIPLICARE
736ITA MOLTO
707DAN MOL(L), MINDRE
707DUT MOL, MINEUR
707RUS MOL, MINORNYY
722ENG MOMENT
722DUT MOMENT
722FRE MOMENT
722POL MOMENT
722RUS MOMENT
722ITA MOMENTO
722POR MOMENTO
722SPA MOMENTO
739DUT MOMPELEN
733DUT MOND
512DUT MONDHARMONICA
596DUT MONDHARP
734DUT MONDSTUK, AANZET
724DAN MONODI
724SWE MONODI

CYRILLIC INDEX